# God is Plural

# God is Plural

## Sermons for an Emerging Church

**Paul Veliyathil**

iUniverse, Inc.
New York Bloomington

*iUniverse books may be ordered through booksellers or by contacting:*

*iUniverse*
*1663 Liberty Drive*
*Bloomington, IN 47403*
*www.iuniverse.com*
*1-800-Authors (1-800-288-4677)*



*ISBN: 978-1-4401-9576-1 (sc)*
*ISBN: 978-1-4401-9577-8 (ebook)*

*Printed in the United States of America*

*iUniverse rev. date: 01/18/10*

# Responses from Congregations

*Paul Veliyathil's sermons are sensitive and thoughtful. Whether you find yourself agreeing with him at all points or not, you will find yourself gently challenged to grow. Paul's thoughts are worth pondering.*

-Rev. Dr. Craig M. Watts, Pastor, Royal Palm Christian Church, Coral Springs, Florida

*Paul Veliyathil's true desire is to bring a more "today" message of Christianity to those seeking a more meaningful and authentic faith. Paul's insights are sure to connect the reader with the mind, heart and spirit of a more modern Jesus, which can ultimately lead to a more meaningful journey of faith.*

-Jack Bloomfield, author of *Celebrating Humanity* and co-founder of *One Planet United*

*An inspirational message in layman's terms that's informative and enlightening, never condescending, delivered with the right touch of humor. Received soulfully, powerfully and sincerely. A true spiritual leader.*

-Connie and Russell Kerr, Pembroke Pines, Florida

*Paul preaches on relevant topics with honesty, sincerity and humor. Through his sermons, he has taught me to live life empowered by the Spirit from within. But most of all, Paul has taught me to think outside the box in matters of religion and spirituality, and it is such a liberating experience.*

-Marian Weber, Board Chair, Resurrection National Catholic Church, Margate, Florida

*I have heard many of Paul Veliyathil's sermons and they always bring light into my life. They are insightful and make the teachings of Jesus real to me. I strongly recommend this book and hope it recharges your batteries like it does mine.*

-Wallace F. Dale, author of *Total Toad*, Coral Springs, Florida

*The essential and maybe only task of spiritual teachers is to teach us how to see properly. Paul Veliyathil invites us to open our eyes and see beyond what we currently see. He inspires us to see that we are human and divine, impermanent and eternal, many and One. He takes us to that place where we become able to see Heaven right here on Earth.*

-Piero Falci, author of *Pay Attention Be Alert,* Coral Springs, Florida

*The diversity and intelligent theology Rev. Veliyathil puts into his sermons and his life is outstanding. His quick wit and ideas reflect a keen analytical mind and an excellent education. I will not duplicate his biography, but will state that he takes complex and difficult social, theological and timely events and makes them come alive and make them relevant to our daily life. His sermons are refreshing, challenging, beneficial and believable because of the man behind them.*

-Jack Woodall, Elder, Faith Christian Church DOC, Hollywood, Florida

*As Moderator and long-time member of Miami Lakes Congregational Church in Miami Lakes, Florida, I have had the privilege to hear Dr. Paul when he fills in for our minister. His sermons have an intense*

*spiritual quality about them, and yet they "hit the nail on the head" relating those thoughts to life here on earth. So many times we sit with heavy hearts about personal problems, and somehow Dr. Paul's message soothes our souls and lifts our spirits with a humanistic emphasis that blends the religious with our reality.*

Nancy L Stander

Educator/Counselor/ChurchModerator,MiamiLakesCongregational Church, Florida

*Rev. Dr. Paul Veliyathil's sermons are biblical, simple and straight to the point. You never have to try to guess where he's going with his message or wonder what he said. He would simply have you believe that God is a nice guy, and that you don't have to work and struggle to win His approval. What a relief! Dr. Paul is a fountain of Jesus' peace and love.*

-Cheryl Caldwell, Elder, Faith Christian Church, Hollywood, Florida

*Dr. Veliyathil has a passion that people come to a deeper intimacy with the true self. His sermons guide you toward the holy center within each one of us where The Divine Presence Dwells. Dr. V speaks with authority borne from contemplative living.*

-Marion Olsen, Miami Lakes Congregational Church, Miami Florida

*I love Paul's Sermons, but I think he teaches more than he peaches. He reads the verses from the bible his sermon is about. Usually, I have read them too, but Paul explains the text differently than I had understood when I read them. He always gives me food for thought. I may not always agree with Paul, but I love thinking about it in a different way.*

-Dolores Millard, Elder, Faith Christian Church, Hollywood, Florida

*If the word sermon implies guidelines for religious life, Dr. Veliyathil's sermons reach deeper. Through his words, the Bible becomes a living document with truths that have lasted for centuries and bridge barriers among diverse human groups. Interpreting these truths through his rich life experiences, Dr. Veliyathil awakens the awareness of our own spirituality and the potential to use it fully in the name of God.*

-Marie-Luise Friedemann PhD, RN, Professor Emerita, Florida International University.

*I have known Paul for many years and heard many of his sermons. I have been moved by his words and actions as a man, husband and father. I have grown by listening to his words and learnt many lessons in life by his actions and how he lives his life which is often talked about in his sermons. He is a gentle man who has faith that God is always love and always part of us. His sermons have been about living life and learning and growing from each situation. I have been blessed by having him in my church.*

-Sharon Schuster, Musician, Royal Palm Christian Church, Coral Springs, Florida

*When Paul Veliyathil preaches at our church, there is never a murmur from the congregation and rarely ever a dry eye. He takes us through a discourse on such practical matters as preparation for death in a calm, non-bombastic manner that leaves all of us nodding our heads.*

-Carolyn Furlong, Miami Lakes Congregational Church, Miami Lakes, Florida

*I always look forward to Dr. Veliyathil's sermons. He is straight-talking, thoughtful, visibly spiritual and with a world view of the many issues of our day. His quiet and honest demeanor is always inspiring.*

-Ruby Holihan, Ex-moderator, Miami Lakes Congregational Church, Florida

*Fr. Paul's message is very insightful and inspiring delivered through a modern intercultural perspective.*

-Nellie and Rodger Bodrug, Toronto, Canada

In Grateful Appreciation to the People of God at Faith Christian Church, Hollywood, Florida (DOC), Royal Palm Christian Church, Coral Springs, Florida (DOC) and Miami Lakes Congregational Church, Miami Lakes, Florida (UCC)

*He who does not see God in the next person he meets, need look no further.*

-Mahatma Gandhi

*Looking for God is like seeking a path in a field of snow. If there is no path and you are looking for one, walk across it and there is your path.*

-Thomas Merton

*We have been endowed with all the resources we need to reach salvation—not in some distant heaven, but right here in the midst of our one and true home, the cosmic creation where the Cosmic Christ is already resurrected.*

-Diarmuid O'Murchu

*There is in our civilization a great deal of ignorance about the human condition, and the more spiritually ignorant you are, the more you suffer.*

-Eckhart Tolle

*To know God, you need only to renounce one thing: your sense of separation from God.*

-Neale Donald Walsch

# Foreword

The members of my church rave about Dr. Paul Veliyathil's sermons. A guest preacher at my church on multiple occasions, his special gift is more than his gifts of erudition, biblical reflection, and presentation. His special gift, although he would not claim it, is the gift of the Spirit, the Word moving in and through him. It is the gift of his contagious spirituality—a spirituality that draws us in and makes us want more.

What we want more of is the Spirit, the presence of God made known in God's love. As Dr. Paul prompts us, we don't just know *about Jesus,* we come to *know* him in a deeply personal way, through the power of his actions and words.

When we open ourselves to the movement of the Spirit, a whole new world opens to us—a world of immense possibilities for love and compassion and for loving our neighbor as ourselves.

In ***God is Plural,*** Dr. Paul offers us a whole range of glimpses into the mystery and wonder of the Spirit. What ***God is Plural*** affords us is the opportunity to make connections and to grasp the deeper meanings of these glimpses.

In sermons like *Your Divine DNA, World Communion Every Day,* and *Seeing the Big Picture*, a universal impulse runs throughout. To the ends of the earth, no matter any of the usual marks of distinction, we are all children of God—all sisters and brothers, all in this life together, all revelations of God's creative hand, all incarnations of the *holy.*

For Dr. Paul, we're not *just* human beings; we are innately spiritual, created in the likeness of God. The implications are gripping and far-reaching. From God's point of view, every human being is an expression of the *holy,* where God's glory is *human beings fully alive*—alive to love, to gentleness of spirit and to living in a spirit of peace and shalom with one another.

A former Catholic Priest and currently a hospice chaplain, Dr.Veliyathil has a whole range of life experiences through which the Spirit moves—all of which serve as a backdrop for the redeeming work of Jesus Christ. God works—not only in Christ—but also in and through us.

I invite us, each one, to spend some time with these sermons. To read them, meditate and reflect on them, and to let them live for a while in our mind, heart and spirit. Over time, they will create in us a greater fullness of God's presence and make us more life-giving disciples of the purposes to which God calls us.

Dr. Jeffrey Frantz, Pastor
Miami Lakes Congregational Church
Miami Lakes, Florida
October 2009

# Introduction

I love stories. Most of the sermons in this book begin with a story. So here is one.

Once upon a time, an elderly pastor decided to take a week off to clean out his closets and reorganize. While going through stuff, he came across a shoe box hidden behind the files and clothes. He was so curious about it and so he opened it. To his surprise, he found three eggs and one hundred dollar bills. He asked his wife what it was all about. She said: "Every time you preached a boring sermon, I placed an egg in the shoe box."

"Three decades of preaching, three boring sermons, not a bad record," thought the pastor. And he said to his wife: "That explains the eggs, but what about the hundred dollars?" The wife sheepishly answered: "*Every time I had a dozen eggs, I sold them for a dollar!*"

Neither my wife nor any one at the three congregations where I have preached these sermons are believed to be keeping eggs in shoe boxes!

"What do you miss the most about *not being a priest*?" I have been asked that question many times in the last 21 years. My answer has always been this: "Losing the privilege of the pulpit."

I was ordained a Roman Catholic Priest for the Archdiocese of Ernakulam, Kerala, India, on October 22, 1975. On that glorious day, I reached the goal of my life as I knew it then. During the next thirteen years of clerical priesthood in a very conservative Church, my ideas about God, Jesus, Church, and life itself began to change. For example, the primary goal of becoming a priest was "the glorification of God and salvation of souls" as explained to us in the sixties when

I joined the seminary at a young age of 15, uncontaminated by the world. My exposure to the West and especially my doctoral studies on Trappist monk and spiritual writer, Thomas Merton, opened my mind and led me to unchartered territories of wisdom and spiritual adventure I had never known before.

After living in North America for 6 years, I returned to India in 1987, with a graduate degree in counseling and a Doctorate in Theology. I returned to a Church that was theologically suffocating and spiritually stifling. The Syro-Malabar Church that I belonged to, is an Eastern Church that is in communion with the Roman Church. It is a very conservative Church that conducts its liturgy facing the altar, away from the people, even today in some Dioceses.

In the eighties, liturgical rivalry was a huge bone of contention in the Church. The leaders of the Church spent hours arguing about "the correct way of making the sign the cross" at the beginning of the liturgy. One group argued that the hand should move from forehead to the left shoulder first, and right shoulder last; another group argued that the hand should move in the opposite direction when making the sign of the cross. It was like discussing how many angels could dance on a pinhead.

My cognitive dissonance with the theological views and liturgical practices of the Church reached a point where I could no longer be an honest representative of that institution. I also had struggles in the area of mandatory celibacy. So, with great sadness, I made the agonizing decision to leave the clerical priesthood in 1988. It caused inconsolable pain and unmitigated disappointment for many. The pain of that decision paralyzed me for nearly two years.

There is a saying that you can take a man out of priesthood, but you cannot take the priesthood out of a man. At the time of leaving clerical priesthood, I had invested 22 years of my life in matters of God and religion. They were formative years that had shaped my identity. In the winter of 1988, I lost my priestly identity and along with it, all the arenas for sharing my knowledge and experience were closed shut.

At the age of 37, I had to start all over again, slowly beginning the process of building a new identity as husband and father. Every time I attended church and listened to sermons, I grieved the loss of being able to preach the Word. As a married father of two children, with life experience in the real world, I had new insights and convictions about God, Jesus and spirituality, but there was no venue to share them.

As a clerical priest, I had to say mass and preach every Sunday. It was part of my job description. And I mostly preached the party line, i.e. gospel message was toned down to align with the teachings of the Church, but I had an audience every Sunday. As a married priest, I had gained new experience and spiritual depth and had really "good news" to preach, but I had no audience.

That changed in 1998 when a local bishop of an Independent Catholic Church invited me to be pastor of one of his parishes. There were only about fifteen families but it was a committed group of Christians. It took me four years to realize that Independent churches are hard to maintain and so we decided to close our church.

I believe that being part of a community is essential to Christian life, because we are companions in a journey of faith. Being part of a community reminds me that my life is not about me.

In our search for a community that would accept us for who we are, my wife and I took our two sons and went to a small church in our neighborhood. During our first visit, we were warmly welcomed and felt instantly at home. Royal Palm Christian Church in Coral Springs, Florida, lived up to its name as an "Embracing Church" when it opened its arms to us. It is a community of believers where the presence of God is palpable, the message of the gospel is lived and the love of Jesus is experienced.

About three months after joining the church, Pastor Craig Watts and I met for breakfast and chat. "Would you like to preach" he asked me. I couldn't believe my ears. During my fifteen years of exile from the pulpit, I had never heard that question, although I had known many pastors and ministers. "Of course, I would love to preach," I told Pastor Craig. "Then the pulpit is yours next Sunday as I have to be away for a conference," he said.

It happened to be the Sunday during the Thanksgiving week. I preached with a grateful heart and tearful eyes for the privilege of returning to pulpit I had left years ago. This time, I was not preaching out of obligation, but because of passion. I was passionate to share my new understanding of God, Jesus and spirituality without fear of being censured or reprimanded by ecclesiastical authorities.

The congregation at Royal Palm Christian Church responded positively to my "new take" on spiritual issues with an "Eastern flavor" mixed with insights from science, psychology and quantum physics. I was invited to preach in two other local congregations: Miami Lakes Congregational Church, in Miami Lakes, and Faith Christian Church, in Hollywood. I have been regularly preaching two Sundays a month at Faith Christian Church for the past four years.

The 52 sermons in this book are born of the deep conviction that sermons should connect with the current life experiences of the people. If the God who spoke to Moses on Mount Sinai 3000 years ago, does not speak to Mr. Mosley in Miami Beach in 2009, we have a theological problem. If the Jesus who healed the sick in Palestine, 2000 years ago, does not heal the sick in Pembroke Pines, Florida, today, we have a Christological problem. If Jesus who calmed the storm in the Sea of Galilee, cannot calm our hearts today, then how can Jesus be our Savior? These are real questions that need answers.

While most preachers solve these problems using the "sinner label" and "eschatological comfort," I address them with the fierce urgency of now. They would preach that we are sinners, born with "original sin" and that we are not worthy to be spoken to by God; that our present life is an effort to be endured in preparation for eternal life later. We have heard these messages from pulpits and believed them and lived them for centuries. No wonder the fullness of life that Jesus promised is a mirage for many, and the world is experienced as a "vale of tears."

It does not have to be this way. If only we could shift from these traditional and familiar paradigms and rise to a new level of consciousness, about who we are and who God is, and how Jesus saves, our lives will be transformed and the world around us will be changed for the better.

As a Hospice Chaplain dealing with death and dying on a daily basis, I strongly believe that this life that God has given us is important and a loving God permeates our being and a living Jesus saves us every moment. I also believe that heaven is more a dimension of our current life than a location for a life after death.

These sermons are born of my experiential faith that God talks to us today and that Jesus heals and saves us now. I believe that we are not "mere humans" with a predominant tendency to sin, but "spiritual beings" with an innate calling to wholeness. However, this truth has not been explained enough from the pulpits, mostly due to ignorance and fear.

More than a preaching style that tells people what to do, I have used a teaching style that encourages readers to use their mind to explore the edges of their faith. Our minds are like parachutes and they function only when they are open. Unlike the Catholic liturgy where the homily plays a minor role, sermons are central to the Protestant worship experience, and these sermons were preached in that context.

I invite you to open your minds and heed the advice of Jesus who told his disciples not to be afraid. Embark on a spiritual journey that will take you on a different terrain than the one you have traveled in the past. You may have to consciously unlearn what you may have unconsciously learnt. I invite you to update the software of your minds and reboot your life to face the challenges of discipleship in the 21st century.

The 52 sermons are for the 52 Sundays of the year; however, they don't follow the liturgical calendar of any particular Church. The sermons address issues about who we are (1-2), who God is (3-7), who Jesus is (8-14), aspects of discipleship and Christian life (15-31), the Lord's Prayer (32-39), and sermons for Christmas, New Year, Epiphany, Lent, Palm Sunday, Easter, Pentecost, World Communion Sunday, Make a Difference Day, and a sermon each on end times and death.

Each sermon is based on a scripture passage. A key verse from the passage is quoted at the beginning of the sermon.

The title of this book is inspired by Dan Brown's latest novel, *The Lost Symbol*. Although I experience God as a divine mystery hiding in plain sight in every human being and the whole of creation, I was not able to come up with a phrase that explains that experience. When I read the novel, the phrase, "God is Plural" hit me like a *eureka* moment. What I mean by "God is plural" is neither pantheism nor polytheism, but more panentheism. It is very revealing that the Hebrew word for God in the Bible, *Elohim*, is a plural. Is it possible that the God who said, "Let us make man in our image, in Gen.1:26, is to be discovered and experienced through a communal experience? I believe that we will get a complete **image of God**, only when we acknowledge, accept and affirm all the **individual images** of God around us.

I am immensely grateful to Rev. Dr. Craig Watts, pastor of Royal Palm Christian Church for paving my way back to the pulpit, to Rev. Kevin McGee for opening the doors to Faith Christian Church in Hollywood, where I have been like a part-time pastor for the past four years and to Dr. Jeffrey Frantz for inviting me several times to his church in Miami Lakes. I also thank him for writing the foreword.

A special thanks to Louise Haggett, founder of CITI, Inc. (Rentapriest.com) and to all my friends for encouraging and supporting me to be a married priest, serving God's people.

I am also grateful to the people God in all three congregations who have listened to me graciously. I also thank my wife Judy for supporting my "married priesthood," for serving as a sounding board for my ideas and for patiently editing these sermons; and my sons, Johnny and Tommy, for serving as inspiration for many of the ideas and analogies.

Rev. Paul Veliyathil, Th.D.
Coral Springs, Florida
October 6, 2009

# Contents

1. **Your Divine DNA** ........ 1

2. **Batteries Are Included** ........ 6

3. **God Is Not a Distant Deity** ........ 13

4. **Does God Talk to Us Today?** ........ 20

5. **The Question Is Not, Whether God Talks to Us, But Who Listens?** ........ 26

6. **God Is Not a Celestial Vending Machine** ........ 32

7. **God Is Plural** ........ 38

8. **Finding the Real Jesus** ........ 44

9. **Knowing About Jesus Versus Knowing Jesus** ........ 50

10. **Salvation Now!** ........ 56

11. **Salvation How?** ........ 62

12. **Seeing the Big Picture** ........ 69

13. **Has Jesus Touched You?** ........ 75

14. **Keep Jesus Awake** ........ 81

15. **Believing as Behaving** ........ 86

16. **Worshipping as Listening** ........ 92

17. **Is Your Faith Working for You?** ........ 98

18. **Remember Who You Are** ........ 104

19. **Namaste!** ........ 110

20. **We're the Ones We've Been Waiting For** ........................116

21. **Living Without Walls** ........................122

22. **How to Be a Disciple in a Post 9/11 World?** ........................129

23. **Look Beyond What You See** ........................135

24. **Blessings Through the 'Least Among Us'** ........................141

25. **The Isness of Life** ........................148

26. **Inconvenient Truths** ........................155

27. **Living in a Dreadful and Wonderful World** ........................161

28. **God Can Only Do for You, What God Can Do Through You** ........................167

29. **Change Is Inevitable** ........................173

30. **Apply Directly to Your Heart** ........................179

31. **`Prayer As Energy** ........................185

32. **Implications of 'Our Father'** ........................192

33. **What Is Heaven's Zip Code?** ........................198

34. **God's Glory Is Man's Wholeness** ........................204

35. **Thy Kingdom Come/My Kingdom Go** ........................209

36. **Surrendering With a Smile** ........................214

37. **Live Simply So That Others May Simply Live** ........................218

38. **A Contractual Prayer** ........................224

39. **Lead Us Not Into Temptation** ........................229

40. **Eight Words That Could Change Your Life** ........................235

41. **Ego-Stripping in the New Year** ........................240

42. **Have a Mind That Is Open to Everything** ........................247

43. **Are You a Barren Tree in the Garden of God?** ...............252

44. **Why Hosanna, Why Not Cheers?**......................................258

45. **If Jesus Is in Your Heart, Notify Your Face**.......................263

46. **Faith Seeking Understanding** ............................................270

47. **What If God Is One of Us?** ...............................................277

48. **Holy Spirit, the Invisible Translator** ...............................283

49. **World Communion Everyday** ............................................289

50. **Doing Small Things with Great Love** ..............................296

51. **Is the End Near?** ...............................................................302

52. **Die Before You Die** ..........................................................308

# 1. Your Divine DNA

Genesis: 1:26-27

*Then God said, "let us make man in our image, in our likeness, and let them rule over the fish of the sea and the birds of the air, over the livestock, over all the earth, and over all the creatures and move along the ground." So God created man in his own image, in the image of God he created him; male and female he created them.*

This is the voice mail message of a pastor from the Mid West: "Hello, this is pastor Williams. At the sound of the tone, please answer the following question: "Who are you and what do you want?" If you think I am inappropriate or even rude, let me remind you that most people live their entire lifetime without answering either of these questions" ...beep.

Who are you? The answer to that question is so important that the kind of answer you give determines the quality of your life. That is why, the greatest advise from Greek philosopher, Socrates, was: **"Man, know thyself**."

We all have answer to that question. But do you have the correct answer? People, who have real inner knowledge, will not stand in line for 14 hours, to buy an I-Phone. You heard stories about the I-Phone mania last week, where some people sold their cars and brought the phone. This is the gadget that in addition to making phone calls, can be used to take pictures, check email, and take your blood pressure!

There was this lady from Boca Raton, who spent the entire night waiting in line in front of a store, bought the phone as soon as the store opened, went home, put it under her pillow and slept all day. What is in her life that is so empty, that she had to fill it with yet another gadget? Why is instant gratification so important that she could not wait one more day?

People who know who they really are will not separate themselves from each other and fight in the name of religion, status or skin color. People who know who they really are, will not spent $5000 for a plastic surgery and refuse to spent $50 for a spiritual retreat.

So who are you anyway? Lebanese poet Kahlil Gibran wrote that there was only one time in his life when he was rendered mute. That is when someone asked him: "Who are you?"

It is a question that is impossible to answer with words, because who we are is formless and timeless and words belong to the world of forms and time. The answer to that question does not come from the physical domain.

You are not your body. The body is nothing more than flesh and blood, and skin and iron and calcium and other materials put together. The world tells you that your body is you and that is why the cosmetic industry is a billion dollar business. You are told to worry about the size and shape of your bodies, spending long hours in front of the mirror, worrying about your hair, height, weight and so on. But that is your false self at work. You own the body, you are not the body. You are not your occupation. However, lots of people spend more time at work than with families. The irony is that, at death bed, I have never heard anyone say:"I should have spent more time at work

You are not your country, race or religion. You are an eternal soul, not an American, African or Chinese. It does not matter what sort of a body you showed up in, where you arrived geographically or what religion you practice. There are no Christians, Hindus, Catholics or

Presbyterians in the realm of the spirit. These are temporary labels we made up to distinguish ourselves during our earthly stay.

If none of this is the real you, then who are you? The answer is simple and profound at the same time. "We are spiritual beings with human experience rather than earthly beings with an occasional spiritual experience." You are a soul with a body, rather than a body with a soul.

What is the difference, you might ask. It is huge. You are spiritual first, and physical second, rather than the other way around. Your soul is part of the universal Soul. And SOUL stands for **S**ingular **O**utput of **U**niversal **L**ife. **You are the localized, custom made, visible, tangible expressions of the Universal Life!**

I had heard it many times before, but I was not convinced about it, because all I see most of the time is my external body; all I feel most of the time are the sinful tendencies of the ego, and the spirit had very little say in my life. Spirit was unseen, unfelt and mostly forgotten while I got busy with life.

Then, one day, it hit me like a rock. It was an epiphany; it was an "Aha moment!" About seven years ago, I got a chance to observe the death of one of my patients. This was the first time I had seen someone actually dying. I had seen dead bodies before, but I had not seen the dying process itself.

I sat at the bedside this patient, who was a very vibrant and vivacious lady when she was alive. She was intelligent, animated, funny and full of life. And I began observing her closely. Her eyes were closed, but she was still breathing. Gradually, the breathing began to be slower and slower, with longer intervals between breaths and finally, she took a deep, last breath. That was the end.

Now, I am looking at a lifeless body. What happened to the wisdom and humor and the vivaciousness of this person? Everything that made her a person was gone. Her soul was gone. She was not a person any more, but just a body.

Now, I want to take you to a scene in the first chapter of Genesis, where God is engaged in the process of creating the first man. I don't take this story literally, but I take it seriously, because there is a profound truth in that story. It says that God formed man out of the clay of the ground and blew into his nostrils the breath of life and so man became a living being.

So what makes us alive is the "breath of God." Breath is also called *Ruah*, in Hebrew, which means spirit. From the moment we come into this world, till the moment we die, we breathe. There is not a moment in our life, when we don't breathe. It does not matter where we are, what we are doing, regardless of time of day, awake or asleep, we keep breathing.

That may be the reason why Apostle Paul said: "We are not far from God, in him we live, move and have our being." God is with us as close and as constant as our breathing. That is why in Eastern religions like Buddhism, the main practice is meditation by focusing on the breath.

When the Bible says that "we are created in the image and likeness of God", we know that God does not have an image or likeness, because God is spirit. And our spirit or soul is part of the Eternal spirit of God. We are cut from the same divine cloth.

So, starting today, introduce yourself as a spiritual being: "Hi, I am Paul, and I am a spiritual being." It may sound funny in the beginning, but make an effort to get that idea engraved in your consciousness. Let it be the template of existence. **Change your awareness from "human being" to "divine being."**

Traditionally, we have identified ourselves as 'sinners', 'depraved' and 'fallen.' Much of Christianity has defined us like that for centuries.

The entire premise of Original Sin, invented by St. Augustine, is that we are born sinners.

The other day, I showed this book titled, *Becoming Like God*, by Michael Berg, to a group of people and asked for their reaction to the title. Many said: 'blasphemous' 'arrogant', 'impossible'. Someone said: "We are sinners, and trying to become like God is the ultimate sin."

Let me repeat a German tale told by Wayne Dyer: There was once a man whose ax was missing, and he suspected that his neighbor's son had stolen it. The boy walked like a thief, looked like a thief, and spoke like a thief. But one day, the man found his ax while digging his valley, and the next time he saw his neighbor's son, the boy walked, looked and spoke like any other child.

There is nothing surprising here, because that is who you are; you are part of God.

Your soul is imprinted with God's DNA. That is why Jesus said: "You are called to be perfect as your heavenly father is perfect." That is why St. Paul reminded the Corinthians: "Don't you know that your body is a temple of the Holy Spirit?"

As most of you know, I am from India and I like to conclude with the traditional Indian greeting: Namaste. *Namaste* is a Sanskrit word which means: "I bow to the divinity within you."

According to the Hindu scriptures, there is no duality between divinity and humanity. God and man are not separate but one. It is this belief that prompted famous Indian poet, Rabindranath Tagore to write to a friend after his visit: "After you had taken your leave, I found God's footprints on my floor."

So, the question this morning is this: **Do you leave God's foot prints where ever you go**? *Namaste*!

# 2. Batteries Are Included

Luke 17: 20-21

*Once having been asked by the Pharisees when the kingdom of God would come, Jesus replied, "The kingdom of God does not come with your careful observation, nor will people say, "Here it is" or "There it is" because the kingdom of God is within you."*

How many of you have seen the movie, *Slumdog Millionaire* which was the movie sensation of the year? It won eight Oscars, including best picture. If you haven't already seen it, I highly encourage you to see it.

Boston Globe movie critic ended his review with these words: "If your heart didn't beat faster and your eyes didn't well up at the end, there is something seriously wrong with you. Check into the nearest hospital."

It is the story of Jamal Malik, an 18 year old boy who grew up in the slums of Mumbai, who is a contestant on the popular game show, *Who Wants to be a Millionaire*? Jamal has no formal education, his father was never in the picture, and his mother was brutally murdered, during a Hindu Muslim riot when Jamal was about 6 years old. So Jamal and his brother, Salim, grew up in the slums, panhandling and basically fending for themselves. When he was a contestant on the show, he was working as a busboy, serving tea to the workers at a Call Center.

On the game show every week, this poor, illiterate, unsophisticated slum dweller gave correct answers to every question. The viewers were mesmerized by his flawless performance. But the producers of the show, especially the host, were suspicious. They wondered how this illiterate slum dog could answer the questions correctly.

The host of the show was convinced that Jamal was cheating and so before the final episode, where he could win the final prize of 20 million Indian rupees, he was turned over to the police. And the police begin the interrogation with some brutal techniques including electric shock. When the police did not get the answers they were looking for, the Inspector took Jamal into his office and played the tape of the show and asked Jamal to tell him how he got each answer correctly.

The answer to every question he was asked had a painful, personal story behind it. I won't go into all of them, but would like to highlight just two.

The first one was both hilarious and sad. He had to answer the question about the most famous Indian movie star. Jamal remembered the day, when he first met the movie star and got his autograph. Jamal was about six years old. He was relieving himself in a makeshift bathroom, out in the open, when news broke that his favorite movie idol's helicopter had landed in his neighborhood.

But he could not get out of the bath room. Other kids had locked it from the outside to trap him. Jamal was intent on meeting his idol, and, so he holds his nose and jumps into the pit beneath him, filled with urine and excrement and runs into the crowd with putrid human waste all over his body and gets the autograph from the movie star. It was that harrowing experience which enabled him to correctly answer the first question

The scene, funny as it is, portrays the lack of sanitation and plumbing in third world countries. While we have our comfortable bathrooms where we can go in with a nice magazine and relax, for half of humanity, their bathroom is the open field, no privacy, no plumbing.

Another question was to name a famous Indian poet who wrote a particular song. That question triggered his memories of spending time in a fake orphanage with his brother. During singing contests, he remembered singing that poem. It was an orphanage, where the eyes of children were gouged, to make them lucrative beggars. Blind children evoked more sympathy from people and thus generated twice the income.

So, one night, Jamal was sent to bring his brother for the gouging; it is a terrifying scene. They ran so fast that night and barely escaped from their captors. It was the harrowing experiences of his life in the orphanage that enabled him to come up with the name of the Indian poet.

There are other interesting questions in the movie, and every answer had a story, an experience behind it.

The point I like to make is this: The correct answer to every question, originated in the crucible of his personal experience.

All of us have questions. Who is God? Where is God? Why there is evil in the world? Why do we suffer? Does God care about our pain? Is Salvation only for Christians? Will others be saved? The questions are endless. And where do you look for answers? Usually in books or from teachers and preachers. We look for answers in the Bible. Yes, there are answers are in the Bible, but they are coming out of the experience of the biblical authors.

The Old Testament is the experience of the Israelite people. The New Testament is the recording of the experience the disciples had about Jesus; the letters of Paul are the product of his experience of the risen Jesus.

Paul says that in Gal: 1:12 “I did not receive it from any man; nor was I taught it; rather I received it by revelation from Jesus Christ.”

**Unless those experiences become part of your life experience, they won't have any transforming value for you. You will feel good reading them, you may be inspired by them, but they won't radically change your life.**

Look at the state of the world. The world had access to the Bible, for 2000 years. But the wars, and killings, the disharmony and hatred have not stopped among those who profess to be reading the book.

You know why? Because the stories that are told in the holy book have not become their stories; the experiences that are described in the Bible have not touched a deeper chord with their experiences. Until that happens, you can do all the bible studies in the world, it won't have any life changing impact on you.

Jesus knew this, and that is why he used simple, ordinary human experiences to teach us about the huge topics of God and His Kingdom.

The story of the prodigal son was the human story of a father who waited every day for the return of his son. When he came back, he is unconditionally loved and welcomed back.

But, there are millions of Christians today, who have not understood that story as part of **their faith experience. They still think that God is somebody far away, up there, who** punishes the wicked and rewards the good.

Look at what he compares God's Kingdom to?

"The Kingdom of God is like yeast which a woman took and kneaded into three measures of flour. Eventually the whole mass of dough begins to rise." This is something that happens in every kitchen in the world. Jesus compares the kingdom to that kitchen experience.

The Kingdom of God is like a buried treasure which a man found in a field; and rejoicing at his find, he sold all he had and bought that field."

Again, "the Kingdom of God is like a merchant's search for pearl; when he found one really valuable pearl, he went back and put up for sale all he had, and bought it."

So, the Kingdom of God is explained through the experiences of a woman in the kitchen, a farmer in the field, a merchant in the market. Ordinary human experiences, extraordinary, divine meanings. Profound questions about God and His kingdom, but simple answers from everyday human experiences such as cooking, farming and shopping.

**So this is the message of Jesus: That we should look for God around us, and within us. We should search for answers to our profound questions about life in our mundane, every day, apparently inconsequential and mostly boring experiences of life.** That is what Jamal did in the movie.

There are two main reasons why we don't experience God in our daily life experiences. First of all, we think of God as this "Almighty Being" who is beyond our reach so that we don't expect to find him in the ordinary experiences. But more importantly, we don't experience God, because we don't trust our experiences. We are told that we are unworthy sinners who don't amount to nothing. I hear preachers telling that our inner thoughts and experiences are from the devil and that we should only trust God, forgetting to mention that God is within you.

Today, November 1st is the feast of All Saints Day. The Catholic Church has a process called canonization by which the Vatican evaluates the lives of those who have lived exemplary lives and make them saints. There are more than five thousand saints and 99.9% are selected from the ranks of clergy and religious. There are only a handful of lay people who are declared saints.

Each day of the year is dedicated to honor a saint. There are only 365 days a year and five thousand plus saints. So, today is All Saints Day, in honor of all the canonized saints.

**None of us will meet Vatican's criteria for sainthood, but all of us meet God's criteria.** I say this not with any sense of arrogance, but with deep humility and a sense of awe, just because we are created by God in his image and likeness. That is why Jesus said that the Kingdom of God is within you and Apostle Paul addressed the Christians in Philippi, Corinth and Ephesus as 'Saints.'

A famous Indian Spiritual teacher, Satya Sai Baba was once asked by a reporter: "Are you God?" Baba responded without hesitation. "Yes, I am." Everyone seemed stunned. After a brief pause, he continued: "And so are you; the only difference between you and me is that, I know it and you doubt it."

In 1981, I was living in Canada. I was this innocent and unsophisticated young priest straight from India. I needed a calculator. So I went to the store and bought one; brought it to my room in the rectory. Opened the package and pushed the ON button. There was nothing on the digital screen. I turned it up and down, pushed all the buttons and still nothing.

Frustrated, I went back to the store, stood in line, brought it to the counter and told the clerk that the calculator did not work. The clerk took it from me and he had this smile on this face. He showed me the two AA batteries on the side of the package. Also there was this message in small print: ***Batteries are Included.***

I didn't see them, because, I did not expect batteries to be included. In India, nothing was sold with batteries included, at least in those days. I had never heard that expression before coming to North America. Also, I did not pay attention.

**You came into this world, *batteries included*!** You are created in the image and likeness of God; The Kingdom of God is within you! You are temples of the Holy Spirit!

When these truths become part of your awareness and life experience, your life will change!

It may not change the circumstances of your life; but it will change your life to meet the challenges of those circumstances.

# 3. God Is Not a Distant Deity

Acts: 17: 22-28

*God is not far from each one of us. For in him, we live and move and have our being. As some of your own poets have said, we are his offspring.*

A couple had two teenage sons who always got into trouble. If there was any mischief in the village, probably, they were involved. No punishment could stop their bad behavior. The mother of these boys was frustrated. Then she heard that there was an elder in town who had great success in disciplining delinquent children, so she asked him if he would speak with her boys. The elder agreed, but asked to see them separately.

So the mother sent the younger son first. The elder, a huge man with a booming voice sat the boy down and asked sternly: "Where is God? The boy's jaw dropped and he had no response. He was questioned in a sterner tone: "Where is God? Boy was shaking, but no answer. Raising his voice, the elder bellowed: "Where is God?"

The boy screamed, bolted from the room, ran home, dove directly into the closet, slamming the door behind him.

When the older boy found him hiding, asked what had happened? Younger brother, gasping for breath said: "We are in BIG trouble this time. God is missing and they think we had something to do with it."

When it comes to God, we are like these boys. The boys mistakenly thought that they were powerful enough to make God disappear. We don't think we can make God disappear but very often we think that we know God, that our definition of God is the right definition, that our God is the right God, that Hindus worship false gods, that Moslems worship a vengeful god, that the pagans have no God etc. etc. As the Pope said the other day, Catholic Church knows the right way to God and other churches have the wrong information and non-Christians have no information.

I am obsessed with God. Not in a negative sense, but in a positive sense. I am obsessed with God mainly for two reasons: First, I was born and raised in a very religious family. We had family prayer every night. When the church bell rang at 7 PM, we knelt down as a family and said the rosary and other prayers. I went to church twice a week, Saturday for special devotion to Mary and on Sundays, of course to fulfill the Sunday obligation.

It is a sin for a Catholic not to attend Sunday mass. During every Sunday mass, I recited the creed: "I believe in God, the father almighty, creator of heaven and earth…" but I had no clue what that meant. I never asked the question: "If God is almighty, why he appears to be so powerless to stop natural calamities like flood, famine, earthquake etc?" My little brain never worked like that. I believed what my parents and priests taught me.

As Marcus Borg describes it, I was in the "pre-critical naiveté stage" of my faith life. It is the childish stage of faith, when you believe everything literally without asking any questions. It is possible that a person could grow to adulthood and still be childish about his faith.

I was surrounded by people who were in the God business: There were four priests and seven nuns in the immediate family: uncles, aunts and cousins including my own sister who is a nun. Because of the influence of such a large group of "God people," I entered a profession in which God was the central focus: priesthood in the Catholic Church.

During the ten years of my seminary training, it was all about God. I had academic courses in bible, theology, philosophy, prayer, spirituality, church history, and I engaged in spiritual practices such as meditation, contemplation, spiritual reading, retreats etc. I was immersed in matters of God. I have to say, it was mainly about the Christian God. There was nothing mentioned about any other theories of God. They were considered wrong or unimportant.

After my ordination, I spent the next thirteen years as a priest preaching about the God I had learned in the seminary. I also spent five years in the University of Toronto, earning a doctorate in theology. A person with a doctorate in theology is supposed to know a lot about God.

After I transitioned from priesthood and got married, I took a break from my obsession with God. Suddenly, I found out that I did not have the luxury of sitting around reading books about God and religion or spending long hours to do prescribed prayers. As a married man, I had new responsibilities; I had to find a job, make a living, pay rent, put gas in the car and deal with the exigencies of regular life in the real world. So my obsession with God went into a remission for a few years.

It perked up back again after September 11, 2001. The horrors of 9/11 and the events that followed after, the mood of the country and the world in general prompted me to think seriously about God again; not as an object of devotion, but more as a subject of serious inquiry and deep reflection.

As you know, one of the planes, United Flight 93, crashed into a field in Pennsylvania. Based on reports, we know that the passengers fought with the terrorists and purposely crashed that plane which was apparently bound for the capitol. According to the cockpit voice recorder, or the black box, the last sounds recorded on it were: "Allahu Akbar" or "God is great."

Osama Bin Laden, in his taped messages denouncing America always invokes God: "May Allah help us to destroy the infidels."

In an interview with President Bush before the start of the Iraq war, a journalist asked President Bush if he had consulted with his father, meaning, George Herbert Walker Bush, about the ramifications of this war. And the president replied: "I consult a higher father", meaning God. So the president bombs a poor country with high tech aircraft and sends 150,000 troops which results in the death of nearly 60,000 Iraqis and 4000 Americans and, God told him to do that? What kind of God is that?

In the 13th century, during the crusades, when the pope ordered Christians to conquer the holy land and kill all Moslems, it was done in the name of God.

In 1993, in a place called Waco Texas, a man named David Koresh, claimed to know the will of God and set fire to the building killing 28 children and 34 adults. Which God was he talking to?

In Afghanistan last year, a man named Abdul Rahman was sentenced to death for converting to Christianity. Do you know why? The Mullahs said that the Christian God is the wrong God, Allah is the only true God.

**The three letter word, God is the most sublime and most dangerous word in the English language**. How we understand and interpret that word has huge implications for our life: personal, national and international. Social reform movements like, women's rights and civil rights have a God dimension.

**Contemporary debates about abortion, stem cell research, capital punishment, global warming, intelligent design, birth control, euthanasia, gay marriage, military policy and foreign policy have a God dimension to them.**

For example, the biblical injunction that women should wear a scarf and they be silent in church, that a menstruating woman is unclean, has a lot to do with denying rights for women for centuries.

When somebody claims that God speaks to him, we have to always qualify that statement by saying: "It is actually, his interpretation of what God said." Because no human being knows exactly how God thinks or talks. No person on this planet, no religion in this world has the direct words of God. Word of God is understood and interpreted by man. **All that we have is, Word of God in words of men.**

**The bible was not written by God, and notarized by Jesus**. All the words, in all the holy books of the world, are God's word in human words, with all its limitations.

Because of my huge obsession with God and my belief that our understanding of God is so crucial to our lives, I began reading a series of books about God. In the last two years, I bought and read twenty five books that had the word 'God' in their titles.

I started with *God: a Biography* by (Jack Miles), followed by *A history of God* ( Karen Armstrong), *God is a Verb* (Rabbi David Cooper), *How to Know God* (Deepak Chopra), *God Talk* (Brad Gooch), *The God of Second Chances* (Stephen Anterburn), *City of God* (E.L. Doctoro), *The Experience of God* (Jonathan Robinson), *The God of Small Things* (Arundhati Roy), *Blue Collar God, White Collar God* (Terry Esau), *Kiss of God* (Marshall Stewart).

*God and the Evolving Universe* (James Redfield), *The God Delusion* (Richard.Dawkins), Left *Hand of God* (Michael Lerner), *Picture of God,* (Barry Kelly), *Becoming Like God* (Michael Berg) and eight books on God by the same author, (Neale Donald Walsch), *Conversations with God, 1, 2, and 3, Friendship with God, Communion with God, What God wants, Tomorrow's God, At Home with God and Happier than God*!

So what do I think after all these readings and hundreds of hours of thinking, reflection and meditation? The more I know, the less I know. It may sound corny, but that is the truth.

Out of curiosity, I also googled God. There are 331 million hits on Google for God. There is a website called *God.com*. It begins with this sentence: "There are six billion people in this world and there are six billion images of God."

As Bishop John Shelby Spong would say, **there is no human word we can speak or an image we can propose, that can fully capture the essence of God. God is beyond our ability to describe and eludes our feeble attempts to control, possess or define. We walk into the mystery of god, we never arrive, if you think you have arrived, you have become idolatrous.**

I believe God is real; I believe that God can be experienced and I also believe that this experience is cross cultural, available to all people, everywhere.

That is why I like the theory of God proposed by apostle Paul in today's reading. Paul was talking to the people of Areaopagus, a town in Greece. Walking around town, he notices an altar with a sign: To an UNKNOWN GOD. Paul thinks they are ignorant about God.

So he tells them that God is the creator of heaven and earth, God does not dwell in temples built by man, God is not served by human hands, God does not need anything from us, because he gives everything to us; that man is supposed to seek God, and perhaps, eventually to find him.

Then, Paul breaks this great news to them: "That God is not far from us: in him we live, move and have our being." God is not just another being; He is the ground of being. God is not a separate being up there, but the very foundation of our being. **We are different**

**from God, but we are not divided from God.** In that sense, God is more of a presence than a person.

There are many images to explain this; my favorite is the image of the Sun. Compare God to the sun. Without the sun's heat, we will freeze to death; without the sun's light, we will choke to death, because there won't be any photosynthesis, and there won't be any oxygen. So the sun is the source of physical life on earth, as God is the source of our life.

The sun is always there, never moves, and never changes his light or heat. As the sun is constantly shining, God is constant in his affection for us. At the end of the day, it feels like the sun is disappearing, but as a matter of fact, we are disappearing from the sun by turning on the axis. When the earth sends clouds up, it blocks the sun; similarly, when we commit sin, we block God's love. When the cloud moves, the sun shines, when we turn away from sin, we experience God.

Just like the sun that does not hold back its light from anybody, God does not withhold his love from nobody. The sun does not say, "I am not going to shine on the pagans because they don't believe in me or on the gays because they are sinful, or on the Moslems, because they worship Allah. God loves everybody.

When we are able to love everybody, and I mean everybody, regardless of their race, religion or sexual orientation, we will start feeling the presence of God all the time.

**Instead of arguing about God, discussing about God, or talking about God, try to act like God**. In other words, be a godly person, and that is the best way to experience God. LOVE EVERYBODY, which is what God does; when we do that we will experience God all the time.

# 4. Does God Talk to Us Today?

Mathew: 1: 18-24

*And this took place to fulfill what the Lord had said through the prophet: "The virgin will be with child and will give birth to a son, and they will call him "Immanuel" which means, "God with us."*

I like to reflect on an important question many people have asked: "Does God talk to us today?

When I listen to some TV preachers, I get the impression that God was a very talkative person three thousand years ago, but he doesn't say much these days. In the book of Genesis, we read that God took evening walks with Adam and Eve in the Garden of Eden and chatted with them on a daily basis.

God spoke to Abraham through his angels, and promised him and Sarah a child in their old age. God spoke to Moses on Mount Sinai and gave him the Ten Commandments. God argued with an unwilling and timid Jeremiah, and convinced him to take the job of a prophet. God spoke to King David and King Solomon. The Old Testament is full of encounters of God with His people.

The New Testament has its own share of stories of a talking God. God spoke to Mary through his angels that she would conceive a child. God told Joseph in a dream that he should not divorce Mary, even though the child she is carrying is not his. God spoke to John the Baptist in the wilderness. God spoke to Peter in a dream and told him that he should not discriminate against the gentiles. God spoke to Saul on the Damascus road and converted him from Saul to Paul.

So the entire Bible is a narrative of God talking to people and the people responding to God. It has been more than 2000 years since the last book of the Bible was written. Since then, we don't hear much about God talking to us humans. So what happened?

Did God stop talking to us after he did all the talking in Biblical times? The predominant opinion seems to be that everything that God ever wanted to tell us is in the Bible and that he does not talk much these days through any other means. A Gallup poll done on this question a few years ago, found that 78 percent of people don't believe that God talks to us today. It is very sad. I saw a bumper sticker the other day: "If you think God talks to you, proceed to the nearest mental hospital".

I had a discussion about this with a pastor. He is a very nice, pious guy, and I respect his opinions on many topics. So I asked him if he believed that God talks to us, and he said: "God does not come for a chat." For him, God is more like the master in the parable who gives his servants five, three and one denarius and goes away to a foreign land, leaving his servants to fend for themselves.

Neal Donald Walsch, author of *Conversations with God* said it well when he wrote: "If someone says that he talks to God daily, he will be called pious; if someone says that God talks to him daily, he will be called crazy; what is crazy is believing that God stopped talking to us two thousand years ago."

So if you believe that God is alive, and always present to us, we have to believe that God communicates with us. But how do you know that it is God talking and that we are not making it up in our selfish minds?

This is a 64K question. This question was asked by our church moderator, Sharon Watkins during a democratic presidential candidate debate two months ago. She asked the candidates: "Do you believe that God talks to us and if so, how do you know that it is God talking?"

None of the candidates answered that question. They evaded the question, as politicians usually do.

The reason why Sharon Watkins asked the question of the presidential candidates is that in 2003 before the start of the Iraq war, a reporter had asked President Bush if he had consulted his father, Bush 41, about the war and his reply was: "I consult a higher father", meaning God. Bush believed that God told him to invade Iraq.

In 1979, in Jonestown, Guyana, Jim Jones, a Disciples of Christ Pastor, thought that God told him to give grape juice mixed with cyanide to a group of 900 of his followers.

The nineteen highjackers of 911 claimed that Allah told them to fly airplanes into buildings and kill the infidels.

CNN aired a three part series called "God Warriors." For three nights in a row, for two hours each, CNN international correspondent, Christian Amanpour told stories of three groups of people from Judaism, Christianity and Islam, who calls themselves, "Warriors for God."

One of those stories was of two young Jewish men who packed an SUV with homemade bombs which they parked in front of an elementary school attended by Palestinian children. They parked the car near the school, the previous night, so that nobody would suspect. Their plan was to detonate the bomb the next morning, from a remote location.

Thankfully, they were arrested before the incident. During the interview from jail, the boys told the reporter: "It was like God telling me to kill those Palestinian children, because they are occupying the land given to us by God." Those young men spoke with such conviction that they had no doubt that it was God telling them to do it.

**None of these, is God talking, because, I don't believe that God will tell any human being to do harm to another human being.**

So our challenge is discernment. This is a term commonly used in spiritual writings for sifting through the mess and finding if something is really from God. Neale Donald Walsch says that discernment is a simple matter with the application of a basic rule.

**When examining your thoughts, feelings, words and actions, check and see if they are your highest thought, grandest feeling, clearest word and purest deed... If so, they are from God.**

The highest thought is always that thought which contains joy. The clearest words are those which contain truth; the grandest feeling is that feeling which you call love. The purest deed is something that is done with compassion.

Joy, truth, love, compassion, these are interchangeable and one always leads to the other.

So next time, you are thinking about something or someone, check and see if that is the highest thought you could have, which is joy, not prejudice.

For example, you look across the street one morning and see a brand new Lexus parked on your neighbor's driveway. If you said to yourself: "Good for him, he deserves a new car," that thought and feeling are from God; on the other hand, if you said to yourself: "Where does he get that kind of money, he must be dealing drugs," that thought is from you.

When you are having a feeling about something or someone, check and see if that is the grandest feeling you could have which is love, not anger or jealousy.

When you are talking to someone or talking about someone, check and see if that is the clearest word you could speak, which is truth not gossip.

When you are doing something, check and see if that is the purest deed you could do at that moment; if not, it is selfish and sinful.

If they pass these criteria, your thoughts, feelings, words and deeds are from God.

Let me give you another example. It is dinner time and your phone rings and it is a sales person with an accent. While listening to that person, you are thinking: "Where do these people come from? You feel annoyed and you say to that person: "Why don't you learn proper English?" and slams the phone. There is no joy, or truth or love or compassion exhibited here and so it has nothing to do with God.

On the other hand, if you were to think, here is a poor immigrant, probably working for minimum wage, struggling to learn a language, and say calmly, "I am not interested in buying anything," and hang up the phone, there is compassion, understanding, truth and love in that experience.

Let us now measure some of the stories I talked about before, against these four criteria. I cannot believe that a God will tell a president to invade a country and kill one hundred thousand of its citizens displacing two million of them, making their lives a living hell. There is nothing loving, compassionate or pure about that.

I can't imagine God telling a minister to poison 900 of his followers. There is nothing loving, truthful or compassionate or pure about that. I cannot imagine God telling 19 men to high jack planes and brutally murder innocent people. I cannot imagine God telling young men to detonate truck bombs in front of elementary schools. These voices are not from God.

Just because there are other voices talking to us, does not mean that God does not talk to us. He does, and we need to listen for them and discern them.

**First step in doing this is to start believing that God talks to us through ordinary and common place events.** We have this wrong notion that if it is from God, it has to be from somewhere up there, or something spectacular, something that belies natural laws. We look for miraculous experiences, similar to what Moses had on Mount Sinai.

When was the last time you had such an experience or anyone you know had such a spectacular revelation? **When was the last time you saw someone part the Atlantic Ocean to go to Europe?** It does not happen.

**Stop looking for the spectacular and start focusing on the ordinary.** That is what the Advent season is about. In a few weeks we will celebrate Christmas again. And what is Christmas? It is the birthday of Almighty God as a simple child; a human being like us, a human being among us, a God with us. That is the meaning of the name the angel gave to Jesus: Immanuel which means, God with us.

If Jesus is God with us, he must be talking to us constantly. I can't imagine Jesus living with us and not communicating with us. If Jesus is God made man, then God is using human beings around us, to talk to us. Look at the people around you with love, listen to them closely, pay attention and you will hear God and discover divinity within you around you. The purpose of the season of advent is just that.

In the next three weeks, spend time in meditation and reflection, try to go within, and check your thoughts, feelings, words and actions and see if they are the highest thought, grandest feeling, clearest word and purest deed you could come up with at any given moment. If they are, you are in touch with God and God is talking to you.

# 5. The Question Is Not, Whether God Talks to Us, But Who Listens?

Luke: 2:8-14

*Today in the town of David a savior has been born to you; he is Christ the Lord. This will be a sign to you: You will find a baby wrapped in clothes and lying in a manger."*

The title of today's sermon was the last sentence of my last Sunday's sermon. I would like to reflect further on it and show you how to listen to a God who is communicating with us all the time, in many ways.

Human beings worry about stuff. We worry about our future: "Will I be healthy, will I have enough money for retirements?" Younger people worry about their jobs, their children. All of us worry about the state of the world, and the list of worries can be endless.

But I have not met anybody to this day, who worries if the sun is going to come up in the morning. We don't go to bed and say, "I wonder if the sun is going to rise tomorrow."

It is guaranteed, it has been happening for billions of years without interruption and it will go on for billions more. Actually if you think about it, the sun does not rise in the east or set in the west. Sunrise and sunsets are myths. It feels like the sun is rising, because the earth is rotating not because the sun is moving or changing. I verified this scientific fact years ago, when I went to India.

It was 6.30 in the morning in India, and I called my wife and told her that it was a beautiful morning there, and the sun was just coming up, and she said it was 8 PM. for her and the sun had gone down. The sun did not come up or go down, we felt that way because we were on different parts of the globe.

As a matter of fact one of my most beautiful divine experiences was watching sunrise from 30,000 feet up. I was taking an early morning flight from Bombay to Cochin, my home town, and I watched this beautiful ball of fire, slowly rising up, in the east coast of the Indian Ocean, caressing the vast blue waters.

I watched it through the airplane's window, and tears began to roll down my cheeks. It was a moment of grace, it was a mystical experience, my heart filled up with gratitude to God for the sun and the moon and the earth and the mysteries of creation, and I prayed: "*Oh God, creator of the universe, guardian of the galaxies, thank you; I live, move and have my entire being in your presence and providence.*"

The sun is a good analogy for God, because God is very much like the sun. Like the sun, God is with us always, he never moves away from us, he does not withhold his presence from us. Also God is personal to each of us, as the sun is personal. Few months ago, I was on the beach in Stuart, Florida and the sun was shining directly in front of me. When I moved, it felt like it was moving with me; you will have the same feeling if you are in another beach in another part of the country or even the world.

Actually, the sun is a symbol of Jesus too. The birth day of Jesus that we celebrate on December 25th, is not the day he was born.

Jesus was actually born some day in April, but thc Church chose December 25th as the date of his birth because that coincides with the birth of the Isis, the sun God of Greek Mythology. Another symbolism of Jesus and the sun is the statement by Jesus himself in the gospel of John: "I am the light of the world; he who follows me will never walk in darkness."

So, just like the sun, God is always with us. Jesus, who is the light of the world, is with us. His name *Immanuel* means, "God is with us." Before his ascension, Jesus promised that he will be with us till the very end.

The presence of God and Jesus with us is not a dead presence. It is an active presence, a relational presence in which they communicate with us, guide and inspire us from within. **So the question is not whether this God is communicating with us, but who listens?**

We live in a noisy world and there are many voices out there competing for our attention. We are surrounded by noise, the TV, the radio, the cell phone, and the iPod, the constant chatter from outside that we have no time or opportunity to listen to the voice of God. Even when people go for a quiet walk these days, they have an iPod attached to their arms and wires hanging out from their ears. In such a cluttered and noisy environment, how do you expect to hear God's voice?

I am a firm believer that God talks to us all the time and if we pay attention, we will hear his voice. I have several experiences of such divine communication, and I would like to share with you one today.

As you know, I was born and raised in India and I have lived in the United States for twenty five years. During these years, very few people have attempted to pronounce my last name. Many have mispronounced it, others have bungled it but majority have just avoided trying. Their usual response is, "I will just call you Paul". Like Madonna, Cher or Prince, I thought of having just one name; I knew it would be risking total oblivion or inviting ridicule.

Every time people fumble over my name, I used to feel uncomfortable, mostly from a sense of alienation, often wondering whether I even belonged in this country. Had I lived in India, nobody would ask me "Where are you from and how do you pronounce your last name?" Sometimes, I have prayed, that nobody asks for my last name.

Many people from India have cleverly avoided this problem by changing their last names or using their middle names as last names. During my moments of confusion and alienation, I have regretted not changing my name early on. I also had fleeting thoughts about changing it to an easy and common name like "Paul Smith."

However, my wife who had a very short maiden name, *Hein*, like in Heinz ketchup, without the 'z' and of course without the money of the Heinz family, wears her married name like a badge of honor. She is from New York, and the name is a conversation starter for her. She says that my name is unique and I should never think of changing it.

One day I tried to test the uniqueness of my name by checking the local telephone directory. And I found that I was the only *Veliyathil* listed. Later, I googled my name, and I was pleasantly surprised to find out that I was the only *Paul Veliyathil* in the whole world, at least according to Google, with 427 hits. *Paul Smith* has 124 million hits!

My wife is right, as usually wives are. I am unique and I don't want to be lost in a crowd of millions. Another advantage is that I am unlikely to be a target for identity theft. No one will dare to use my name or pretend to be a *Veliyathil.*

I received the greatest blessing of my last name from an Alzheimer's patient few months ago. It was an unforgettable moment of divine grace.

As a hospice chaplain I work with elderly and terminal patients. I believe that every human being that I meet has a lesson to teach me if I listen with a third ear, and a gift for me, should I remain open to it. **This is especially true of hospice patients who will bestow upon you parting gifts, before they pass over to the other side.**

I met such a gift giver in Dolores, who was 79 years old. She was pleasantly confused and not oriented to time and place. She would tell me that she was 30 years old and that her husband was 35 and she had a 40 year old daughter. When I tell her that is impossible, she would squeeze my hand and tell me that I don't know what I was talking about.

**During visits, I sit next her, looking intensely into her twinkling eyes, always wondering what an adventurous life she might have had before Alzheimer's set in. I consider my elderly patients who have gone through the depression and the wars, and many other unfathomable life altering experiences as mysteries to be contemplated and miracles to be approached with reverence.**

Dolores asked me what my name was, a question she asks during every visit. But that day, she was more animated and playful. When I told her "Paul" she asked for my last name. I did not want to burden her with a name, that average people have a hard time figuring out or pronouncing.

But since she insisted, I lifted my badge and held it up in front of her eyes. Dolores looked at it intensely for a few seconds, looked at me and asked, Paul VERY FAITHFUL?

I was instantly elevated to a moment of grace. My jaws dropped, tears welled up in my eyes and I was overcome with emotions of gratitude and joy: Through the innocent eyes of an old lady, going through her second childhood.

**I felt as if Dolores was peeking into my soul and I was beholding divinity**. I experienced a powerful affirmation of who I am, and an invitation to proudly own my name, to live up to its meaning as Dolores saw it, to be faithful to my job, my family and to life itself.

God spoke to me through Dolores that day and in that blessed moment, the discomfort associated with my last name was erased forever. My feeling of alienation about living in a foreign country was instantly gone. I finally felt at home.

This is how God communicates with us: through simple, mundane, day to day experiences. Look for them in your daily life. Get away from the chatter and listen closely, you will hear them. That is what today's reading confirms.

Almighty God was born of a simple peasant woman; He did not choose the richest and the most gorgeous woman to be his mother; Look at the simplicity of the surroundings; it is a manger not a palace; God is surrounded by animals not security guards; God is wrapped in swaddling clothes, not velvet silk; no dignitaries representing the rich and the powerful are present; just simple and ignorant shepherds.

This is how God comes to us, and talks to us, through ordinary, run of the mill events and experiences. If you look closely and listen carefully, every mundane experience can be an encounter with God.

That is the message of Christmas; it is the story of Immanuel, God with us; **Christmas is about the closeness of God to human events; Christmas is about the ordinariness and simplicity of God; it is about the availability of God to everyone, everywhere.**

If Christmas is about God becoming man, then, wherever there are human beings and human experiences, there has to be God. Advent is a time to open our eyes and find that God among us.

Advent season is a time to listen to Jesus who is walking beside us, behind us and in front of us. Christmas is not a date on the calendar that we are waiting for once a year. Christmas is meeting Jesus and listening to him on a daily basis.

**So the question for you today, is not whether God talks to us, *but who listens*?**

# 6. God Is Not a Celestial Vending Machine

Mathew: 6: 5-8

*And when you pray, do not keep on babbling like pagans, for they think they will be heard because of their many words. Do not be like them, for your Father knows what you need before you ask him."*

A man was walking on a California beach, deeply in prayer. Suddenly, there was a voice from above: "Because you have tried to be faithful to me I will grant you one wish." "Build me a bridge to Hawaii so that I can drive over there any time I want," said the man.

The voice said: "Your request is very materialistic. Think of the enormous challenge of such an undertaking. The support required to reach the bottom of the pacific. The concrete and steel it would take; I can do it, but it is hard to justify your desire for material things. Take a little more time and think of something related to spirituality, love, or relationship."

The man thought for a while, and said: "Lord, I wish I could understand my wife; I want to know how she feels, what she is thinking when she gives me the silent treatment, why she cries, what she means when she says 'nothing is wrong'; and how can I make a woman truly happy?"

The Lord replied: "Do you want two lanes or four on that bridge?"

The moral of the story is that even God can be stumped by some of our prayers.

Prayer is such an integral part of our lives as Christians and so, I would like to share with you some personal reflections about this very important topic.

Over the centuries, theologians and preachers have written so much about prayer. According to St. Thomas Aquinas, there are four kinds of prayer: prayer of adoration, prayer for forgiveness, prayer of supplication or petition and prayer of thanksgiving. Have you heard the yuppies' prayer? It goes like this:

*Now I lay down to sleep, I pray my e-mail to keep;*

*I pray my stocks are on the rise and that my therapist is wise;*

*That all the wine I sip is white and that my hot tub is water tight.*

*That racket ball won't get too tough and that my sushi is fresh enough;*

*I pray my cell phone always works and that my career won't lose its perks;*

*That my microwave won't radiate and my condo won't depreciate.*

*I pray my health club does not close and that my money market always grows;*

*And if I die before I wake, I pray my Lexus they won't take"*

It may sound like a silly prayer, but in some form or another, many people pray like this. The words may be different, but the sentiments are basically the same.

The shortest definition of prayer is that it is a conversation with God. Examine those words: "Conversation with God," which implies that we are talking with someone out there. God is understood as someone 'up there' who listens to our prayers and answers them. There is a problem with this understanding of prayer. Let me give you some scenarios.

There is a nurse on my hospice team. She is a very religious person and always talks about the power of prayer. She told us a story about how God heard her prayer about selling her house. She was so thankful to God that she was able to sell the house two weeks before hurricane Wilma hit the area and buy another house in Georgia.

The house she sold was totally destroyed by the hurricane. What about the prayers of the new owners of that house? I am sure they prayed for a happy life in their new home. How come God did not hear their prayers? Some people said, may be they did not pray, but how do we know that?

Bishop John Shelby Spong talks about his wife's cancer and how all the priests and people in his diocese prayed for her. The doctor had given her two years to live after the diagnosis. However, the bishop's wife lived six more years. His congregation took pride in the fact that it was their prayers that prolonged her life. The bishop, while being very appreciative of the support and prayers of his people, did not believe that God extended his wife's life due to prayers.

He asks: "What about the garbage collector's wife who also had cancer, but since no body prayed for her she died within a year of her diagnosis?" He says that this kind of thinking makes God an ego maniac who can be manipulated; or God as partial to some and punitive to others.

Let us take another example. It was reported that the 19 highjackers of 9/11 said their prayers before they set out for the airport. Should we believe that God answered the prayers of the highjackers? Because it looks like their prayers were answered.

What about the prayers of the passengers and thousands of their family members who prayed for a safe flight that Tuesday morning? Did the prayers of the highjackers reach God first and they were granted and the prayers of the passengers were late reaching heaven?

Very confusing, right? Let us get some clarity on this issue from Jesus. How did Jesus pray? What did he pray for? And what did Jesus teach us about prayer?

There are numerous instances in the four gospels where the New Testament writers tell us that Jesus went to pray, but rarely do they tell us how Jesus prayed or what he prayed for. So, it is logical to conclude that for Jesus, prayer was spending time alone with his father. There was not much chatter, but just being with his father, in deep closeness and quiet.

Jesus told his disciples this: "When you pray, go into your room, close the door and pray to your father in private; do not rattle on like the pagans. They think their prayers will be heard, by the sheer multiplication of words. Do not imitate them; your father knows what you need before you ask him."

When the disciples asked Jesus to teach them to pray, he said, "When you pray, first of all, say **Our Father**." It is important to note that the disciples did not ask Jesus to teach them **a** prayer, but teach them **to** pray. They knew so many prayers, such as the psalms.

What they were asking was teach them to be prayerful people, and Jesus said, if you want to be prayerful, the first thing to do is be aware that God is your father. There is a very important ramification to that awareness. If God is **our** father, then the whole humanity is our brothers and sisters, because God is the father and creator of ALL people.

So what Jesus is saying is that you cannot really have a prayer life, if you don't include all the six billion people of this world in your circle of concern. In other words, if you are angry, upset, prejudiced or hateful towards any group of people, you cannot pray effectively.

You may be saying prayer formulas, but they won't connect you to God, the ultimate source of love and peace. About such people

Jesus said: "These people honor me with their lips, but their hearts far from me."

So, prayer for me, is awareness that God is my father, that every human being is my brother or sister,

That I am connected to God through my connection to people,

That when I am separated from my fellow humans, I am separated from God,

That loving my neighbor is same as loving my God,

That I have all the blessings I need, before I even ask for them,

That God loves me unconditionally, even when I don't love God,

That God is present to me always, even when I am not present to God.

Apostle Paul understood prayer as awareness and that is why he advises us to "**pray ceaselessly.**" None of us can utter prayers, 24/7, none of us can be in church or in a prayer room 24/7, but all of us can cultivate the awareness of God 24/7 and that is what praying ceaselessly means.

The holy book of the Hindus called the *Bhagavad Gita* has a story that illustrates this. A man named Arjuna has to fight a battle. So he prays to Lord Krishna, for victory in battle. Krishna appears to him and says: "Your enemy also has prayed to me for success in battle."

So, there are two options: "I can give you 5000 chariots, 5000 horses, 5000 soldiers and 5000 arrows to fight your enemy and I will join your enemy and fight along his side. Or, the second option is: "I can grant all these resources to your enemy and I will fight on your side? Which do you want?

Arjuna thought for a moment and said to Krishna. "**I don't want any resources; I just want you to be on my side, fighting with me**." He made the right choice; he won the battle.

When you pray, do you want a few blessings from God, or do you want God? Do you just want one safe trip when you travel, or do you want a safe journey through your entire life, with God on your side, so that any obstacles you may face, you will face them with God's help.

Do you want one healing for your illness, or do you want God to be with you so that you can deal with all the illnesses with acceptance and peace. **When I pray, this is what I say to God: "Lord, I don't want your blessings, I want you."** because, "if God is with us, who can be against us?"

It is like asking to ride on the back of an elephant through the forest where there are all kinds of snakes, and potholes and wild animals, rather than, asking for a stick so that we can use it to defend against the animals.

**So for me, God is not a celestial vending machine and prayer is not pushing the button of that machine.**

Prayer is knowing, feeling and experiencing that God is with me always, and making my choices and arranging my priorities in such a way, that I am radically available to God, ready to forgive, eager to love, willing to reach out and embrace life with enthusiasm.

Prayer is knowing deeply that the Lord is with you **Always and All Ways!**

# 7. God Is Plural

1Jn 4: 7-21

*No one has ever seen God; but if we love one another, God lives in us and his love is made complete in us.*

At a church harvest festival, the pastor put a sign in front of a pile of freshly baked cookies: "Please take only one cookie, God is watching." At the other end of the table was a basket of newly picked apples. A small boy put a sign in front of it saying: "Take all the apples you want, God is watching the cookies."

The story implies that God cannot do two things at the same time. But that is not true. Early in our religious education, we were taught that God is all powerful. Our prayers usually start with the phrase: "Almighty God." According to St. Thomas Aquinas, the three characteristics of God are: Omniscient, Omnipotent, and Omnipresent which means, all knowing, all powerful and present everywhere. You have heard the expression, "Our God is an Awesome God."

The concept of God is so huge, so beyond the reach of man and that is why atheists don't believe there is a God; agnostics would say that there may be a God, but we cannot know him, and the faithful would say: "Just believe in God, because it is impossible know or experience God."

Who is God? How do we know Him, or Her, or It? Does God even have a gender? Is it even possible for us to know God? These are some of the questions I like to reflect on today.

According to the Old Testament, God is a distant and scary figure. Look at the encounter Moses and the people had with God, on Mount Sinai. You can read it in Exodus chapter 19: The Lord asked Moses to prepare the people to see God in the mountain. The Lord would appear in the cloud and speak to them. But Moses was specifically told to "put limits for the people around the mountain" and tell them to "be careful that you do not go up to the mountain or touch the foot of it, whoever touches the mountain shall surely be put to death." (V.11-13)

*On the morning of the third day, there was thunder and lightning, with a thick cloud over the mountain, and a very loud trumpet blast. Everyone in the camp trembled. Then Moses led the people out of the camp to meet with God and they stood at the foot of the mountain."*

*Mount Sinai was covered with smoke because the Lord descended on it in fire. The smoke billowed up from it like smoke from a furnace, the whole mountain trembled violently. Then Moses spoke and the voice of God answered him.*

Do you know what happened then? The people did not get to see God after all. When the people saw the thunder and lightning and heard the trumpet and saw the mountain in smoke, they trembled with fear. They stayed at a distance and said to Moses: "Speak to us yourself and we will listen. But do not have God speak to us or we will die!" For the ordinary folks, direct contact with God was a death sentence!

So God spoke through Moses and gave them the Ten Commandments. Then again in chapter 33 of the book of Exodus, Moses has another meeting with the Lord where he requests God to show him his glory. But God said to him: "You cannot see my face, for no one may see me and live."

So do you know what God did? God puts Moses in between two rocks and covers the face of Moses with one hand. And when the glory of God passed by, God removed his hand from Moses' face and Moses saw the back side of God. I have no idea how God's behind looks like.

You can speculate on that all you want, but the point is that the God of the Old Testament is a mysterious figure who is distant, overpowering and frightening. Philosopher, Rudolf Otto describes this God as "mysterium tremendum et fascinance" a tremendous and fascinating mystery.

Over the centuries, theologians and saints have talked about approaching and experiencing this mysterious God. According to them, one way to experience God is through contemplation and prayer. Saints like St. John of the Cross and St. Theresa of Avila have spent years in contemplative prayer and have written books about their experiences of God.

But none of us live in monasteries. I don't think any of us have any immediate plans to leave this world and enter a monastery. So how do we experience God? Is there a way? Yes, there is a way, very easy way, but we have not given much thought to it. Yes, there is an easy way to see, feel, know and touch this majestic and mysterious God. I found that out only a few years ago, although I was in the God-business for a long time.

When I was in the seminary, the focus was on experiencing God in prayer and bible study and I spent months and years doing that. Looking back, I have to say, I did not really experience God those days. I still had my fears and anxieties; I was prejudiced and judgmental of others. I did not know God in such a way that knowledge would affect my life in any significant way.

All that changed when I really understood the God of Jesus, the God revealed in the New Testament. Before I understood and embraced the God of Jesus, I had to do some deconstruction work. I had to realize that God is the same yesterday, today and tomorrow. **God does not change, but our ideas about God change. So, I rejected**

**the Old Testament idea of God as a scary figure and embraced the New Testament idea of God as a loving father**

You see that God fully described in the 15th chapter of Luke's gospel: The story of the prodigal son. Jesus told that parable not to tell us about the son's sinfulness, but to tell us about the mercy and kindness of God.

The God of Jesus is "Abba," a Hebrew word which means, daddy. The God of Jesus is a loving father who loves us unconditionally. His face is not hidden from us. If you look at his face we will not die. Jesus said: "I and the father are one; anyone who has seen me has seen the Father"

So if we want to see the Father, we have to look at Jesus. Looking at Jesus is looking at God; Knowing Jesus is knowing God. Where is Jesus today that we can look at him? That is the tricky part.

Our faith tells us that Jesus is risen and that he is alive, but for most people, he is nowhere to be found. There are millions of Christians who believe that Jesus is somewhere "up there" and he is going to come again at the second coming. I won't totally blame people for believing that because, they have been told that by preachers and theologians.

The other day, I was listening to 89.3 FM, and these two guys were talking about where is Jesus now. And they said that Jesus can be found in the book of Revelations, chapter one. This is the picture of Jesus that Revelations paints:

*Son of man wearing ankle length robe, with a sash of gold about his breast; the hair of his head was as white as snow and his eyes blazed like fire. His feet gleamed like polished brass refined in a furnace, and his voice sounded like the roar of rushing waters. In his right hand, he held seven stars. A sharp, two edged sword came of his mouth and his face shone like the sun at is brightest.*

It is a scary image of Jesus. This is not the Jesus I find in the four gospels. And for me, the book of Revelations is the last place I will look for Jesus. For me, Jesus is right here, in front of me. For me, you are Jesus. That is how I understand the mystery of incarnation. God becoming man; yes, in theory, every human being is Jesus. That is why Jesus said: "whatever you do to the least of my brothers, you do it to me."

St. John understood it so well and that is why he takes the whole mystery of seeing and experiencing this "Almighty God" to the level of love. In today's reading, he proclaims that God is love. "Everyone who loves has been born of God and knows God. Whoever does not love God, does not know God, because God is love."

If anyone says, "I love God" yet hates his brother, he is a liar. For anyone who does not love his brother, whom he has seen, cannot love God, whom he has not seen. So knowing and loving the human being in front of you, whom you can see and touch, is the pathway to knowing God.

That statement hit me like a brick a few years ago, and it led to a huge insight and opened a new pathway to experience God.

My wife Judy loves Jigsaw puzzles. She would open a puzzle box of a 1000 pieces and lay it on the dining table and each day she would put a few pieces together. It would take a week for her to complete the entire picture. Every morning when I come down the stairs, I would look at the puzzle, and I will notice that many pieces are still missing. Without all the pieces in place, the picture is incomplete. Then one day all I will find that all the pieces are in place and the picture is complete.

My experience of God is something like that jigsaw puzzle. There are six billion pieces of God, scattered around this planet, because every human being, regardless of his race, religion or sexual orientation, is created in the image and likeness of God. **Every human being is a piece of God.**

When I mentally hold them all together as part of one big puzzle, when I embrace all those pieces as part of one family, I experience the fullness of God. John says it beautifully: "No one has ever seen God; but if we love one another, God lives in us and his love is made complete in us."

Dan Brown, in his latest novel, *The Lost Symbol*, makes a profound statement: "God is Plural." Even though I had experienced what that means, I had never heard anyone put it that way. "God is found in the collection of many…rather than in the One."

He goes on to explain that the very first passage of the Bible refers to God as a *plural* being*: "Elohim.* The Almighty God in Genesis was described not as One … but as Many." I know many believers have no problem in thinking of God as plural as far as it limits to Trinity. But do we have to limit there. If we take Gen. 1:26 seriously, "Let **us** make man in **our** image, in **our** likeness let us make him," doesn't it mean that every human being is an individuation of divinity? **Is it possible that we get a full image of God only when all His images are acknowledged, accepted and affirmed?**

So when you embrace the entire humanity in love, you embrace God completely. When you accept all people as God's children, you experience God; when you consider all people as your brothers and sisters, you know God.

The main reason why many people don't experience God or feel so dry and frustrated and angry and upset in life is, because of their inability to embrace all of humanity. Issues of nationalism, racism, sexism and homophobia raise their ugly heads in us. And when that happens, we ignore, denigrate, judge, separate or hate some pieces of this God puzzle from our circle of love.

Humanity gets divided, love becomes eroded, God remains incomplete and we become fragmented inside and outside.

**Always remember that holiness is wholeness.**

# 8. Finding the Real Jesus

Luke: 6:27-36

*But I tell you who hear me: Love your enemies, do good to those who hate you, bless those who curse you, pray for those who mistreat you. If someone strikes you on your right cheek, turn to him the other also. If you love those who love you, what credit is that to you? Even sinners love those who love them."*

There is a book called *The Third Jesus* by Deepak Chopra. The title implies that there is more than one Jesus. So then the logical question is, if there is more than one Jesus, who is the real Jesus and where do we find him?

In my search for the Real Jesus 25 years ago, I stumbled on something that has stayed with me ever since. That something is a scene from a novel called *The Brothers Karamazov* written by Russian Novelist, Fyodor Dostoyevsky. It is a 900 page novel, and chapter five is called "The Grand Inquisitor."

You know what the Inquisition is? It was that period in Christian history in the middle ages, when those who questioned the teachings of the official Church were branded as heretics, rounded up, interrogated, tried and publicly burnt. The scene is set in 15$^{th}$ century Spain, in a small town called Seville, where heretics were burned, and Jesus walks into the town and he is immediately surrounded by a crowd. This is not the second coming, but just like he was on earth 1500 years earlier.

He came down to the southern town in which on the day before, almost a hundred heretics had been burnt by the Cardinal, the Grand Inquisitor, in the presence of the king, the court, the knights, the cardinals, most charming of ladies of the court and the whole population of Seville.

It was done for the glory of God.

*He came softly, unobserved, and yet, strange to say, everyone recognized him. The people are irresistibly drawn to him. He moves silently in their midst, with a gentle smile of infinite compassion. The sun of love burns in his heart, light and power shine from his eyes, and their radiance shed on the people, stirs their hearts with responsive love. He holds out his hands to them, blesses them, and a healing virtue comes from contact with him, even with his garments. Children throw flowers at him and cry Hosanna; "It is He; it is He," all repeat.*

*He stops at the steps of the Seville Cathedral, when weeping mourners are bringing a little white coffin. In it lies a child of seven, the only daughter of a prominent citizen. The dead child lies hidden in flowers, "He will raise your child," the crowd shouts to the weeping mother. The priest coming to meet the coffin, looks perplexed and frowns, but the mother of the child throws herself at His feet with a wail: "If it is you, raise my child", she cries, holding out her hands to Him.*

*The procession halts, the coffin is laid at his feet: he looks at them with compassion and his lips once more softly pronounces: "Maiden, arise," and the maiden arises; the little girl sits up in the coffin, and looks around, smiling with wide open wondering eyes, holding a bunch of white roses they had put in her hand.*

*There are cries, sobs and confusion among the people, and at that moment, the cardinal himself, the Grand Inquisitor, passes by the cathedral. He is an old man, almost 90, tall and erect with a withered face and sunken eyes in which there is still a gleam of light.*

*At a distance behind him come his holy guards. He stops at the sight of crowd and watches them from a distance: he sees everything; he sees the child rise up and his face darkens; he knits his thick grey brows and his eyes gleam with sinister fire. He snaps his finger and asks the guard to take Him.*

*And such is his power, so completely are the people cowed into submission, and trembling obedience to him that the crowd immediately makes way for the guard and in the midst of deathlike silence, they lay hands on Him and lead him away. The cardinal blesses the crowd in silence and passes on.*

After this Jesus is locked up in a dark room. And the Cardinal comes into the dark prison room alone and closes the door behind him. He gazes into Jesus' eyes and asks him:

"Why did you come back? And he goes into a long lecture about how his message had failed, that loving one's enemies does not work, that the Kingdom of Heaven is a pipe dream, that showing the other cheek is so dumb, and that "blessed are you poor for you will inherit the Kingdom" is such a fairy tale.

He tells Jesus that he was such a fool not to succumb to the three temptations in the desert where he could have obtained, riches, power and domination. And then he asked Jesus:

"Why did you die such a miserable death on the cross? Why didn't you come down from the cross and show the world how powerful you are? You died like a criminal; you should have fought like a man and defeated your enemies."

After a long lecture from the grand inquisitor spanning many pages, basically excoriating Jesus for being such a failure, the Cardinal basically told him that the Church was under his control and he will run it the way he saw fit and asked Jesus not to interfere.

When the inquisitor ceased speaking, he waited for an answer from Jesus. His silence weighed down upon him. He saw that the Prisoner had listened intently all the time, looking gently in his face and evidently not wishing to reply. The old man longed for Him to say something, however, bitter and terrible.

But Jesus suddenly approached the old man in silence and softly kissed him on his bloodless, aged lips. That was all his answer!

The old man shuddered. His lips moved. He went to the door, opened it, and said to Jesus: "Go, and come no more...come not at all, never, ever!" And let him out into the dark alleys of the town. The Prisoner went away…

And the old man? The kiss glows in his heart, but the old man adheres to his idea!

Is it possible that we have this "nice feeling in our hearts" about Jesus, but when it comes to behaving like him, are we like this Cardinal?

Now let me read to you again, the passage I read in the beginning: "To you who hear me, I say: Love your enemies, do good to those who hate you; bless those who curse you and pray for those who maltreat you."

"When someone slaps on you one cheek, turn and give him the other. When someone takes your coat, let him have your shirt as well. Do to others what you would have them do to you. If you love those who love you, what credit is that to you? Even sinners love those who love them."

"If you do well to thosc who do good to you, how can you claim any credit? Sinners do as much. Love your enemies and do good. Then your reward will be great."

Now that is the real Jesus. It is very hard to follow him; so what did we do? We wrapped him up in creeds and dogmas, set him up on a high pedestal and began to worship him as Lord and Savior, instead of following his teachings. We didn't do that personally but the Church did. **Worshiping Jesus is easy, following him is hard.**

**In the fourth century, something bad happened to Christianity.** That is when Emperor Constantine elevated Christianity to the status of a state religion. Christianity as a way of life until then became a religion with all the trappings of pomp and ceremony.

For a moment, I want you to imagine something. On one side is the Pope with glittering garments, the mitre on his head, the golden staff in his hands, the golden chain around his neck, traveling on a pope mobile fitted with bullet proof glass. And he is cheered by adoring fans.

On the other side, a naked man hanging on a wooden cross, with a crown of thorns on his head, exposed to the elements, abandoned by his followers, bleeding to death. And he is jeered by a hostile crowd.

I have a very hard time identifying one with the other. But that is what happened. **Emperor Constantine took Jesus off the cross, cleaned him up nicely, put glittering garments on him, and gave him a golden crown and a staff and made him the founder of a religion in a way Jesus never imagined.**

An itinerant preacher from Nazareth, who preached against the power structures of his time, was made part of the power structure of Rome. A poor carpenter from Nazareth who said, "Foxes have holes, and birds of the air have nests, but the son of man has no place to lay his head," was given the royal palace. And Christianity that started as a way of life was changed into a religion with, dogmas, doctrines and rituals.

In the year 325 A.D., in a place called Nicea, Emperor Constantine convened a council of all the bishops of the Church. During that council there was a fierce argument about the nature of Jesus. One group argued that the humanity of Jesus should he emphasized, while another group argued that the divinity of Jesus should be emphasized. There were fierce arguments and divisions during that Council.

At the end, the divinity side prevailed and they wanted their ideas put into a creed so that nobody could change it later. So, a long creed was promulgated and it is called the *Nicene Creed.*

This is what the creed says about Jesus: "I Believe in Jesus Christ, Son of God, the only begotten, light from light, God from God, begotten not made, one in essence with the father, through whom all things were made. For us and for our salvation, he came down from heaven and was born of the Holy Spirit and virgin Mary; He was crucified under Pontius Pilate, died and will rise again."

The human Jesus was reduced to a dogma; His humanity was diminished and divinity was given prominence.

**Look at the words of the creed again: It says, "He was born of the Virgin Mary; He was crucified and died."** What happened to his three years of ministry?

**The creed jumps from birth to death, with no reference to his life. Repeating that creed will not transform our lives. We need to get to know the Jesus who lived between his birth and death, what he did and what he taught during those three years.**

For that, we need to focus on the gospels and you will fall in love with the person you meet there. **It is not an idea, or a dogma; it is a fascinating and powerful person, the human Jesus.**

So, if you want to know the real Jesus, start reading the gospels, which again is a portrait of Jesus as the gospel writers saw him, but it is the closest to the original Jesus we can get. Start by reading the Gospel of Luke which is the most comprehensive and detailed. And the Jesus you meet there will transform your life.

# 9. Knowing About Jesus Versus Knowing Jesus

Mathew: 16: 13-20

*"Who do you say I am?" Simon Peter answered, "You are the Christ, the son of the living God." Jesus replied, "Blessed are you, Simon son of Jonah, for this was not revealed to you by man, but by my Father in heaven."*

A man wanted to join a church. First, he walked into a Catholic Church. Met with the priest and asked about requirements to join the church: "Rite of Christian Initiation of Adults (RCIA,) six months of instruction, learn the Apostle's Creed, and receive the sacrament of baptism." The priest wanted to make sure that the man had the basic knowledge about Jesus. So he asked the man: "Where was Jesus born? Man said: "Pittsburgh." "Get out of here; you don't deserve to be a member of this church."

So the man walks into a Baptist church: The pastor tells him that the requirements are daily reading of the Bible, remembering the verses and baptism by immersion.

This pastor also wanted to test his basic knowledge and so asked him: "Where was Jesus born?" and the man said: "Philadelphia." "Get out of here; you don't even know the basics."

He walks into a Unitarian church. The minister told him: "We have no special test for membership; we have no dogma or creed; we support total individual freedom. Just sign a membership card." The man was happy that there was not even a test question from the minister.

He was curious, so he asked the minister: "But tell me sir, where was Jesus born? "Why, Bethlehem, of course." The man's face lights up: "*I knew it was some place in Pennsylvania*."

I am sure you know more about Jesus than his place of birth. But how much do you know? Or the crucial question is, does your knowledge about Jesus impact your life? Because, an atheist or a student of religion can know a lot of things about Jesus, but that may not have any influence on the way they live their lives.

So the question is not how much you know *about* Jesus, but whether you *know* Jesus. There is a huge difference between knowing about a person and knowing a person. The first is book knowledge or hearsay knowledge and the second is experiential knowledge.

Let me give you an example: As a former priest, I knew a lot about the last Pope, John Paul II. He was born in Poland, his parents died when he was young, he was an actor, he was conservative in his views, he has traveled many countries, he was media savvy etc. but all that factual information had no impact on my life.

That changed in 1985 when I had the chance to see him up close, kiss his ring and listen to him while he was visiting Canada. From that day onwards, my attitude to the pope totally changed. Every time he was on TV, I would watch him, and I had a new perspective and opinion about the man. I had a personal connection. I began reading his biography and I was more open to listening to his teachings.

This is true not of persons, but of places too. For example, when I hear about LAX, Los Angeles International Airport, I have no real concept of it, because I have never been there.

But when I hear about London's Heathrow Airport, I have a different feeling. I have been there many times during my trips to India. I know all four terminals, the signs posted there, the shopping mall, the very smell of the airport, and it is a totally different knowledge.

So knowing Jesus and knowing about Jesus are very different.

I like to present to you two scenarios. Listen carefully. Both are taken from the lives of my hospice patients. Patient number one is Emma, and she is 96 years old and lives in an Assisted Living Facility. She is five feet tall, moves around with a walker, a former teacher from New Jersey, and very funny. She is still is very sharp and I have fun visiting her, listening to her stories.

She gets along with everyone, she talks to her fellow residents, and she has a very positive attitude about life. She always asks me about my life and my family.

Emma has a daughter who lives in another town. When I asked her how often her daughter visits, her response was: "She comes when she can, I am an old lady, I lived my life, but she still has to live hers; her husband needs her more than I need her." Emma has a very selfless attitude about it; rather than demanding that her daughter visit her, she has this selflessness about her. Emma does not have any sense of entitlement or "it is all about me" "or "poor me" attitude.

When I ask her about her aches and pains, she would say: "What do you expect, I am an old lady, and things fall apart when you get to my age." When I asked her if she was afraid of dying, she became very philosophical:

"I am 96 years old; I think I have over stayed my welcome on this earth. I had a great life, I am ready." "So what happens after you die?" Emma laughed and said: "You go six feet under and that is it." "What about going to heaven? "I think I had some glimpses of heaven here."

"What is the secret of happiness? This is a question I ask all my patients, because these elderly people have a lot to teach, and the answers are always a reflection of their personality. Emma told me that the secret of happiness is to “follow the golden rule.”

Let me now tell you about another patient. His name is Michael and he is 95. In his younger days, Michael was a contractor. His second wife died in 2001. He has two daughters and they visit him every day.

Michael is very angry and depressed. During my first visit, he said to me: “Until two years ago, I was fine. I drove my car, lived in my own home and ate what I wanted. Now I am in this pit; this should not be happening; why is God doing this to me?”

Responding to my question about happiness in life, Michael said this: “What happiness, you think this is a happy life? You must be kidding?”

His daughters called me and said it was getting very frustrating to visit their dad, because he is mean and nasty. He won’t take his medications, he gets angry with them for little things; he told them that if he had a gun, he would shoot himself and end his miserable life. He is so selfish and demanding that if his daughters fail to show up one day, he gets upset and makes them feel guilty. The daughters feel helpless and worried about their father. “He is not pleasant to be around” they said.

So, we have 96 year old Emma, who is pleasant, loving, peaceful, realistic, selfless, patient, funny, happy to be alive and not worried about dying. And then there is 95 year old Michael, who is miserable and unhappy, selfish, moody, demanding of others, frustrated with life, and wants to kill himself.

Now let me ask you a question. “Who do you think really know Jesus: Emma or Michael?

Emma? The irony is that Emma is Jewish and Michael is a Christian, member of a Presbyterian church. He attended church every Sunday, listened to the sermons, he followed the teachings of his church, he said his prayers, he read his Bible; he has a Bible sitting next to his bed, he knows a lot of things about Jesus, but I don't think he knows Jesus.

I am telling you these stories not to argue that being non-Christian is a better way of life, but to highlight the point that knowing a lot of things about Jesus does not guarantee inner peace or give the tools to deal with the struggles of life.

**For Jesus, knowing him personally was more important than knowing about him from others and that is why he asked his disciples, the crucial question we read in the gospel today.**

"Who do you say that the son of man is? They responded by quoting others: "some say, John the Baptist, others Elijah, still others Jeremiah or one of the prophets." Jesus did not care about what others thought of him, Jesus did not want his disciples to know him through the opinions of others.

He wanted them to know him through personal experience and that is why, after they gave all the hearsay answers, he asked the question directly: "And you, who do you say that I am?"

And Peter answered on their behalf: "You are the Messiah, the son of the living God."

Over the centuries, Christians have repeated Peter's answer. But for most, it has not become their personal answer. Christians believe that Jesus is their savior. If everyone who claims to be saved by Jesus behaved as such, there would be no poverty in the world, there would be no wars in the world, and there will be no sexism, racism, terrorism or any of the things that we describe as problems. The planet would be paradise.

So what happened? **My theory is that Christians know about Jesus, but majority of them don't know the real Jesus. If you**

**really know Jesus, your life will be totally transformed. You will become a "new creation."**

That is what happened to Saul. He was transformed from Saul, a persecutor of church, to Paul, the greatest witness to Christ. On the way to Damascus to persecute Christians, something happened to Saul. He experienced Jesus personally and his life was changed forever.

It is fascinating to know the real Jesus; it will change your life and I like to do that in a series of sermons about the real personality of Jesus. Marcus Borg, in a book titled, *Meeting Jesus Again for the First Time*, talks about how he grew up into adulthood without really knowing Jesus. And he wrote about the real transformation that happens in a person's life when he or she knows Jesus.

In the coming weeks, I like to invite you to embark on an exciting journey of finding the real Jesus and maybe, *meet him again for the first time*.

# 10. Salvation Now!

Mathew: 21:1-11

*The crowds shouted: "Hosanna to the Son of David!" "Blessed is who comes in the name of the Lord!" "Hosanna in the highest!"*

A minister delivered a sermon in ten minutes one Sunday, which was about half the usual length of his sermons. He explained: "I regret to inform you that my dog that is very fond of paper ate that portion of my sermon which I was unable to deliver this morning." After the service, a visitor from another church shook hands with the preacher and said: "Reverend, if that dog of yours has any pups, I want one to give to my pastor."

I don't have a dog, so the sermon is going to be 20 minutes!

In our continuing search for the real Jesus, I like to reflect on one of the most important, perhaps the most important title of Jesus: "Jesus as Savior."

Every Christian, when asked about Jesus, would say: "He is my personal savior." As a matter of fact, the only question that is asked of new members at our church is: "Do you believe that Jesus is your Lord and Savior, and the Savior of the world? And people say "yes," but I have often wondered if they really understand what they are saying, or mean what they say!

So I took a mini survey: I posed the question to a group of people. None of them could explain what 'Savior' meant in their own words. They talked about it using words they had heard from preachers or learned in religion classes. A 13 year old boy told me: "It means that Jesus will save me when I die, I guess."

Another one said: "I think it has something to do with going to heaven, after we die." But nobody knew how that worked, except to say that we have to take that in faith. It is hard to explain.

There is a huge problem here: In order to explain something, we have to either experience it or understand it. Many people don't experience Jesus as savior now, because, they are hoping to experience it when they die; so they are not looking for salvation now.

In our interactions with the world, there are four things happening always: they are experiencing, understanding, judging and deciding. For example, while you are sleeping, you experience a sound. You understand it is your alarm clock, you judge that it is six in the morning, and you decide to get up.

Or, you are driving, and you experience a squeaky sound when you turn the corner. You understand it is coming from the tires, you judge that it is due to low air pressure, and you decide to go to a gas station. Or you experience attraction towards a person, you understand it is because you feel there is something special about that person, you judge that it is something worth exploring and you decide to ask that person for a date.

These four stages of dealing with realities happens all the time, and they happen so fast in our mind that we don't see them as separate, but these four part mental process happens all the time.

Now, what has this to do with Jesus as Savior? Do you believe that Jesus is your Savior because the Church teaches that, or is it because you experience his saving power in your daily life and you understand how he saves you?

**Most people neither experience it nor understand it; no wonder Jesus as Savior often remains a dogma to be believed or a title to be repeated.**

One of the primary misconceptions about Jesus as Savior is that the salvation Jesus brings about is something that happens after we die.

I am reminded of a story: Father Murphy walks into a bar and asks to the first person he meets: "Do you want to go to heaven? The man says: "I do, Father." "Then stand over there against the wall." Then the priest asked the second man: "Do you want to go to heaven? "Certainly, Father," he replied. "Then stand over there with him."

Then father Murphy walked up to Mr. O'Brien and asked: "Do you want to go to heaven? And Mr. O'Brien said: "No, I don't, Father." "I don't believe this: you mean to tell me that when you die, you don't want to go to heaven?" And Mr. O'Brien replied: "Oh, when I die yes, I thought you were getting a group together to go right now."

As I mentioned earlier, when I ask people how Jesus saves them, the first thing they say is that Jesus will save them after they die: "Jesus helps me get to heaven" or variations of that theme. If that is how you see Jesus' saving activity, you are missing the whole point of the Jesus story. **If the salvation that Jesus offers is only after death, then there was no need for Jesus to come into this world.**

He could have just sat with his Father in the heavenly kingdom, and wait for us to die. When Jesus said, "I came that you may have life and have it abundantly," he was not referring to eternal life after death.

The word *life,* as it is used in the Gospel of John means, 'fullness of life now and a continuation of it after death.' **It is so tragic that we have to go through life on earth, struggling, suffering, frustrated, jealous, tired, revengeful, upset, angry and mad, and somehow get into heaven at the end.**

**This life is not just a dress rehearsal for the next; it is for real; a once in a life time chance to be on this beautiful planet, were love is experienced and shared, where compassion is given and received, where joy is manifested, kindness is demonstrated and peace is felt.**

The focus of Jesus' teaching was not to help us get to heaven in some faraway place, but how heaven can come to us. In the Lord's Prayer, he taught us to pray: "Thy kingdom come on earth as it is in heaven." **We don't pray to take us into heaven**.

If you examine the gospels, you will find that Jesus rarely talked about life after death. He was a Jewish teacher and the Jews had no concept about an afterlife. The Jewish scriptures, I mean the Old Testament, rarely talks about an afterlife.

When he appeared to Moses on Mount Sinai, God did not ask Moses to prepare the Israelites to go to heaven; He told Moses to lead them to the Promised Land, flowing with milk and honey, a land on the face of the earth, a land called Palestine. That is a piece of real estate in the Middle East, on this earth.

**The commandments that were given to Moses on Mount Sinai were rules to follow on this earth to make life heavenly, rather than prescriptions for life after death.**

You know I am a hospice chaplain. I have a lot of Jewish patients. I always discuss death, and after life with them.

When I ask them what happens after death, most of them say, "You go six feet under and that is it." "Then what happens? I ask. "Nothing; you are dead; end of the program." When I tell them that many people believe in life after death in heaven, they say: "if it makes them feel better, more power to them, but we think it is a fairy tale."

The other day I attended the death of a 91 year old Jewish lady. Her three grown daughters were distraught; one of them was lying next to their mother's dead body holding on to it and weeping. "I will never see her again," she said. She had no hope of a spiritual reunion.

In the book called *The Power of Now*, Eckhart Tolle says that "true salvation is a state of freedom from fear, from suffering, from a perceived state of lack and insufficiency and therefore from all vanity, needing, grasping and clinging. It is freedom from compulsive thinking, from negativity, and above all from past and future as a psychological need."

Your mind is telling you that something needs to happen or you need to become this or that before you can be fulfilled or saved. You see time as the means to salvation; in fact it is the greatest obstacle to salvation.

Jesus always talked about the importance of living in the present. He told us not to worry about the tomorrows. Salvation is instant when you find him.

Look at the story of Zacheus. This is the story of a tax collector who climbed on a tree to see Jesus. He was considered a sinner, despised by people and considered unworthy of the Kingdom.

Jesus enters his house and says: **"Today, salvation has come to this house." Jesus did not say that Zacheus will be saved some time in the future; Jesus did not say, Zacheus had to die before he attains salvation. Salvation is today, now, instantly, in the presence of Jesus.**

In John 17: 3, Jesus explains eternal life: "Eternal life is this: that they may know you, the only true God and Jesus Christ whom you have sent." Jesus does not say, eternal life is life that we will have with God in heaven after we die. **Eternal life is knowing Jesus now!**

On the first Palm Sunday, when the crowd shouted Hosanna to Jesus, they were pleading with him to save them from political oppression. When Jesus entered Jerusalem on a donkey, the crowd shouted: "Hosanna, to the Son of God." "Hosanna" is a Hebrew word which means "Save us Lord." It is used today as a greeting, but actually it means: "Save us." The crowd was not asking Jesus to save them when they die, they were asking Jesus to save them now, from the oppression of Rome. They were pleading for political freedom.

But Jesus made it clear to them that he was not a political leader interested in saving them from political oppression, because even if they are saved from the Roman Empire, there is no guarantee that they won't be enslaved by another emperor, or enslaved by the same empire another time. Jesus knew that physical freedom or salvation is only temporary.

He was interested in spiritual freedom or salvation, and the way to achieve that is by dying to self. He said: "Unless a grain of wheat falls to the ground and die, it remains just a single grain; but if it dies, it bears much fruit."

The path of Jesus is the path of death and resurrection, understood as a metaphor for spiritual life. When we die to our old way of being, the ways of sinfulness and selfishness, we will be born into a new way of being; we will be saved. When our ego, with its pride, arrogance and vengeance dies, and the spirit takes over, we will experience love, peace and joy and that is salvation now!

So I invite you to change your mind set: You don't have to suffer, struggle, be unhappy and miserable in this life and hope to enjoy heaven later. In other words, **you don't have to go through hell to get into heaven. Heaven is not a place to go to, but realizing that you are already there, and that is salvation.**

# 11. Salvation How?

Mathew: 1: 20-21

*But after he had considered this, an angel of the Lord appeared to him in a dream and said: "Joseph son of David, do not be afraid to take Mary home as your wife, because what is conceived in her is from the Holy Spirit. She will give birth to a son and you are to give him the name Jesus, because he will save his people from their sins."*

In our quest for the Real Jesus we reflected on the most important title of Jesus: "Jesus as Savior" that was about three weeks ago, and the title of the sermon was: "Salvation Now." What I said was that the salvation Jesus offers is to be experienced NOW not later, after we die. Life after death is actually a continuation of what we have now.

Today, I like to reflect on "Salvation HOW?" How does Jesus save us?

"Jesus saves" is the very basis of Christian faith; the name 'Jesus' means 'Savior.' Peter proclaimed it in Acts: "There is no other name given under the sun by which man may be saved."

But what does that really mean? What does the title Savior mean? The traditional meaning is: "Jesus saves us from our sins; he died for our sins."

I hear that all the time from church pulpits, from radio and TV preachers and ordinary faithful. They all repeat it; it has been repeated for two thousand years.

If somebody who is a Hindu or a Moslem, who does not know anything about Jesus, asks you to explain to them HOW Jesus 'saves', what would you say? You might give the standard reply: "Jesus died for our sins." But how does that work?

Let us say, I break into my neighbor's house and steal his money: money for his mortgage, food, tuition, gas, etc. I really sinned against him. I broke the 7th commandment.

How, does Jesus save me from that? How does Jesus dying on the cross 2000 years ago, save me from that sin today? I asked this question in a Bible Study group and no one could answer that. You see the problem. You wonder why we cannot attract more people to Christianity; because we have these formulas that we repeat, but we have not experienced or understood what that means and so we cannot have a convincing conversation.

I asked this question to an elder in my church who is supposed to know these things. She said: "Jesus saves me from the wrath of God; He washed me in his blood; it is like a blood bath every day; God sees me, washed and clean in His son's blood"

**If I were a non-Christian, and if somebody explained the saving act of Jesus to me like that, similar to a blood bath, I would run so fast and very far, never wanting to talk about Jesus again**. The imagery of a wrathful God, who needs to be appeased with the blood of his son does not appeal to me; I have no interest in Christian life as a blood bath!

So I asked this elder: "Other than just repeating 'Jesus washed me in his blood', or 'Jesus died for our sins,' what does that really mean in layman's terms? She could not explain that.

It is important to understand the meaning of what you believe. You must be curious about 'faith seeking understanding.' You have to be able to articulate in your own words what you believe; otherwise it will have no impact on your daily life and behavior. Unless your belief becomes personal, it has no life changing power. A belief that is not understood, is like undigested food. It goes through your system, but it does not nourish your body.

Let me explain to you the traditional explanation of the phrase: 'Jesus died for our sins.'

"Before Adam ate the apple, everything was fine. When he disobeyed God and ate the apple, man's relationship to God was broken; he was thrown out of the Garden of Eden. God was so angry with man and He wanted payment for his disobedience. But no man could do that to God's satisfaction. So he sends his only son, Jesus, who appeases God by sacrificing his life on the cross, which is expiation for the sins of humanity."

This is called the substitution theory of salvation; Jesus substituting his life for us. This is what is meant, when people say: "He died for our sins."

You see this phrase in letters of Peter and Paul. Even the gospel of Mark has this phrase: "His life was given as a ransom for many." How did they come up with this idea? From the Old Testament. It is a theological explanation based on the images of the sacrificial lamb in the books of Exodus and Leviticus. It also has references to the suffering servant of Second Isaiah.

Exodus is the story of the Israelites leaving Egypt under the leadership of Moses. Plagues were unleashed on the country hoping that Pharaoh would soften up and let the people go. After nine plagues he did not budge, so the tenth plague was killing all the first born children of Egypt.

To save their children, Israelites were told to slaughter a lamb and smear its blood on the door posts of their houses. And the angel of death would spare those houses and the children living in them. So the understanding was that the blood of the lamb saved the children. (I always wondered why the Angel needed to see blood on the door steps; an angel should have already known which house belonged to the Israelites).

The same imagery is in the book of Leviticus chapter 16. Once a year, the Israelites had to atone for their sins. It was called the "day of atonement." Jews today celebrates it as "Yom Kippur." On the Day of Atonement, Aaron was asked to kill a bullock and sprinkle its blood for the atonement of his sins and his family's sins.

The blood of the goat was for the sin-offering of the people. V. 18 says: "taking some of the bullock's and the goat's blood, he shall put it on the horns around the altar, and with his finger sprinkle some of the blood on it seven times. Thus he shall render it clean and holy, purged of the defilements for the Israelites."

So that is where the lamb theology comes from. Just like the blood of the lamb saved the Jewish people of their captivity, the blood of Jesus saves us from our sins. That is the meaning of the expression in John's gospel: "Behold the lamb of God who takes away the sins of the world."

It still does not explain, how that happens, but that is a matter of faith. We have grown up with this understanding of faith during our life time; Now, if you want to believe that way, and if that works for you, that is perfectly fine with me.

But for me, this Old Testament imagery of the lamb and the blood does not make much sense today in the 21st century. Do I believe that Jesus is my savior, of course I do, but I like to explain that in a way that makes more sense today. I like to share that with you. You don't have to believe it, but I invite you to reflect on it.

First of all, Jesus never referred to him as the sacrificial lamb. There are seven I am statements in the gospel of John, such as "I am the light of the world, I am the way, the truth and life, I am the good shepherd, I am the resurrection and the life," but "I am the sacrificial lamb" is not one of them. That was a title the Church gave him, and as Church, I think, we can give him another title that is more contemporary, and meaningful. John the Baptist referred to Jesus as the Lamb of God, but does that have to the last word about his identity?

I think it is imperative to replace the image of Jesus as a sacrificial lamb for several reasons. First of all, it is a two thousand years old imagery which has no resonance today in many parts of the world. In the ancient world, animal sacrifice was part of worshiping God. In the modern world, it is considered very primitive.

It is practiced in tribal cultures in some parts of Africa, but no civilized society practices it as part of worship. Members of Santeria religion that originated in Haiti and Cuba, sacrifice chicken as part of their worship. As a matter of fact, two years ago it was done in the backyard of a home in Kendall, Florida, and the city got involved and it was forbidden.

Secondly, this image of blood sacrifice, postulates an "angry God up there" who needs to be appeased by the sacrifice of his son, shedding his blood. Such a God does not appeal to me. The God of Jesus is a loving father not a blood thirsty deity who demands atonement through bloodshed.

Thirdly, this type of thinking has no personal impact. For example, how does the priest sprinkling the blood on people remove their sins? If anything, it only makes more stains on them. Or how does Jesus dying on the cross 2000 years ago, remove my personal sins today? It seems to absolve us of any personal responsibility for our sins. "Since Jesus has already paid for my sins, I don't have to do anything," attitude.

The phrase, "Jesus died for our sins" gives the impression that Jesus loved to die on the cross, and that he walked to the cross and died with a smile on his face. As a matter of fact, he was brutally killed; he was executed by the government. The people behind his killing, Pontius Pilate, the Romans and the high priests, were all afraid.

Pilate was afraid he would lose his position as governor, the Romans were afraid they would lose a province and the high priests were afraid that Jesus would change their ideas of God, which would cause them to lose their livelihood made from serving a God "up there."

Another issue is that when we say Jesus died for our sins, it refers to the past and focuses on the sins, the negative side of our life. It is a memory. It addresses only part of our humanity, the sinful part. But Jesus is much more than a memory; he is not a figure of the past, he is very much alive and his focus is not on sin, but life itself, life in its fullness.

Life is not lived in the past; the past is over; life is experienced in the present and I need Jesus with me right here, right now, to save me now, today. As a matter of fact, Jesus said that, but nobody pays attention to it; because they enjoy living in the past focusing on his death.

So, instead of the phrase, "Jesus died for our sins," I like to say: "Jesus lives to save us." Death and sin are replaced by life and salvation. And how does Jesus save me today?

When I wake up in the morning and the problems of the day begin to weigh on me, Jesus reminds me about the birds of the air and lilies of the field who live without worries and that lifts my spirits up. When I get anxious about hurricanes, terrorism, or accidents that could happen to me or my wife or children, Jesus tells me: "Let not your hearts be troubled; trust in me and trust in my father."

When I feel angry towards someone for cutting me off the road, call me derogatory names, or act unjustly towards me, Jesus gives me the strength to "love your enemies and do good to those who hate you." When I feel physical pain from my arthritis or emotional pain from rejection or disapproval, the cross of Jesus gives me perspective on my sufferings. **The cross of Jesus assures me that life with all its sufferings and pain is redemptive with Jesus on my side.**

Going back to the example of the sin of breaking into my neighbor's house and stealing his money: how does Jesus save me from that sin? Jesus who lives in my heart would not even let me think about stealing my neighbor's money, let alone make me do it; if anything, the Jesus who lives in me, will make me give some money to the neighbor rather than steal from him.

**For me, the best experience of salvation is, being constantly aware of the final promise of Jesus: "I am with you always, till the end of times." He did not say, I WAS with you in the past, he did not say, I WILL be with you in the future, but I AM with you. When you become fully aware of that presence and latch on to Jesus, you are saved.**

You will be able to say with Apostle Paul: "It is no longer I, but Christ lives I me." And, that is salvation!

# 12. Seeing the Big Picture

John 8: 1-12

*If any one of you is without sin, let him be the first to throw a stone at her." Again he stooped down, and wrote on the ground."*

A young boy had just gotten his driver's permit. He asked his father who happened to be a preacher if they could discuss the use of the car. His father took him to his study and said to him: "I will make a deal; you bring up your grades, study the bible a little each day and get your hair cut and we will talk about it."

After a month, the boy came back and asked his father if they could discuss the use of the car again. They went to the study. "Son, I am really proud of you; you brought up your grades, you studied the bible diligently, *but you did not cut your hair*."

The young man thought for a moment and said: "You know dad, I have been thinking about that; Samson had long hair, Moses had long hair, Noah had long hair, and even Jesus had long hair." And his father replied: "*Yes, and they walked everywhere they went.*"

The human mind is a funny thing. It has a tendency to zero in on what it wants to think or gain at any given moment. The young boy wanted to keep his long hair and yet drive the car and so he looked for an argument in that area, just focusing on the long hair of biblical figures.

The father on the other hand, wanted to deny the request, and he focused on the fact that, there were no automobiles in biblical times.

Both the boy and the father were right; but neither of them was happy, because neither got what they wanted.

This is very true of our life in general. We are unhappy, unfulfilled, and frustrated, because our minds are narrow or closed. We often see only portions of the reality in front of us; we rarely see the whole picture. If reality can be compared to a pizza, we only see separate slices; we don't see the whole pie. These slices could be our religious views, our political views, our ideas about God, neighbor, or any other idea or issue that affect our lives, which is basically everything under the sun.

Clinging adamantly to our own point view without the broadness of mind that is required to see the other side is the root of all the problems in the world. Let me give you a couple of examples.

Let us take the issue of creationism versus evolution. There is a segment of the population that strongly believes that the biblical story of creation is a historical fact; that God created the world in six days and that is it; there is no room for discussion about it; case closed; end of story.

There is a another segment of the population which believes that the world came into being through millions of years of evolutionary process and the creation story is a metaphorical narrative trying to explain the unexplainable in human terms.

A mind that is open, a mind that can see the big picture, would ask the question: "Can I reconcile both these theories?" I think we can. If you say that Almighty God is the source of all life and started the very process of evolution, one could reconcile both creationism and evolution.

Let me give you another example. A few years ago, a young man named Mathew Sheppard was brutally murdered in Kansas. He was gay. He was beaten and strapped to a barbed wire fence by a group of people who believed that homosexuality is a sin and that God hates gays.

They got that idea from the book of Leviticus where it says that a man lying with another man is an abomination. That is just one slice of the pie, or let us says, one book of the bible, that was written about 3000 years ago when no research about the biology and psychology of sexual orientation existed.

If those men who had killed Mathew Sheppard had expanded their mind and looked for the big picture, they would have found out that killing is against the very commandment of God. They would also have found that Jesus had said not to judge other people. Jesus also said: "Be compassionate as your heavenly father is compassionate." Had they looked at the big picture, they would have also found out that, Jesus never said a word about homosexuality.

Every problem in the world starts with one track thinking; or the inability of the mind to see the big picture. We see it in politics as the fight between liberals and conservatives or Democrats and Republicans. In the religious arena, it shows up as religious arrogance, the claim that one religion is better than another religion. In personal lives, it shows up as impatience, intolerance, frustration and making mountains out of molehills.

Few weeks ago, we had a boil water advisory in Coral Springs. Tap water had to be boiled for three minutes before use. Some of our neighbors got very upset about that. While they were complaining about it, I was thinking of the millions of people in the world who have no drinking water.

When I get impatient about waiting in line at a fast food restaurant, I say to myself: "At least there is food at the end of the line, but three million people will go to bed hungry tonight."

When there was a 692 point drop in the stock market, I looked at my 401(K), and realized that I had lost $3000 that day. As soon as I began to get depressed, I thought about a TV program I had seen about the war in Congo, where two million people were killed and women were raped and shot. I said to myself: "At least I have food to eat, a roof over my head and money for all my needs. If my 401(K) which is my retirement income 15 years from now, has less money in it, I will still be OK. **When millions have no money for their daily bread, I should not worry too much about my bread in the year 2023!**

In all these cases, it was my awareness of the big picture that helped me deal with the situation calmly.

Jesus had this uncanny ability to see the big picture. His mind was open to see all the sides of an issue and that is why he was such a loving, compassionate and peaceful person. Let us examine the story of the woman caught in adultery that I read today.

This woman is brought before Jesus by the Scribes and the Pharisees. They are totally focused on punishing the woman according to the Law of Moses, which is stoning her to death. Follow the law; kill the woman; case closed; end of story.

Jesus was saying, not so fast. He must have been thinking about all aspects of this incident. So he sat down and began doodling on the ground. Jesus must have been thinking why they brought only the woman! Where is the man who also was a partner in this crime?

But of course, the Pharisees did not accuse him, because the Law said only the woman should be stoned. It was a patriarchal society where the men made all the laws and the women had no rights. Jesus must have been thinking about the cruelty and injustice of that law.

Jesus also thought about the need for compassion rather than the need to punish. Jesus must have thought about the experiences in her life that led this woman into adultery: Was it abuse at home? Was it for survival? Or, did the man force her into it?

While the accusers focused their attention solely on the accused, Jesus looked at the accusers; their self righteousness, their lack of compassion, their tendency to follow the law at the expense of human kindness. That is why Jesus said: "Let the one without sin among you throw the first stone."

Examine the way Jesus deals with this situation. He does not give a direct, cut and dry answer to their question. He does not say, stone her to death or don't stone her to death. These are the two choices they thought they had. And depending on his answer, they could trap him.

If Jesus had said: "don't stone her," they could accuse him of not following the law; if he told them to stone her, they could accuse him of being not compassionate. They could only think in terms of "either, or," "black and white." Their minds could not handle ambiguities or different possibilities and viewpoints at the same time.

Jesus has a different mindset. He thinks about all the sides of an issue. His mind can handle a variety of options and possibilities. He wants them to come up with an answer. He challenges the Pharisees to probe their conscience, examine their motives, reflect upon their attitude, and reassess their behavior.

And look at the transformation that occurred: no arguments, no discussion, no debate, no trial, no cross-examination; nothing; the crowd just left, one by one.

I am sure Jesus helped them explore the situation from all angles, not just from the angle of the Law, and they were forced to see the big picture, and when they did, they could not stone the woman. Even a strict law written in the Scriptures was superseded by other considerations.

When the big picture was taken into account, an emotionally charged situation was diffused, a tragedy was averted, a life was saved, and hearts were transformed.

This is what happens every time, when we see the big picture of a situation. **Think of all the situations in your life when relationships were strained, tables were pounded, names were called, blood pressure rose, prejudice was felt, arrogance was displayed, tragedy took place, pain was caused, and you will see that narrow mindedness, or your inability or unwillingness to see the big picture, was the problem.**

So, the next time you have to deal with an issue, make a choice, give an opinion, or take action, spend a few quiet moments in prayer, and try to see all sides of the issue; see the big picture; when you do that, you will be putting on the mind of Christ. As apostle Paul says: "Let the same mind be in you that was in Christ Jesus."

# 13. Has Jesus Touched You?

Luke: 7:11-18

*Then he went up and touched the coffin, and those carrying it stood still. He said "Young man, I say to you, get up." The dead man sat up and began to talk, and Jesus gave him back to his mother. They were all filled with awe and praised God. "God has come to help his people".*

As most of you know, I have a day job as a hospice chaplain and I deal with death and dying on a regular basis. When I am "on call" during the night, I could be dealing with multiple deaths on the same night. Few weeks ago, I was on call from 8 PM to 8 AM, on a Sunday night and I was called out to attend three deaths during that period. The first one, forty year old woman with breast cancer, and the second one was a 55 year old man with throat cancer.

Walking into a home where someone has just died, regardless of his age or diagnosis, is always an emotional experience. The body will be in one of the bedrooms, and sometimes in the living room; there will be family, friends and neighbors milling around, crying, sobbing, talking, and sometimes drinking. In one family almost everyone including women had a beer in their hand. I think that was their way of coping with the loss.

The third death I attended that night was the hardest. It was a young boy who was few days away from his 18th birthday. He had brain tumor. The tumor grew so much in his head that his right eye was pushed out and he had a patch on his eye socket. It was a Haitian family and there were a lot of people in and around the house. Cars parked all over the streets, people wailing and weeping all around. He was the oldest of five children.

The mother of this boy was literally clinging to her son's lifeless body. Four men had to pluck her away from the bed because she was fiercely holding on to the body. The father had to be restrained. The siblings and cousins were weeping. It was a very emotionally draining and painful scene.

I have a gift for wild imagination. During situations like these, my imagination goes on overdrive. While I was witnessing the pain, and the loss and the crying and the weeping of the mother and family members of this young man, I wished, hoped and prayed that I could just walk up to the bed and touch the boy, and he would wake up and sit on his bed.

What a wonderful scene that would be! I don't want that miracle for my fame or glory, but just to take away the pain and suffering of the grieving family. In many other situations, I have imagined that, but obviously it has never happened.

It is like my fantasy to go the Hollywood Beach on a Sunday morning and walk on the water in front of the beach goers. Obviously all the people on the beach would come around to watch that miracle and then I could tell them about the importance of attending church on a Sunday morning.  I wish I could show them the power of Christ, but no such luck.

When I read the story in today's gospel, Jesus raising a widow's son, my experience at the death of this young Haitian boy came to my mind. According to the gospel story, Jesus was going through a town called Naim, and he saw a funeral procession. The only son of a widow in town had died. And the gospel says, "The Lord was moved with pity and told the woman not to cry."

And then he stepped forward and touched the coffin and the pallbearers stood still. And Jesus said to the young man, "I tell you get up" and the dead man sat up in his coffin and began to speak. We have no idea what he said, but I leave it to your imagination to figure out what this young man must have said, sitting in a coffin, surrounded by people.

Anyway, according to the story, "fear seized them and they began to praise God. And they said: "A great prophet has arisen among us, God has visited his people."

What is the meaning of this miracle story for us today in the 21st century, in Hollywood, Florida? Once we were discussing this story in a bible class and one of the participants asked: "Why did this raising of the dead happen only thrice in history?"

He was referring to the three miracles of Jesus raising the dead. The first one is the most famous, the raising of Lazarus, the second one is the raising of Jairus' daughter which is recorded in Mark, Mathew and Luke, and the raising of the widow's son that I just read. Why did it happen two thousand years ago, when Jesus was around but why not now?

We may have to say that it never happened, as some bible scholars think. Or we have to admit that Jesus is not alive today, because if he were, why doesn't he raise dead people, especially the young ones? These are wrong questions. That kind of thinking takes us away from the message of the story.

Last week I was attending the death of a 75 year old man. After I did the initial prayers, and hugging family members and offering condolences, there was a lot of time, waiting for the funeral home to arrive to pick up the body. So this widow and I struck up a conversation. She said: "We had a wonderful marriage, he never said a bad word to me, we always got along and now God took him, and I am alone and it is not fair." And then she popped this 64 million dollar question:

"Why do people have to die?" I have heard that question too many times. I wanted to immediately ask her a question: "Why do babies have to be born? Or "Why the sun has to set?" But I didn't, because that is being insensitive. But during our conversation, I made her realize that death is part of life; that without death, there is no life either.

If you want life, you have to embrace death, because it comes in a package, you cannot have one without the other. The fact of the matter is that about five hundred thousand people die in the world every day, and about the same number are born daily. All of us will die one day and Jesus is not going to bring us back to physical life after we die, like he did it for this young man in today's story.

So this story has to have another meaning. What does it mean? It is a spiritual meaning. To understand its meaning, I want you to focus on two sentences in the story: First, "Then Jesus stepped forward and touched the coffin." Jesus touched. The second sentence is v.16. "God has visited his people." When Jesus touched the coffin, everything changed; the young man came alive; and then the people felt as if God has visited them.

If Jesus touches our hearts and God visits our lives, we will come alive. Today, there are lot of "dead people" in the world. They are physically alive, breathing through their nose, their hearts are beating, and blood is flowing through their veins, but they are spiritually dead. It is like the movie, Dead Man Walking. They are spiritually dead, because they lack love, compassion, joy, peace, patience, kindness and goodness in their lives.

**Ask yourselves: "Has Jesus touched my heart and has God visited my life?"** How does Jesus touching my heart, make me different? How does being a part of a church make me different? In other words, what is the sign that God has touched your life?

These are important questions. If we have no answer to these questions, we should be troubled by that fact. After all, Jesus said that he came that we may have life, and have it abundantly. He did not say that he came so that people could have more 'stuff.' The abundant life that Jesus promised us is not a matter of having, but being. **How is your life fuller, richer, joyful and peaceful because Jesus has touched you and God has visited your life**?

When God visits your life, he leaves traces. There is no way your life will be visited by God and the terrain of your life will be left unchanged. It never happens, and I will show you so many examples from the bible. When I say this, I am reminded of my office at home.

I have a room at home used as an office. There is a computer in there. Four of us including my youngest son, Tommy, use the computer. I know when my son has visited the office, because he leaves traces: his socks will be under the table, his iPod will be hooked up to the computer, and there will be potato chips on the floor. When my son visits the computer room, he leaves traces. I know Tommy has been here.

When God visited Abraham he changed his name from Abram to Abraham and blessed him with a son in his old age. When God visited Mary, that young girl was totally transformed to become the mother of God. When God visited Saul on the way to Damascus, Saul was converted from a persecutor of Christianity to a preacher of Christianity and he became St. Paul.

When God visited Peter in jail, he was set free from bondage. When God visited the home of Zacheus, a tax collector who was considered a sinner, was transformed into a generous and outgoing man, and he probably became a follower of Jesus.

**Has God visited your life? Has he left traces of that visit in your life?**

Jesus came to make a difference. He came to make a difference in our individual lives and he calls us together as a church to make a difference in the world. We use a variety of words to name the difference he makes: hope, love, peace, community, kindness, support, compassion, and the list goes on and on.

Jesus, who raised the widow's son 2000 years ago, is waiting to touch our hearts and visit our lives. Are we ready to be touched by Christ? Notice that, in the story, when Jesus touched the coffin, the pall bearers stood still. If we let Jesus touch our lives, our lives will be much calmer and serene and peaceful, as opposed to being anxious, worried, distracted and disturbed.

We have to slow down from the fast pace of life, stop, be still and spend time in prayer and meditation and allow Jesus to touch us. And when Jesus touches us and God visits us, our lives will be transformed.

# 14. Keep Jesus Awake

Mark: 4:35-40

*He got up, rebuked the wind and said to the waves, "Quiet! Be still! Then the wind died down and it was completely calm. He said to his disciples, "Why are you so afraid? Do you still have no faith?"*

There are only two emotions in life: fear and love. All other emotions are derived from these two. Today I would like to talk about fear and next week about love because of Valentine's Day.

But first a story: Once a robber broke into a house and began ransacking it. When he reached the bedroom, a couple sleeping there, woke up frightened. He drew the gun and said: "I am going to shoot you, but before I do that I want to find out your names." First to the woman, "What is your name? "Elizabeth." "That is my mother's name, I can't kill you." To the man, "what is your name?" Trembling, he said: "My name is Philip, but everybody calls me Elizabeth."

Fear can make us do funny things. As Dan Quayle once said, "Fear is a scary thing." We all have our fears. (*Ask audience about their fears*)

According to psychologists, the top ten fears are: Arachnophobia (fear of spiders), sociophobia (social situations), aerophobia (flying), agoraphobia (of open spaces), claustrophobia (confined places), emetophobia (vomiting), acrophobia (heights), cancer phobia (cancer), brontophobia (thunder and lightning), and necrophilia (fear of death).

There may be other fears you may be dealing with, such as fear about the future of this church for example.

There are physical or external fears such as fear of spiders, snakes, and psychological fears. Physical fears are easy to deal with, for example, if you are afraid of dogs, stay away from them. But psychological fears can be paralyzing.

Some of the famous people of the Bible were fearful people. Take for example the story of Abraham in the 12th chapter of Genesis where he was asked by God to leave his father's house and go to a land that God would show him. And there was this promise: "I will make you a great nation, and I will bless you; I will make your name great so that you will be a blessing." During this journey, Abraham had to pass through Egypt.

When he was about to enter Egypt, he told his wife Sara: "I know you are a beautiful woman. When the Egyptians see you, they will say: 'She is his wife.' Then they will kill me, and take you. Therefore, please say, you are my sister, '*so that it will go well with me on your account and my life may be spared.*'

This is one of the biggest acts of selfishness, cowardice and lie in the Bible. As you know, fear and lying always go together. When you are afraid, you lie. Children do this all the time.

Even though Abraham was chosen by God to be the father of a nation, even though he had special blessings on him, he was a fearful man, because his faith was not strong enough at that point.

Now let us look in the New Testament. The disciples are great examples of fearful people. When Jesus was arrested, they all fled in fear. Peter sneaked into the courtyard of the high priest, and sat near a fireside. The gospel of Luke says: "A servant girl saw him sitting in the light of the fire; she gazed at him intently and said: 'This man was with him.' But Peter denied by saying: "Woman, I do not know him."

A little later, someone else saw him and said: "You also are one of them", But Peter said: "No sir, not I". An hour later another spoke more insistently: "This man was certainly with him, because he is a Galilean" and Peter said: "My friend, I don't know what you are talking about."

What do you think is going on here? Peter, who was supposed to be the leader of the pack, was shivering in his pants. He was deathly afraid. He lied three times, denying Jesus, because he was filled with fear. We have another incident, in the gospel of John where the disciples locked themselves in a room "for fear of the Jews."

So, we know that the disciples of Jesus did not have a great record on bravery. And we see that clearly in the gospel story I read today. Let us examine it closely.

It was late in the day, Jesus was with the crowd and he wanted to go the other side of the lake to have some quiet time and they got into a boat.

Now for those of you who have never been on a boat, it may be hard to imagine. We are not talking about the Carnival Cruise Line's "Fantasy of the Seas" or Royal Caribbean's "Ocean_Princess" which can take 2000+ passengers in comfort. It is small boat, more like a big canoe, which can carry ten to fifteen people.

I have been on one them; it can be a scary feeling even when the water is calm because you can feel every movement. If there is a storm, or a squall, forget it, you could tip over, and that is exactly what seems to have been happening.

There was a huge squall and the boat began to shake and the waves were breaking over the boat and the disciples were terrified and shaking with fear. And Jesus, in the midst of all this chaos, was sound asleep on the stern on a cushion. Nothing bothers him.

The story says, "They finally woke him up" which means that for a while they thought they could handle it themselves, but when they realized that they could not rely on their power, they woke him up. He awoke, rebuked the wind and said to the sea: "Be quiet, be still;" the wind fell off and everything was calm. Then he turned to the disciples and asked them: "Why are you so terrified? Why are you so lacking in faith?"

The gospel says that "they took him with them." It does not say, Jesus took the disciples with him. They had him *with them*, and at the beginning of the journey, I am sure, Jesus was awake for a while, and there were no problems, things were quiet, and it was smooth sailing. And then Jesus fell asleep.

When they took the focus away from him or forgot that Jesus was with them, they saw trouble. They focused on the waves around them, and they were terrified. This is a great analogy for our life.

Our life is like a small boat in this vast ocean called life: The problems in life, such as pain, suffering, fears, anxieties, illness, frustrations and hopelessness are waves and squalls that send us on a roller-coaster ride through life, and sometimes it feels like our boat is going to turn over and we are going to drown.

All of us have experienced situations like these and most probably, like the disciples, we have tried to face them by ourselves, using all the skills we have, and most likely, it was a difficult ride.

We proclaim Jesus as our Lord and believe in him. Theoretically, that is true. But on a practical level, it may not be true. When we were baptized, we were baptized into Jesus, when we take communion every week, we take Jesus into our hearts, **but it seems like Jesus is sleeping in the boat of our lives, most of the time.** If Jesus is awake, the boat of our life should be steady.

So, the best way to have a smooth navigation through the sea of life is to keep Jesus awake in our lives and the way to do it, is to be quiet, be still. Every day, find some time to be quiet with God, stop all the busyness of life, all the activities of life and be still. Practice the art of contemplative prayer or meditation, just thirty minutes a day and your life will calm down.

Try to keep Jesus awake in your life this week!

# 15. Believing as Behaving

Mathew: 7:21-29

*Not everyone who says to me, 'Lord, Lord' will enter the kingdom of heaven, but only he who does the will of my Father who is in heaven. Many will say to me on that day, "Lord, Lord, did we not prophesy in your name and drive out demons and perform many miracles? Then I will tell them plainly, "I never knew you, away from me, you evildoers.*

When you hear the word 'belief' what comes to your mind? You believe in God, you believe that Jesus is the son of God; you believe that Jesus rose from the dead; you believe that the Bible is the word of God, etc. Believing is mostly understood as an intellectual exercise.

The other day I walked into a house to visit a patient. The first thing the care giver asked me was: "Are you a believer?" She was a staunch Baptist, and she wanted to make sure that I believed what she believed. There are patients, mostly Jehovah's witnesses, who have refused prayers from me because our beliefs are different.

Two years ago, at the local church where I am a member, we had some problems based on who believed what. There was a group of Elders who were very conservative. They did not take kindly to some of my views and beliefs about theology and the Bible. So one of them took me aside, sat me down and said: "I want to ask you this straight:

"Do you believe in the resurrection? Do you believe that the Bible is the true word of God? Do you believe that Christians have a better chance of going to heaven? I said "yes" to all of these, because I did not want to argue with that person, because we believe the same truths, but understand and interpret them differently.

What is funny about this line of questioning is that the Elder thought that what we believe is the most important thing; that believing is an intellectual exercise. She is not alone in this. As a matter of fact, majority of people in all religions think that believing is more important than anything else, and that it is an intellectual ascent to a set of truths.

Look at the Apostle's Creed. There are 12 affirmations in it. It contains the belief system of the Church. "I believe in God the father almighty, I believe in Jesus Christ his only son, I believe that he was crucified, died and was buried... a long list of 12 affirmations. Unless you study them, and are able to recite them, you are not considered a good Catholic.

Look at the history of the early Church. The reason for the first division in the Church, between the East and the West was a fight over the Holy Spirit. One group said the Holy Spirit emanated from both the Father and the Son, while another group said that the Holy Spirit emanated from the Son only, and they divided into two groups, which later became two Churches, the Western Church and the Eastern Church.

In the fifteenth century, the main reason for the breakup of the Church, that began with Martin Luther in Germany, which gave birth to Protestantism, was the 95 Theses he posted on a church wall. He began by challenging the practice of selling indulgences. It was the belief that if you said certain number of 'Our Fathers' and 'Hail Marys,' the same number of souls would go from purgatory to heaven.

There was a huge argument about what happens to the elements of bread and wine when the words of institution are uttered by the priest. Catholics call it "transubstantiation," and Protestants believe it is only "trans-signification." Transubstantiation is based on the Aristotelian theory of substance and accidents. So when the words are said, the substance of the bread and wine are changed into the body and blood of Christ, while their accidental qualities remain.

That is why there are tabernacles in Catholic churches, where they keep the hosts that are left over after communion. They worship that host in a monstrance and it is called adoration of the Blessed Sacrament.

Few years ago, I had a book study group at my house. The meetings began with a prayer. The person, who said the prayer one day, began the prayer by saying: "God our mother," instead of the usual, "God our father." This person referred to God as a "She" instead of a "He," and it caused a huge problem for one of the participants. He was offended that God was called a mother. He believed that God was male. He argued with the group, went to the pastor and demanded that the group be banned, just based on his belief.

If you look at the different religions in the world, it is beliefs that set them apart. Christians believe in Jesus, Hindus believe in Krishna, Moslems believe in Allah and Buddhists don't believe in a personal God. Moslem terrorists believe that if they kill an infidel they would go straight to heaven to be greeted by 72 virgins.

Christians believe that if you do that, you will go straight to hell. If you live a lukewarm life, you will go to purgatory, and if you are a child who dies before baptism, you will go to a dark place called limbo. Hindus believe that after death, you are re-incarnated, but Christians believe that there is only one life to live and at the end of it, is either heaven or hell.

It is the difference in beliefs that cause all the problems in the world. It is at the root of all the religious animosity and fighting. **On the**

**level of beliefs, religions are very different. But on the level of behavior, they are all the same.**

Every religion talks about Love. Loving God with all your heart and loving your neighbor as yourself is the essence of Christianity. The golden rule, "do unto others, what you want them to do to you," is the essence of Judaism. The five pillars of Islam, faith in Allah, praying five times a day, giving alms, fasting during Ramadan and making a pilgrimage to Mecca, are behaviors, not beliefs. The Essence of Hinduism can be summarized in one word: *Dharma*, doing one's duty: i.e. behaving properly in the world, not believing in some truths.

**Jesus knew that he could not monitor people's beliefs and that is why he did not focus on them. He was interested in changing behaviors, not beliefs**. That is why Jesus never asked his followers to believe in him, but he asked them to follow him. Following is a behavior.

When he saw Peter and his Brother John fishing, he did not tell them to believe in his teachings. He asked them to follow him; when he called Mathew the tax collector, he did not discuss his teachings with him and asked if he believed in them. Instead Jesus said: "Follow me."

You might say, but sometimes Jesus asked people whether they believed in him: But you have to always remember, that Jesus was not asking them to believe in certain truths, or statements or facts. He was asking them to believe in his Person. Let us look at a few:

In John 9: 35, we have the story of the blind man. Jesus asked him if he believed in the Son of Man. "Who is he, sir? The man asked: "Tell me so that I may believe in him." Jesus said: "You have now seen him; in fact, he is the one speaking to you." Then the man said: "Lord, I believe" and he worshiped him.

In John, 6: 68, when many followers left him, Jesus asked his disciples if they too wanted to leave, and Simon Peter answered: "Lord, to whom shall we go: you have the words of eternal life. We believe that you are the Holy One of God."

Yes, Jesus asked his followers to believe in HIM; believing in Jesus is following Jesus. In the Bible,"belief" is a personal commitment to Jesus, to behave like Jesus, to commit one's allegiance, loyalty and love for Jesus: For Jesus, belief and behavior are the same.

That is why, in today's reading we hear Jesus say: "None of those who cry out Lord, Lord will enter the Kingdom of Heaven, but only the ones who does the will of my father." He is talking about behaving, not just repeating formulas or prayers.

"Anyone who hears my words and puts them into practice is like the wise man who built his house on the rock." Jesus does not say any one who hears my words and believe in them. If you just intellectually believe in his words, you will be like foolish men who built their house on sand.

So, I invite you to change the template of your consciousness. Believing is not assenting to certain teachings of the Church, or a set of statements like God exists, that the Bible is the word of God, that Jesus is the son of God that he was born of a virgin, that he will come again, etc. Believing is actually behaving like Jesus.

If you are in a bible study group and you hear someone say things that don't make any sense to you, don't make a big deal out of it. Focus on the behavior of the person saying those things you disagree with. If his or her behavior is full of love and compassion, he is actually a believer in the biblical sense.

**The tragedy today is that we have too many believers and too few followers;** that people have separated their beliefs from their behaviors. If you listen to TV evangelists, you will see that they are great believers, but their behavior don't match the example of Jesus.

Jerry Falwell, one of the so called believers of our time, once said: "You've got to kill the terrorists before they kill us. If it takes ten years, blow them all away in the name of the Lord." **Kill in the name of a Lord who said: "Love your enemies!"**

A senator had introduced a bill in the Florida legislature this year to have a specialty license plate with the words, I BELIEVE with a cross and a stained glass window as background.

Placing an "I Believe" tag on your car does not make you a believer; reciting the creed does not make you a Christian; attending church does not necessarily make you a disciple; baptism does not guarantee salvation.

**When we start behaving like Jesus, we will become believers.**

# 16. Worshipping as Listening

Luke: 9:28-36

*While he was speaking, a cloud appeared and enveloped them, and they were afraid as they entered the cloud. A voice came from the cloud saying, "This is my Son, whom I have chosen; listen to him.*

One Sunday morning, a pastor spotted a young boy gazing intensely at a large plaque that hung in the church foyer. The plaque was covered with names, and small American flags adorned each side of it. After observing him for a few moments, the pastor walked over to the boy and said: "Good morning, Tim."

"Good morning, Reverend" said the boy, still focused on the plaque. "What exactly is this: what do all those names mean? "Well Tim," explained the pastor, "It is a memorial to all the young men and women who died in the service."

The young boy nodded silently and asked the pastor: "Which service, 9.45 or the 10.30?"

We don't have such confusion. We know that service in the context of the church means worship service. There are millions of church services around the world, every Sunday. Worship service is the central act of the Church. Worship is number one among all the activities of the Church. It is the only activity that all the members participate, unlike other activities such as bible study, choir, men's group women's group etc. which only some people participate.

Every church has a worship committee that carefully plans and puts together the service each week. Cheryl, the church secretary, does a good job; she makes sure that I send her the sermon topic by Wednesday, and prepares the bulletin with the order of service, announcements, prayer requests etc. It is a huge deal.

Congregations everywhere have done it for nearly two thousand years; we have worshipped all our lives that we don't really think about it. Today, as part of our series on understanding the mind of Christ, I like you to join me in reflecting on the real meaning of worship.

**These are some of the questions I want you to think about. Did Jesus worship? Did he want us to worship him? How does he want us to worship? What is the purpose of worship?**

Answers from the gospels might surprise you. But I like you to listen carefully, till the end.

During the time of Jesus, Jerusalem temple was the center of Jewish life. It was the most sacred place on earth. Every devout Jew went to the temple, participated in services, and paid the temple priest to offer sacrifices on their behalf on special occasions.

Did Jesus go the temple? According to the gospels, Jesus went to the temple only twice. He did not go there to worship or offer any sacrifice.

The first time he went, he was only 12 years old, according to Luke. Luke is the only one who records this incident. This is the time during the Passover when the whole family went to temple, and Jesus stayed back. Mary thought he was with Joseph and Joseph thought he was with Mary. In those days, men and women traveled separate. They did not go in the same car; of course they had no car.

When they finally found him, he was not worshiping in the temple. He was sitting in the midst of teachers, listening to them and asking them questions.

The second time we see Jesus in the temple is towards the end of his life. Here again, he was not worshiping or offering sacrifice. It was again during the Passover and the temple was filled with people, pilgrims from all over the world, coming to offer sacrifices. What does Jesus do?

He gets mad. He makes a whip of chords and drives out the oxen and the sheep out of the temple area and knocks down the tables of money changers. He yells at them: "Get them out of here, stop turning my Father's house into a market place."

This is the last straw that broke the back of the camel. The Jewish authorities were not happy with the teachings of Jesus, but this incident was on the top. He was challenging the temple worship and sacrifice. He was telling them that going there once a year and sacrificing animals was not the kind of sacrifice God was looking for.

He was telling them that his God is a loving father who does not need animal sacrifice. He was telling them that God is not a blood thirsty tyrant somewhere in the clouds, who needs these animals to be slaughtered so that he can be pleased.

It was a direct challenge to the religious authorities. It was a threat to the kind of God they worshiped. They could not understand that or handle that. And that is why they crucified him.

**Jesus was not a pious Jew, who went to the temple to do traditional worship and offer sacrifice. If he were, he would never have been crucified.**

Now to the second question: Did Jesus want to be worshiped? If you really study the four gospels, the answer is no. Jesus never asked his disciples to worship him. **There are numerous scenes in the gospels, where Jesus asked his disciples to follow him; there is no incident where he asked them to worship him.** As a matter of fact, there is an incident where he told them not to worship him and that is where today's reading comes into focus: The story of transfiguration on Mount Tabor. I had the privilege of being on the top of mount Tabor in 1984. If you go on a tour of the holy land, they will take you to the Church of Transfiguration on that mountain.

Two thousand years ago, something mystifying and magnificent happened on the top of that mountain.

The story says that Jesus took Peter, James and John and went to a mountain to pray. While praying, his face changed in appearance and his clothes became dazzlingly white. What it means is that there was a special glow on his face, and he almost looked like an angel. Then there were two men talking to Jesus.

These are the most prominent figures in Jewish history: Moses and Elijah; Moses is the greatest lawgiver and Elijah is the greatest prophet. It is like the President and the Prime Minister flanking the King. There is nobody above them.

The story says that they appeared in "glory," and glory is a term always associated with God. Luke writes that Peter, James and John fell into a deep sleep. They could not handle that glorious sight. They were dazzled and dumb founded by the experience that they fell into a trance.

When they woke up, the disciples knew that it was the place to be. Something very special has happened here; their master, who they thought was a human being, is really the Son of God. He is the fulfillment of the Law and the Prophets. He is God. So they don't want to leave that mountain top.

They want to stay; they want to pitch three tents. They want to put Jesus, Moses and Elijah in three separate tents, and worship them. Enjoy their presence, be in the light, share in their glory, and have a great spiritual life. What could be more noble, worthwhile and spiritual than being in the presence of God?

If Jesus wanted to be worshiped by his followers, this was the perfect time to make that argument. He was on the top of the mountain, in full divine glory, flanked by the godliest men in history. He could have received and enjoyed their worship forever. But that is not what happened.

What happened is very significant. Luke says that Moses, Jesus and Elijah were overshadowed by the cloud. Now, in the Old Testament, cloud symbolizes the presence of God.

And a voice was heard from the cloud and it was God speaking: "This is my beloved son, my chosen one, listen to him." Examine those words carefully, it says; this is my beloved son, **LISTEN** to him. It does not say, this is my chosen one, *worship* him. If that was the purpose, it would have been the perfect time to let us know that.

**Is it possible that over the years, we are too busy worshiping Jesus, that we have forgotten to listen to him?**

So if the fact is that Jesus never worshiped in the temple and that he did not want to be worshiped by us, what is the point of coming here every Sunday for worship? It is a very legitimate question.

First off, let me say, it is very important that we go to church every Sunday and worship. But also understand the real meaning of worship and how to do it properly.

Here again, Jesus has the answer. Do you remember the scene in John's gospel where Jesus talks with the Samaritan woman at the well? For Jesus, it was not just an occasion to ask for some drinking water. It was a great teaching moment. He taught that woman a lot of things, and where and how to worship, was one of them.

The woman said that Samaritans worshiped on the mountain and Jews worshiped in the Jerusalem temple. Jesus said to her: 'Believe me woman; an hour is coming, when you will worship the father neither on this mountain nor in Jerusalem. The hour is already here, when authentic worshipers will worship the father in spirit and truth, indeed it is such worshipers that the father seeks."

God is Spirit and those who worship him must worship in Spirit and in truth. So, that is the answer. We come **here** to worship God, so that we can worship him **everywhere.** God, who is Spirit, is not confined to these walls. He is everywhere.

**Our eyes that see God here, must see Her everywhere; our ears that listens to God here, must listen to His voice out there; our hearts that are open to God's word here, must open them to the words that come from others out there. Our arms that embrace God's people here, must embrace people in the streets. When you leave this holy ground, prepare your hearts in such a way, that every ground you walk on, will feel, as if it is holy.**

In other words, the worshiping that we do here with bells and whistles is not an end in itself. It is not a program that we participate every Sunday for its own sake. It is a glorious mountaintop experience that should take us down to the valley to LISTEN to HIM, there.

# 17. Is Your Faith Working for You?

Phil: 4: 4-8

*Do not be anxious about anything, but in everything, by prayer and petition, with thanksgiving, present your requests to God. And the peace of God, which transcends all understanding, will guard your hearts and your minds in Christ Jesus.*

It was the height of summer and a fearful drought threatened the crops throughout the land. One hot, dry Sunday, the village pastor told his congregation: "The only thing that will save us is to pray for rain. Go home, pray, believe, and come back next Sunday ready to thank God for the rain he will send."

The people went home, prayed hard, and returned to church the following Sunday. But when the pastor saw them, he was furious. "We can't worship," he raged. "You do not yet believe that God will send us rain, perhaps this very day."

They protested: "We prayed and we do believe." "Believe," he responded. "Then where are your umbrellas?"

All of us are believers; we are baptized Christians; we are members of this church; we come here to worship every Sunday; we read the bible, we are disciples of Christ. The question is, does all that really help us in our daily life?

When you drive behind a slow driver, if your blood pressure goes up and you start getting mad, your faith is not working for you.

If you become sick and the pain becomes insufferable and you become angry with God, you have not understood the meaning of faith. If you are a married person, but you are not being loving to your spouse, your faith is not working for you. You say you are a Christian parent, but if you don't discharge your parental duties, your faith is not working for you.

If you claim to be a disciple, but harbor hateful thoughts about other people, then your faith is not working for you. If you have people in your life who have offended you but you have not fully forgiven them, your faith is not working for you. If you get easily offended by the behaviors of others, and your tolerance level is so low, your faith is not working for you. You say you have deep faith in Christ, but when the rubber meets the road, if you become frazzled, fearful and anxious, and totally fall apart, your faith is not working for you.

If any of this is applicable to you, it is time to take a serious look at your faith. Because, if your faith does not help you navigate the frustrating and difficult areas of your daily life, it is no faith at all. If your faith does not play a serious role in how you feel towards others and how you behave in particular situations, especially the challenging ones, your faith may not be useful. That is why it is so important to ask the question: "Is my faith working for me?"

A colleague of mine was forced to ask this question recently. A nurse on my hospice team had ovarian cancer. Her name was Susan and she died last month at age 52. After she was diagnosed, she had three surgeries and a few chemotherapy treatments. But when her doctor told her that she had only six months to live, she stopped chemo, because she did not want to go through the pain and nausea of extensive chemo therapy.

She signed up for hospice care. As a hospice nurse, she knew exactly what was coming. But she was very brave. She went and bought a new sports car. She said, "I am going to enjoy the days I have left." She went on line and ordered an urn for her ashes; she went to a cemetery in Boca Raton, taking her 18 year old daughter with her, to make funeral arrangements.

This is one of those modern cemeteries where the inside of the crypt is visible from the outside. Unlike the usual ones, where there is just a name and date of birth and death outside, these have glass doors. The size of the slot depends on how big your urn is and what objects of yours you want to display along with the urn. Susan bought a 10x10 inch slot where her ashes would be placed, along with her cell phone, which has been her life line for years, and other personal items.

Susan also wrote her obituary. She did not want her children to have that responsibility. Only one little line was blank on that obituary, the date of her death.

Susan was a very charming woman. I sat next to her during our staff meetings every Wednesday, along with sixteen other team members who are nurses, CNAs, social workers and a doctor. On my first day of work I was sent into the field with Susan. She met me at the Assisted Living Facility she was working. When a patient asked her who I was, she said: "Oh, this is Paul, my new husband."

Susan had a great sense of humor. She is one of the bravest women I have come to know. She was not afraid; a month before death, she told me: "I know I am going to die, there is nothing I can do about it; I have no regrets; I had a good life."

There is one very important piece of information, about Susan that I have not told you yet. Susan was an atheist. She had no faith; she did not think there was a God. She thought God was a man made reality and that heaven was a fantasy land; she did not read any holy books; neither did she say any prayers or attend any temple.

I told you Susan's story to tell you the story of another person on my team who was forced to examine her faith in light of Susan's terminal cancer. Marci is a Nurse's Aide on my team. She is from

Jamaica and a member of a Seventh Day Adventist church. She attends church twice a week: On Wednesdays for bible study, and on Sundays for worship. She also sings in the choir. Basically her every sentence ends with the phrase: "Praise the Lord."

Marci is one of these people who wear their religion in their sleeves. She is very serious about converting the whole world to Christ, because she thinks that non-Christians will not be saved. When she visits Jewish patients, she would turn their TV channel to TBN so that they could hear the word of God. She got into trouble for this from some Jewish families, but Marci is very proud of her religion. I know when Marci is in the building because I know the car she drives. It has a special plate in front which says: "Jesus is Lord."

Two weeks before Susan died, Marci broke down and made a confession to the team: "I am embarrassed to admit this, I am kind of ashamed of myself, but I have to say that I am so afraid of dying. Here I thought that I had so much faith in Jesus, but I am scared of death, and I look at Susan, who has no faith in God, let alone in Jesus, and she is facing her death bravely and calmly. I am ashamed of myself; I say I believe in Jesus, but when it comes to my fear of death, I am not relying on Jesus. My faith is not really helping me to deal with my fears and anxiety."

Marci who was always worried about Susan's soul began taking a second look at her own faith, which she thought was strong, but actually was not. She thanked Susan for helping her re-examine her own faith.

I think there are lot more Marcis in this world than Susans. The Susans are at least honest with themselves, they don't claim to know God; they don't profess their faith in Jesus and they deal with what life brings, in their own way.

Is your faith in Jesus working for you in all areas of your life?

One of the best ways to find out is to check your anxiety level. Are you anxious or worried about anything? There is no shortage of problems out there that can provoke anxiety. There are health problems, money problems, relationship problems, natural disasters, national and international problems, the list goes on. And then there is the ultimate question of facing one's own death.

There will always be problems around us. The question is: "How do you react to them?"

Jesus said: "Let not your hearts be troubled; trust in me and trust in my father?" Do you think about that promise of Jesus when you get anxious? Does that promise of Jesus calm your nerves? Or do you say: "Yes, it is in the Bible, but..."

Or how does this one sound? "Dismiss all anxiety from your minds; present your needs to God in every form of prayer and in petitions full of gratitude. Then God's own peace, which is beyond all understanding, will stand guard over your hearts and minds in Christ Jesus."

I get goose bumps when I read those words of Paul to the Christians in Philippi. Paul is telling us to dismiss all anxiety from our hearts; it doesn't matter what kind of anxiety it is, dismiss them all; don't be paralyzed by fear. Let the Lord take care of you!

Is the peace of God which is beyond all understanding, guarding your hearts and minds in Christ Jesus?

I am sure you have heard the story of a man who thought he had deep faith in God. He fell over a cliff and was clinging dearly to his life, holding on to the branch of a tree. He could see the deep ravine beneath him and he knew that if he fell, he would die.

He began to cry for help and he heard a voice from top: "Do you believe in me?" "Of course I believe in you," said the desperate man. The voice asked again: "Are you sure, you really believe that

I can help you?" "Of course, Lord I believe in you." Then the voice said, "If you really believe that I am God, and that I can save you in this desperate situation, then, let go off the branches."

And the man asked: "Is there anybody else up there?"

**We can claim to have all the faith in the world; but if it does not help us to be calm and peaceful in real life situations, especially during the challenging ones, our faith may not be working for us.**

# 18. Remember Who You Are

Gen: 1: 26-27

*Then God said, "Let us make man in our image, in our likeness, and let them rule over the fish of the sea and birds of the air, over the livestock, over all the earth, and over all creatures that move along the ground." So God created man in his own image, in the image of God he created him, male and female, he created them.*

How many of you have seen the Disney movie, *The Lion King*? It begins with a dedication ceremony for Simba, the baby lion born to the current king, Mufasa and his wife, Serabi. When his father retires, Simba would be heir to the throne. But Mufasa's brother, who is Simba's uncle, Scar, wants to be king too. So he looked for a chance to eliminate young Simba from the scene.

One day, he tricked Simba by taking him to a place where he would be attacked by Hyenas. When the attack happened, his father, Mufasa, fought off the Hyenas, but he was killed there by being pushed off the cliff by Scar. Simba was heartbroken and traumatized, witnessing his father's death.

Scar convinced Simba that his father's death was Simba's fault. Young Simba began to cry. To avoid shame and guilt, and as penance for his mistake, Scar told Simba to run away. "Run away and never come back."

While Young Simba ran, Scar gave orders to the Hyenas to kill him. But Simba ran fast, the Hyenas gave up, and Simba ended up in a place outside the kingdom. There he met two friends, a warthog named Pumba, and a meerkat called Timon. He grew up with them. Even though he was a lion, he didn't act like one; he was timid and quiet, and began to eat bugs and vegetables like his two friends.

Years passed when the spiritual master from his old kingdom, Rafiki, the guy who had done the dedication ceremony, realized that Simba was still alive. He located Simba and asked him to return and take his place as king, in a kingdom which was deteriorating under Scar's rule.

Simba said he did not want to do that. He did not believe he could do that, because even though he looked like a lion, he did not feel like one, or act like one. He did not have the self esteem or the courage to fight and defeat his uncle Scar and take the kingdom back. He began to sulk and feel sorry for himself. **He had forgotten who he really was.**

At that time, Rafiki hit Simba hard on his head and asked: "Are you crazy?" You are born to be king and you are acting like a coward? What is wrong with you? He took him to a lake and asked him to look into the water. When he looked, Simba found his own image reflected in the water, and then his father's. At that time, he heard his deceased father's voice:

"*Simba, you have forgotten who you are; you are more than what you have become.*

*Remember who you are.... Remember you are my son, the one true king..... Remember!"*

When he remembered who he really was, he returned to his kingdom, defeated his uncle who was illegally occupying the throne, recaptured the land, and restored the kingdom. It is a beautiful and inspiring story of self realization and self discovery.

When I first saw that movie, I thought that the young Simba, who was exiled from his kingdom, is a paradigm for us human beings, who are also exiled from our true identity. Two things have happened to us spiritually: First, we are not told who we really are. Secondly, even if we have been told, we have forgotten.

**When I was growing up, I never heard from the priests or religion teachers that I had the image of God within me,** even though it says in bold letters in Gen. 1: 27: "God created man in his image; in the divine image he created him, male and female he created them."

This verse was never emphasized. Instead, I was taught about the fall. That Eve ate the wrong fruit, and gave it to Adam and that they disobeyed God. So, they were thrown out of the Garden of Eden, cursed by God, and the rest of their lives was a punishment. Every person born after that shares in the sin of Adam and Eve.

**The central theme of Christianity has been sin and evil. In sermons and classes, we have heard more about hell than about heaven, more about the devil than about God**. Man has been always pictured as a miserable sinner.

This idea came from the theology of Original Sin developed by St. Augustine, and that idea has stuck with the Church for centuries.

Matthew Fox, in his book *Original Blessing*, says: "There is no question whatsoever in my mind that among those who call themselves Christians, 99% know about original sin, and barely one percent have ever in their lives heard about original blessing."

Herbert Haag, former president of the Catholic Bible Association of Germany and author of *Is Original Sin in Scripture,* writes: "Original sin is not found in any of the writings of the Old Testament." He goes on: "The idea that Adam's descendants are automatically sinners because of the sin of their ancestors is foreign to holy scripture."

We enter a broken, torn and sinful world; no doubt about that. But we do not enter this world as sinful creatures. We burst into this world as "original blessings." Anyone who has joyfully brought children into this world knows this.

I remember being in the delivery room at Coral Springs Medical Center for the birth of my two sons. It was one of the most awesome and spiritual moments of my life. No sane person can look at an innocent baby and call him a sinner. **Sin is a choice we make, not something that we are born with.**

Children have no sin, original or otherwise, and that is why Jesus made children the primary inheritors of the kingdom: "Unless you become like little children, you will not enter the kingdom of heaven." If they were born with sin, Jesus would not have said that. Jesus did not say that they would enter the kingdom after they are removed of their original sin.

So the Church made up the theory of original sin and made baptism a requirement to remove that sin. That is the beginning of infant baptism in the Catholic Church. In olden times, seven days after the baby was born, he was baptized, for fear that if he died, at least his soul was saved.

It was too cruel to send infants who died without baptism to hell; so the Church invented a middle place between Heaven and Hell, and called it Limbo. Last year, the Pope removed Limbo as a place of punishment for children.

According to professor Haag, "No man enters the world a sinner. As the creature and image of God, he is from his first hour surrounded by God's fatherly love. Consequently, he is not at birth a sinner as is often maintained, an enemy of God and a child of God's wrath. A man becomes a sinner only through his own individual and responsible action."

Imagine that you are the parent of a small child. You tell that child every day that he or she is a "wretched sinner." "You are hopelessly lost." "You are incapable of doing anything about your destiny."

"You are lazy and ugly. "You will never amount to anything." Would that create a healthy adult? Obviously not.

Yet, that is the message people have mostly heard from their pulpits, in their prayers, and in their hymns. The hymn "Amazing Grace", thanks God for saving a "wretch like me."

According to a Hindu legend, there was a time when all men were gods, but they so abused their divinity that Brahman, the chief God, decided to take it away from men, and hide it where they would never again find it. Where to hide it became a big issue.

When the lesser gods were called in council to consider this issue, they said: "We will bury man's divinity deep in the earth," but Brahman said: "No, that will not do, for man will dig deep down into the earth and find it."

Then they said: "Well, we will sink his divinity into the deepest ocean." But again Brahman replied: "No, not there, for man will learn to dive into the deepest waters, will search out the ocean bed, and will find it."

Then the lesser gods said, "We will take it to the top of the highest mountain and hide it there." But again, Brahman ruled that out, for man will eventually climb every mountain on earth. He will sure find it someday."

Then the lesser gods gave up and concluded, "We do not know where to hide it, for it seems there is no place on earth or in the sea that man will not eventually reach."

Then Brahman said: "Here is what we will do with man's divinity; we will hide it deep down within man himself; he will never think of looking for it there."

Ever since then, the legend concludes **"man has been going up and down the earth, making pilgrimages, visiting holy places, asking**

**teachers and preachers, desperately seeking for something that is already within himself."**

Two thousand years ago, a man named Jesus found it and shared that secret with us. To his bewildered disciples who were looking for the kingdom here and there and everywhere, looking for miraculous signs of the Kingdom, Jesus said, "The kingdom of God is within you."

Unfortunately, many people still don't believe that. **Unfortunately, in the religion that sprang up in Jesus' name, the divinity of man has been the best kept secret of the ages.**

Today, I invite you remember that truth: that you are created in the image and likeness of God. When young Simba of the *Lion King*, remembered that he was in fact a lion inside, everything changed for him. He became aware of his true identity, realized his potential, restored his dignity and, reclaimed the kingdom for himself and for the service of his fellow animals.

When you truly believe, beyond a reasonable doubt that you are created in the image and likeness of God, and start behaving based on that belief, you will start seeing magnificent changes in your life. You will be transformed into a godly person, and when you act like a 'godly person,' everything around you will change.

# 19. Namaste!

1Jn: 2:7-11

*Whoever loves his brother lives in the light and there is nothing in him to make him stumble. But whoever hates his brother is in the darkness and walks around in the darkness; he does not know where he is going, because the darkness has blinded him.*

A rabbi once asked his students: "What is the exact moment when darkness ends and light begins?" One student said: "When you can see an animal at a distance and tell whether it is a sheep or a dog." "No," said the rabbi. Another said: "It is when you look at a tree at a distance and tell whether it is a fig tree or a peach tree."

"No", said the rabbi again. "Then what is it," the students asked: "***It is when you can look on the face of anyone and recognize him or her as your brother or sister; if you cannot, you are still in darkness."***

That is what John says in today's reading. Anyone who claims to be in the light but hates his brother is still in darkness; he does not know where he is going, because the darkness blinds him.

Existentialist philosopher, Fredrick Nietze, was once asked about hell and he said, "Hell is other people." The expressions we use when we are upset with people, "the hell with them" or "go to hell," come from that definition.

What is your view of other people? Your neighbors, your colleagues, people you see on the streets or in the shopping malls; people of different color, people with different sexual orientations, people of the opposite sex, people from other religions, people from other countries, people with disabilities.

Surveys show that we don't have favorable opinions about other people. Racism, sexism and homophobia are alive and well today. Let me give you some examples. One of the questions that are often asked during this election season is "Is America ready for a black president?" Racism is implied in that question.

Forty years after Martin Luther King's speech where he dreamt of a nation where his children will be judged by the content of their character rather than the color of their skin, why is that question asked? Every time I hear that question, I cringe because it is literally, a peripheral question asked by people whose level of consciousness is only skin deep. **Selecting a president, based on his pigmentation is like children selecting M&Ms based on their color.** So racism is alive.

There was a news item last week coming out of the Anglican Church in England that some bishops were going to break away from the Church because the Church decided to ordain female bishops. They feel that females are unworthy to be leaders of the church. So sexism is alive.

The American branch of the Anglican Church is the Episcopal Church. They are having a rift in this country, because of the ordination of Gene Robinson, a bishop in Rhode Island, who is openly gay. Somebody commented, "There are many gay bishops in the Church, but he is the only honest gay bishop." So homophobia is alive.

You remember the story of Matthew Sheppard, a homosexual man who was brutally beaten and tied to a fence to die in Wyoming.

So we have the blacks, who are less than equal, the females who are deficient and the homosexuals who are sinners, and of course the illegal immigrants who always get beaten up because they are not even supposed to be here, to begin with.

Examine your attitude towards all these groups of people; actually, examine your attitude towards all people out there, and sincerely answer to yourself, what you really think of them.

If we really believe that God is the creator of every person in the world, and if we really mean the first words of the Lord's prayer, 'Our Father,' by which we are acknowledging the brotherhood of all people, we have no choice but to love and embrace every human being on this planet regardless of his color, race or sexual orientation.

**Racism, sexism and homophobia should be completely erased from the dictionary of a disciple.**

I know it is so hard to do that. I know we mean well. I know we want to love everybody, but it is so hard, because people irritate us, they challenge us, they go against our expectations, they behave badly, they do a lot of things we just don't like. They don't even fit into the preconceived notions that the Church has taught us about them for centuries. So, I know it is not easy to love everybody.

Let me share with you some insights and truths that have helped me to love everybody.

First of all, we have to get over the illusion that other people are separate from us. It is called the "separation illusion." We mistakenly think that the other person is so different from us. The "other" is not that different at all. As a matter of fact, the other person is different only in the packaging. The other is actually me, in a different package. The other person is actually an extension of my soul. We are both cut from the same cloth. Each of us is a chip of the old block, meaning God. It is not just an opinion; there is science to back it up.

A few months ago, I was watching CNN and there was this story about a National Geographic study called the "Genographic Project." "It is titled: "The Greatest Journey Ever Told: The Trail of Our DNA." New DNA studies have shown that all humans descended from an African ancestor who lived about 60,000 years ago.

Population geneticist, Dr. Spencer Wells who is leading this study said: "The human genetic Code or genome is 99.9 percent identical throughout the world. What is left, .1 percent, is the DNA responsible for our individual differences; the color of our skin, race, etc."

I fell out of my chair when I heard that. I had thought that 50 percent of DNA accounts for our similarities, and 50 percent for our differences. That is what my friends thought. When I told them about this study, their jaws dropped, their eyes popped out, and they said: "You cannot be serious." I told them that I read this in the National Geographic, not the National Inquirer.

I have no intention to prove to you that we are all connected. It is like gravity, whether you agree with it, or not.

The fact of the matter is that we are the same genetically, 99.9 percent. Only .1 percent of our genes account for our differences. All the anger and jealousy is about the .1 percent! All our divisions and acrimony, is about the .1 percent! All our prejudices and fighting, hatred, killings, terrorism and war are about the .1 percent!

Mind boggling, right? It is happening because we are not conscious of our basic identity as human beings and our connectedness to each other.

We often live superficial lives, at the level of our five senses. The world around us is experienced and interpreted using our five senses. However, our senses can be very deceptive. For example, the senses tell us that the earth is flat, but that is not true; our eyes tell us that the sun rises in the east and sets in the west, but we know that the sun neither rises nor sets.

It is the same with our view of people. On the physical level, people look different: different colors, different races and religions, but at the level of the soul, they are all the same, members of one human family, each one intimately connected to the destinies and dreams of the other.

A single mother of four living in Africa looks up at the same stars and moon that shine down on an elderly French man in Paris. A Tibetan monk living in India, a newborn infant in China, and a young couple saying their marriage vows in Indiana all breathe the same air, by the same process.

We have all been hurt and we all have cried.

No matter what our political views, we all love to laugh. Regardless of how much or how little money we have, our hearts pump blood through our bodies in the same way. With all this in common, it is clear we are each individual members of the same family: the human family.

St. John's observation that whoever hates his brother is in the darkness, and walks around in the darkness, is very profound. What is true about darkness is that we cannot see anything. John says that what makes us dark is our dislike for others. That is right, if you don't love other people, you turn dark. When you love others, you turn into light.

So according to John, when you look at another human being, and you don't recognize him or her as your brother or sister, that means you are dark. It is not because he or she is in darkness, but because you are in darkness. In other words, your ability to recognize others as your brothers and sisters has nothing to do with who they are, but has everything to do with who you are.

I think that is very true of life in general. We see the world not as it is, but as who we are. What you see around you is actually a reflection of the light in you.

The other day, I met one of my chaplain colleagues in the hallway of our office. I gave her a hug and told her: "I see grace on your face." And she said: "What you see is a reflection of your grace on me." It was a very humbling experience.

The recognition of divinity in others comes first from remembering who you are. When you remember that you are created in the image and likeness of God, you will recognize that in others too. Like Apostle Paul, you will recognize that others are "temples of the Holy Spirit."

I like to end with the traditional Indian greeting, *Namaste*, which means "I bow to the divinity within you."

Dream of a world in which the divinity within you is always affirmed and the divinity within others is never denied. When we do that, the darkness around us will be removed and we will recognize everyone as our brother and sister.

# 20. We're the Ones We've Been Waiting For

Mathew: 5: 13-17

*You are the salt of the earth. But if the salt loses its saltiness, how can it be made salty again? It is no longer good for anything, except to be thrown out and trampled by men. You are the light of the world. A city on a hill cannot be hidden. Neither do people light a lamp and put it under a bowl. Instead they put it on its stand, and it gives light to everyone in the house. In the same way, let your light shine before men, that they may see your good deeds and praise your Father in heaven.*

In our reflections on the three "R"s of discipleship, today, I would like to talk about the third R which is "Revealing the Christ within you". The first was 'Remembering' who you are and the second was, 'Recognizing' who others are.

If we have to reveal Jesus to the world, the logical question is where is Jesus now? Is he a statue we have to unveil? Is he hiding in churches? Or is he hiding in the Bible? Some say, Jesus is in heaven, sitting at the right hand of God. I don't think any of these answers are true. **I think that Jesus is hiding in plain sight; Jesus is hiding in you... and in you... and in me**. We have to reveal him to the world, and if we don't, Jesus will not be revealed.

There is a story about what happened after Jesus ascended to heaven. As we know, after three years of ministry of teaching, preaching and bearing witness to the Kingdom of God, Jesus died and was buried and rose again and ascended into heaven. When he reached there,

God the Father asked Jesus: "What about all the good work you did in the world? Who will continue that?

Now that you are here, don't you think all that will fall apart?"

And Jesus said: "I have selected a group of people and entrusted them with the task of continuing my work." And God replied: "But they are humans, they are fickle, one of them betrayed you, another denied you and another one was a doubter! What if they fail? Do you have a backup plan?" Jesus fell silent for a moment and replied: "I have no other plans."

So, we are it. You and I; we who call ourselves Christians. If we cannot to reveal Jesus today, we have failed Jesus. It is a huge responsibility; but it is a privilege too.

Unfortunately, there are still many Christians who think that they don't have the power to reveal Jesus today. The title of this year's Vacation Bible School was "Power Lab." The purpose of the program was to teach the children how powerful Jesus was. Jesus had the power to heal the sick, Jesus had the power to walk on the water, Jesus had the power to forgive, Jesus had the power to raise the dead, Jesus had the power to rise from the dead, etc.

The program never talked about our power as disciples. I was in charge of the adult class during VBS. I asked my class if they had any power. Four out of ten said they had the power too, but six out of ten said that we humans have no power. All power is with God,, and we are weak and sinful. Our role, according to those six people is to be receptors of God's mercy and forgiveness, and our goal is to be ultimately saved by Christ.

We know that Jesus of Nazareth is not with us in flesh. He is the risen Lord and we cannot see the risen Lord with our naked eyes. The Word that became flesh 2000 years ago in Jesus must become flesh again in our lives. Jesus wants to use our lives: our hands and feet, our eyes and ears, our hearts and minds, to reveal him to the world today. And how do we do that?

Jesus used two symbols to explain our role in the world: the symbols of light and salt. In the Sermon on the Mount, Jesus made two very powerful statements to his followers: "You are the salt of the earth. You are the light of the world."

He did not say, you should be the salt of the earth, or you should be the light of the world, but *you are*. Jesus was pointing to the inherent dignity of his followers. The inherent dignity of being created in the image and likeness of God, which I spoke about in the first 'R' of discipleship: 'Remembering who you are!'

In Mt. 5:14, Jesus says: "You are the light of the world." But in John 8:12, Jesus says of himself, "I am the light of the world." Who then is the light of the world, Jesus or his followers? This apparent contradiction is resolved by another passage in John 9:5 where Jesus modifies the statement about himself: "As long as I am in the world, I am the light of the world."

**As long as Jesus is physically present in the world he is the light of the world, but when he is no longer physically present, his followers assume the role of being the light of the world**.

The imagery of the light is very easy to understand. What does a candle or a light bulb do? They light up the room. The candle does not blame the darkness, the candle does not curse the darkness, the candle does not judge the darkness; it just comes into the dark room, and the darkness disappears.

Darkness does not stand a chance in the presence of a lighted candle or a burning bulb. A Christian is supposed to do just that. A light, shining with love, and compassion and kindness and non-judgmental attitude, and he or she would light up the place.

But that is not what we normally do. We criticize the world for being a difficult place to live. We are upset with the crime and immorality around us. We fault the government for not doing enough. When we become upset and angry about the situation, we are only adding to the darkness that is already there. Jesus does not want us to do that. He wants us to be the light in the darkness. It is better to light a candle than curse the darkness.

As light, we are called to show the way. As disciples, we have this huge responsibility and calling to be an example to the world around us. We are a city on a hill. We are a lamp that should be kept on a lamp stand, not to be hidden under a bucket.

And we are called to be salt in the world. Now what is it salt does? It adds taste to the food. In Jesus' time, it was also used as a preservative, because they did not have refrigerators. So, as salt, we have the calling to keep the world from being putrid; we have the vocation to add the flavors of love, and kindness, to a world that is filled with anger, and hatred, and jealousy and unkindness.

Salt must be different from the food before it can be of use. If salt loses its taste, than it is useless and can no longer make a difference. Light must be different from darkness in order to be of help. A flashlight with dead batteries is no good for someone in the dark. So, being salt and light of the world means being different from the world.

If believers have nothing that distinguishes them from unbelievers, then they are like salt that has lost its saltiness and therefore cannot make a difference. What distinguishes us from non-believers should not be our title as Christians or the badges and pins and crosses we wear, but the lives we live. As Jesus says in John 13:35, "By this everyone will know that you are my disciples, if you have love for one another."

**Love is the distinctive mark by which you can distinguish true Christians from the false ones.**

What do you think is the greatest hindrance to Christianity in our country? This is a question that is bound to elicit a variety of answers depending on who you ask. Possible answers would include: the mass media, popular culture, materialism, bad government policies, other religions, etc.

A missionary had the occasion to put this very question to the great Mahatma Gandhi, "What is the greatest hindrance to Christianity in India?" Gandhi's answer was swift and decisive: "Christians."

It is said that the world would be a better place today were it not for the Christians. The Christians who are a hindrance to Christianity are not the real and committed ones, of course, but those who describe themselves as Christians in name only. Most often, their behavior has very little to do with Christ.

Being a Christian or being salt and light is not a complicated thing. Ask yourself one simple question: Do I bring the flavor of love and joy to my surroundings? My family, my neighborhood, my church, my town? Does my presence bring a sense of peace and lightness to the environment or do people consider me a burden or pain in the neck? When I interact with people, do I bring a taste of joy into their lives or do I leave a bitter taste with them? When you leave, do people say: "Thank God he is gone" or do they say: "What a nice guy or girl?"

There is a flip side to these symbols. Too much light can be blinding. Too much salt can make the food bitter. Do not impose yourself on others. Also salt in the wrong place, such as an open wound can be very painful. Being the right amount at the right place is the key.

Being light and salt does not require you to be an expert in theology. It does not demand that you by heart verses from the Bible and proclaim them from a hill top. You don't even have to tell others that the Bible is the word of God or argue with them to prove your point. You don't even have to tell people that unless they become Christians, they will not be saved. Leave that to God.

You just have to behave like a disciple. Francis of Assisi, one of the great missionaries of all time, understood this so well. He gave his monks this advice: **"Preach always; use words, if necessary".**

**For many people, your life is the only bible they will ever read**. That is why I like to repeat the quote I always printed on the bulletin of my last church: "If you have Jesus in your heart, notify your face."

Let your light shine before people so that they may see goodness in your behavior and give praise to your heavenly father.

# 21. Living Without Walls

Luke 13: 22-30

*People will come from east and west and north and south, and will take their places at the feast in the kingdom of God. Indeed there are those who are last who will be first, and first who will be last.*

A man arrives at the gates of heaven. St. Peter asks him: "What religion?" and the man replies: "Methodist." Peter looks through the list and says: "God to room #24, but be very quiet as you pass room #8." Another man arrives, and Peter asks for his religion, and he says: "Baptist." "Go to room #18, but be very quiet as you pass room #8." A third man arrives at the gate and he is Jewish: "OK, go to room #14, but be very quiet when you pass room #8." The man said to Peter: "I can understand having different rooms for different religions, but why must I be quiet when I pass room #8? Peter told him; "Well, the Catholics are in room #8, and they think they are the only ones here."

I was reminded of this story when I read the news item in the paper last week: "Roman Catholicism is the Only Way, Pope Asserts." The Pope released a document last week in which he said that protestant churches are "mere ecclesial communities" and not "true Churches" and they did not have the "Means of Salvation."Only the Catholic Church has the "fullness and the means of salvation."

Let me give you some background. Until 1965, the Catholic Church taught that "outside the church there is no salvation"(*extra ecclsia nulla salus*). I grew up believing this teaching. But I was not very comfortable with it because my neighbors were Hindus, some of the nicest people I have ever met. They worked hard, sent their kids to school, said their evening prayers, went to their temple for worship but they did not believe in Jesus. I could not fathom that they would go to hell because of that.

In 1962, Pope, John 23rd convened the second Vatican Council. Pope John was a generous and open minded man. In that council, it was decided that, the Church should stop teaching that "outside the Church there is no salvation. The council removed that phrase from church teachings."

The council went one step further and released another document called "The Declaration on Non-Christina Religions" in which it said that people who do not know Christ for no fault of theirs, could be saved. That Council also changed the language of Mass from Latin to native languages.

So, 42 years after the second Vatican council, Pope Benedict has gone back to the pre-Vatican II days by restoring Latin Mass and calling for salvation exclusively through the Catholic Church. By the way, the revival of the Latin Mass made the Jewish people so angry, because there is a prayer in it for the "conversion of Jews."

The pope is not the only one doing this. The other day I was listening to a Christian radio station 89.3 FM and a preacher called Dr. Michael Yousa was giving the sermon. He said: "Anyone who does not worship Jesus is worshiping the devil; all those who worship Buddha are worshiping the devil; all those who claim to worship their inner being is worshiping the devil; when I say this, people might call me a bigot, but I wear that title like a badge of honor for Jesus Christ my Lord."

What do you think of these teachings? The Pope is more exclusive than the preacher. According to the Pope, only Roman Catholics will be saved; that is about 1.2 billion people in the world. You and I are not included in that group. According to the preacher, only those who believe in Jesus will be saved, and that is about 3 billion people. Thank God, you and I are included in that group!

I don't heed the teachings of neither of these men or anyone who preaches exclusivism. There are six billion people in this world. God created all of them. God placed them in different parts of the planet. I cannot believe that God would send 1.3 billion Chinese, and one billion Hindus and one billion Muslims into hell, because for no fault of theirs, they did not hear about Jesus and believe in him.

Then what about John 14:6? "I am the way, the truth and life, and no one comes to the father, except through me?

First of all, that phrase is only in the gospel of John, and not in Matthew, Mark or Luke. If it was such a crucial statement, why wouldn't all four gospels record it? Think about it.

As a matter of fact, in the Gospel of John, there is another way for salvation: In John 3:3, Jesus said to Nicodemus: "Unless you are born from above, you will not enter the Kingdom of heaven." In Mark 10: 13, Jesus says: "Unless you become like little children, you will not enter the Kingdom of heaven." According to Luke 10:27, the way to heaven is through love. And according to Mathew Chapter 25, you inherit the kingdom through service. So which is it?

Let us say, Jesus actually said that he is the only way to the Kingdom, and if so what does it mean? Does it mean that one has to get to know the historical Jesus, the Jesus who lived in flesh and blood two thousand years ago, or does it mean, knowing and following the teachings of Jesus?

Pay attention to the text's central metaphor: Jesus is the **way**.

**The way of Jesus is a path to be followed, not a creed to be believed.** For John, the way is the path to death and resurrection. That way, the path of dying to an old way of being, and being born into a new way of being is the only way to God. The way of Jesus is about loving others as Jesus did, and if you do that, you will be saved. In that sense, no one can come to the father without following the way of Jesus, which is love.

To understand this better, let me take you to the scene where a lawyer approaches Jesus and asks the question: "Master, what must I do to gain eternal life?" Or, what should I do to be saved? What does Jesus say? He does not say to the lawyer that he had to believe in him as the only way to the father.

Instead, Jesus said: "Love God with all your heart, all your mind, and all your soul, and love your neighbor as yourself."

Let me take you to another scene, the scene of the last judgment in Matthew chapter 25. When all the people are gathered for the final judgment, what are the criteria for salvation there? Jesus does not say: "Because you believed in me, and because you were baptized and had membership in a church, enter heaven."

Jesus says "Come and inherit the kingdom that has been prepared for you from the creation of the world; For I was hungry you gave me food, I was thirsty you gave me drink, I was stranger, and you welcomed me and I was naked and you clothed me...whatever you did to the least of my brothers, you did it for me."

Here again, it was love for one's neighbor that makes one eligible for heaven. There is nothing here about knowing the historical Jesus, but it is all about walking the way he showed, the way of the cross, practicing sacrificial love for your neighbor. In that sense, Jesus is the way, the truth, and the source of eternal life.

There are many Christians who believe that non-Christians will not be saved. They have not understood the mind of Jesus or studied the life of Jesus.

In Luke 9: 51, there is an incident where Jesus was going to Jerusalem, and he had to pass through a Samaritan village. The Samaritans did not welcome him, because there was so much hostility between the Jews and the Samaritans. The Samaritans took Jesus for just another Jew, and they were not receptive to him. So, how do his disciples, James and John, react to this? They wanted to destroy that town by calling down fire and thunder from heaven! That is why James and John called the 'sons of thunder.'

So what does Jesus do? He turns to James and John and reprimands them. The text does not say, what Jesus said, but I am sure he must have said something like this: "Are you crazy, you will incinerate an entire village because they don't welcome me?" And Jesus moved on.

Jesus is the most inclusive person you will ever find in history. He loved the Samaritans whom the Jews hated and acknowledged a Samaritan, as the greatest example of neighborly love. He spoke to a Samaritan woman at the well, even to the chagrin of his disciples. He included women in his close circle of friends, in a culture where women had no value. He touched the leper whom the people of his time abhorred and banished from society.

He forgave the prostitute who was going to be stoned to death by the Pharisees. He visited and ate in the homes of people whom the society called sinners and prostitutes. Nobody was outside the inclusive love of Jesus.

**As followers of Jesus, we have no right to exclude anyone whom God created, and Jesus loved. It may be an inconvenient truth, but it is a truth that we must embrace if want to be true disciples.**

There was a protestant minister in Tulsa OK, who embraced this truth late in his ministry. His name is Bishop Carlton Pearson. He is a graduate of Oral Roberts University, which is a very conservative school. Oral Roberts was his mentor. During his ministry, Bishop Pearson preached exclusive salvation through Jesus Christ. He said to his congregation that only those people who believed in the bible and accepted Christ their personal savior, would be saved. His congregation grew, and he had six thousand people in his church and had plenty of money.

Then one day in August 2005, Bishop Pearson, while watching ABC News, saw a segment about the poor people in Darfur. Most of the people in Darfur are Muslims and there is abject poverty everywhere. He saw those poor people who had no food to eat, no clothes to wear, no houses to live in, but barely existing in thatched huts. He was horrified at the sight of malnourished children with sunken eyes and bones sticking out through their rib cage.

And he said to himself: "I can't imagine these people are going to hell, just because they don't believe in Jesus; they are already in hell." It was a moment of conversion for this narrow minded pastor with a huge prejudice towards the non-Christians.

So, the next Sunday, he began preaching about inclusive salvation. He said that he could not believe in a God who is partial to Christians. **He told his congregation that God loves and saves everybody.**

Guess what happened. People started leaving his church. They could not believe in an inclusive God. They began leaving in droves. Within a few weeks, a congregation of 6000 people shrank to a group of just 300 people. The pastor lost his nice church building, because he could not pay the bills.

Oral Roberts wrote him begging him to change his mind about inclusive salvation. When he refused, he was denounced.

The leaders of his Church denomination called him a heretic, and the members of his congregation called him a betrayer. Bishop Pearson rented space from the local Anglican church and held services for his supporters, preaching a gospel of inclusion. Bishop Pearson says, he has never been happier. His congregation is slowly growing.

And the bishop wrote a book about his experience. It is called *The Gospel of Inclusion.*

At the end of our life, when we face God, it is not belief that matters, but behavior. As the last judgment shows, there is no mention of what they believed. Jesus does not say, because you believed in me, inherit the Kingdom . Instead, he says: "Whatever you DID to the least of my brothers, you DID it to ME! It is our BEHAVIOR towards others that makes us eligible for the Kingdom.

So be kind, and compassionate towards everybody, and I mean everybody, and lovingly embrace the six billion people on this planet.

Tear down any walls that you may have built to exclude people from your circle of love. Remove any feelings of prejudice, elitism, exclusivism and holier than thou attitude from your thinking. When you do that you will see the face of Jesus on every face.

**Then, you don't have to worry about your future salvation. You are already saved!**

# 22. How to Be a Disciple in a Post 9/11 World?

John 17: 20-23

*My prayer is not for them alone. I pray also for those who will believe in me though their message, that all of them may be one, Father, just as you are in me and I am in you. May they also be in us so that the world may believe that you have sent me. I have given them the glory that you gave me, that they may be one as we are one: I in them and you in me. May they be brought to complete unity to let the world know that you sent me and have loved them even as you have loved me."*

Joe Smith started the day early having set his alarm clock (made in Japan) for 6 AM. While his coffee pot (China) was perking, he shaved with his electric razor (Hong Kong). He put on a dress shirt (Sri Lanka) and designer jeans (Singapore) and tennis shoes (Korea). After cooking breakfast in his new electric skillet (India) he sat down with his calculator (Mexico) to see how much he could spend that day.

After setting his watch (Taiwan) to the radio (Japan), he got in his car (Germany), filled it with gas (from Saudi Arabia) and continued his search for a good paying American job. At the end of another discouraging and fruitless day of checking his computer (Malaysia), Joe decided to relax for a while. He put on his sandals (Brazil), poured himself a glass of wine (France), and turned on his TV made in (Taiwan), and then wondered why he can't find a good paying job in America!

This story is used to illustrate the negative aspect of globalization. I am going to use it to show you how interconnected we are with the whole world, for our existence and survival. Being connected and interdependent is not a bad thing; in fact it is a good thing. This is what God wants us to do and Jesus wants us to understand and put into practice in our daily lives. Because, as Apostle Paul says in Ephesians: "We all are children of the same God, and Christ came to make us one new humanity from divided humankind."

On this 6th Anniversary of 9/11, I like to reflect on our common humanity and connectedness to each other. I also want to show you how our thinking about nationalism and patriotism can be often opposite to the mind of God.

On that fateful day, six years ago, a terrible thing happened not only to our country, but to humanity itself. Nineteen mad men who hated the United States boarded four planes, destroyed nearly three thousand lives, and negatively affected the lives of thousands of others.

It is a day etched in our memory. I am sure all of you remember what you were doing on that Tuesday morning six years ago. The anniversary falls, on a Tuesday this year. I was driving to work, listening to the radio, and I heard the news that a plane had hit the World Trade Center. But it was not clear why. When I reached the office, I saw my colleagues glued to the TV and a horrific event began to unfold right before our eyes.

As tragic as the event was, it also united us as a people for a while. Someone wrote a poem about that day, called, ONE.

*As the soot and dirt and ash rained down, we became one color.*
*As we carried each other down the stairs of the burning building, we became one class.*
*As we lit candles of waiting and hope, we became one generation.*
*As the firefighters fought their way in to the inferno, we became one gender.*

*As we fell to our knees in prayer for strength, we became one faith;*
*As we whispered words of encouragement, we spoke one language;*

*As we gave our blood in lines a mile long, we became one body;*
*As we mourned together the great loss, we became one soul.*
*As we retell with pride of the sacrifice of heroes, we become one people.*
*We are... one color, one class, one generation, one gender, one faith,*
*One language, one body, one family one soul, ONE PEOPLE.*

That day also changed the character of America as an open and loving country to that of a nation gripped with fear of strangers, and suspicion of Muslims. The Department of Homeland Security came into existence after 9/11. Then we had different levels of terror alerts. Air travel became a nightmare.

Then came the war in Afghanistan and the invasion of Iraq, which still continue. Slogans like "United we stand," "We should fight them over there, before they fight us here," became common. The phrase, "War on terror" is etched into the national psyche.

In the last six years, we have changed from a nation of freedom to a nation of fear. The notion of "Us versus Them" has become very popular. "We will destroy you before you destroy us," has almost become the national slogan, filled with emotions of anger, hatred and vengeance.

In this context, what is a Christian supposed to do? How are we disciples of Christ supposed to think? Should we join the crowd and fight the enemy? Then what happens to our discipleship which calls us to love our enemies? How does Jesus' command to turn our right cheek to the person who strikes us on the left cheek make sense in this context?

Is God on our side when we fight the enemy? Are our national interests and divine interests the same? If they are different, how do we conduct ourselves as citizens and disciples at the same time?

These are difficult questions for a disciple. We should not stop asking them, but ponder them prayerfully.

Let us turn to the first disciple, Peter, for some guidance in this matter. Peter was not a courageous man; in fact he was a fearful man. That is why he denied Jesus three times, in front of a maid. Peter also was a narrow minded, staunchly Jewish man. He was not open to gentiles, and he did not want to associate with them. He thought he was specially chosen by God and the gentiles were outside the love of God.

Then Peter went through a life changing experience. An awakening happened in his life that changed his whole perspective about gentiles and so called outsiders. It is described in chapters 10 and 11 of the Acts of the Apostles. I strongly encourage you to read it.

Let me summarize for you what opened Peter's eyes. Peter was staying in the house of a man named Simon, the tanner, in a town called Joppa.

At noon, Peter went to the roof terrace of the house to pray and he fell into a trance. He saw the sky open and a canvas being lowered in front of him, by its four corners... Inside it, were all the Earth's four legged creatures, and reptiles and birds of the sky. A voice said to him: "Get up Peter, slaughter them and eat!"

Peter said: "Sir, it is unthinkable, I have never eaten anything unclean or impure in my entire life." The prospect of eating unclean food was against his religion. It was a horrifying thought for Peter. But then, he hears a voice from heaven: "What God has purified, you have no right to call unclean." This happened three times and then the canvas was snatched up into the sky.

While Peter was still thinking about the meaning of this vision, two men came to invite him to the house of Cornelius. Now, you have to remember that Cornelius was a gentile and Jews and gentiles are not supposed to mix and mingle. Peter was a bit confused, but since he was invited by the gentile, he went to his house.

When he arrived, he said to him: "You must know that it is not proper for a Jew to associate with a gentile or to have dealings with him; but God has made it clear to me that no one should call any man unclean or impure; that is why I have come in response to your invitation without raising any objections."

And then Peter addressed them in these words: "I begin to see how true it is that God shows no partiality. Rather, the man of any nation who fears God and acts uprightly is acceptable to God."

**God shows no partiality. God does not love one nation more than any other. God is not a partisan. He wants all his children to be united, beyond borders, beyond nationalism. That is why the last prayer of Jesus was for Unity**.

Just before his arrest and crucifixion, Jesus said a series of prayers. Unlike other times, when Jesus prayed in silence and the gospels don't tell us what he prayed for, this time the content of his prayer is spelled out. So it must be very important.

You can read the entire prayer in the 17$^{th}$ chapter of John's gospel. **And Jesus prays for is unity, not just unity among his disciples, but unity among all peoples.** "I pray that they may be one, as you Father are in me, and I in you. I have given them the glory you gave me, that they may be one, as we are one that their unity may be complete."

Jesus wants the whole humanity to be united as he and the father are united and the closeness of the unity between the father and son is the model of the unity between all God's children. **So, unity of humanity is the last will and testament of Jesus.**

We take great effort in fulfilling the last wishes of our loved ones. I see this all the time in my work as a chaplain. I had this lady whose mother wanted a nice funeral with expensive casket and a lot of flowers. But when the mother died, the daughter was in very hard financial straits.

So, the funeral home suggested cremation which will cost only $500 as opposed to the five thousand which is the cost of a burial in the ground. The woman begged and borrowed from family and friends and took a credit card loan to give her mother the burial she wanted. It was about fulfilling the last wishes of her mother.

Unity of humanity was the last wish of Jesus. Jesus must be broken hearted watching the divisions, disunity, separation and hatred that we have created in the world. **It must be so painful for a God to see his children building walls between them in the name of race and religion.**

We live in a post 9/11 world. Our national tendency is to become more isolated, fearful and suspicious of others. We may be tempted to support and cheer our political leaders when they say that we have to fight and destroy our enemies before they destroy us.

But what is a disciple to do? We have no choice but to follow the advice of Jesus. If we want o be disciples that is what we have to do. We are called to unity by our Lord Jesus. Thoughts of separation, isolation and division are sins we need to eliminate them from our thinking. **We have to open our hearts and minds to forgive our enemies, include them in our concerns and hope and pray for a peaceful world. I don't know how to be a disciple in any other way.**

Apostle Paul realized that when he proclaimed: "There is neither Jew, nor Greek, neither woman, nor man, neither slave nor free, we are all one in Christ Jesus." If Paul were to write that today, he might say: "There is neither Muslim nor Christian, neither gay nor straight, neither white nor black, we are all one in Christ Jesus."

When we sincerely believe that proclamation and change our thinking and behavior to match that belief, we will become true disciples of Christ.

# 23. Look Beyond What You See

John: 9: 1- 41

*Jesus said, for judgment I have come into this world, so that the blind will see and those who see will become blind." Some Pharisees who were with him heard him say this and asked, "What? Are we blind too?"Jesus said, "If you were blind, you would not be guilty of sin; but now that you claim you can see, your guilt remains.*

In the Disney movie *Lion King One and a Half*, Timor, a meerkat, leaves home to find a life for himself.

On the way, he meets Rafiki, the wise baboon, who asks him where he was going. Timon tells the baboon "I am looking for a life without worries." The monkey asked: "So you are looking for *hakuna matada*." Rafiki gave Timon this advice: "If you are looking for a life without worries, look beyond what you see."

All of us are looking for a life without worries; a peaceful life, a harmonious world, a united planet, but it seems to elude us all the time. *Looking beyond what we see* can be a beneficial exercise in achieving that goal.

We often live superficial lives, at the level of our five senses. The world around us is experienced and interpreted using our five senses. However, our senses can be very deceptive.

For example, the senses tell us that the earth is flat, but that is not true. Our eyes tell us that the sun rises in the east and sets in the west, but when we look beyond what we see, we know that the sun neither rises nor sets.

It is the same with our view of people. On the physical level, people look different: different colors, different races, religions, but on the level of the soul, they are all the same, members of one human family, each one intimately connected to the destinies and dreams of the other.

As an observer of life, I feel that most people are sleep walking through life; Deepak Chopra calls it the "hypnosis of social conditioning." According to Neal Donald Walsch, author of *Conversations with God*, "the world is in the condition it is in, because the world is full of sleepwalkers, living in a dream and watching that dream turn into a nightmare."

We need to wake up, look around us, look beyond the obvious and then, we will be introduced to a higher level of consciousness. There is a bed time prayer that we usually say: "Lord, don't let me die before, I wake up." We should reverse it and pray: "Lord, wake me up, before I die"

I like to share with you some stories about how I look beyond what I see and how it has helped me become aware of our connectedness and its wonderful benefits.

When the school reopened last year, my sons brought home registration cards from the school. Judy filled them out, with their names, date of birth, and social security number, but when it came to *race,* she stopped and asked me what shall we put for race? There are four choices: White, Black, Asian or Other. Our children don't fit into any one of those. They are not 'White,' because I am brown, they are not 'Black' because Judy is 'White,' they are not 'Asian', because Judy is Caucasian.

If you strictly want to follow the race definition, my children should be called *Amerasians*. That is a term used for children born of Asian women and American men during the Vietnam War. I didn't like to call my children *Amerasians*; it sounds like the name of a laxative. So we wrote, *Human* on the registration card and sent it to school.

You have seen birth announcements on mail boxes. When a child is born you see a balloon tied to a mailbox and it would say: "It's a Boy "or "It is a Girl." It never says: "It is a White American Catholic Boy" or a "Brown Mexican Methodist Girl." A week after we are born, we get the birth certificate; it is our first label of nationality. A few months later, we get a baptism certificate which gives the second label of religion. Later we acquire labels such as Conservative, Liberal, Republican, Democrat, etc. Some labels may be necessary for civic purposes, but they should have no place in our enterprise called life.

According to Neal Donald Walsch, all our problems are due to our desire to be in separate groups: *Every sadness of the human heart, every indignity of the human condition, every tragedy of the human experience, can be attributed to one human decision: the decision to separate ourselves from each other; all of our rage, all of our disappointments, all of our bitterness, has found its birth, in the death of our greatest joy: the joy of being one.*

The reason why we don't feel this unity and connection is because we don't pay attention or we are always in a hurry. We don't have the time or the patience to look beyond the peripheral and the obvious.

Let me share with you story. A year ago, I was at a church fair promoting VITAS Hospice. I had a huge banner behind me and a lot of literature about VITAS on the table. I was standing behind the table with this nice name tag with VITAS in big letters. This nice lady came up to me and said: "I have a bone to pick with your company. My husband was in hospital for a week and ever since he came home, your company is sending me these huge bills." I told her that our company does not send out bills to individual patients, and there must be a mistake. She became angrier, accusing me of not knowing the policies of the company.

Angry and frustrated, she threw an envelope on the table. "Look at these outrageous amounts of money they want from me." I opened it and looked at the stationary and I had to smile. It was a bill from VISTA, a medical insurance company. VITAS and VISTA, just one letter, placed differently, big difference. She was embarrassed, and apologized to me profusely.

**Walk in wakefulness, and move with mindfulness and you can avoid a lot of troubles in life.**

It is about raising our consciousness to a higher level; it is about expanding our minds so that we transcend the distinction between self and others and embrace a greater cause, the universe itself; it is about realizing that strangers are family we have not yet met. It is about experiencing the world around us with spine-tingling amazement. It is not about learning anything new, but remembering what you already know. It can do a world of good for you, and it is good for the world.

We live in a moving universe. It appears like we are sitting still, but if you become aware of it and look beyond the sensory experience, we know that we are spinning 66,000 miles per hour around the sun. Everything in our body is moving: our lungs, our hearts, the blood flowing through our veins. The billions or neurotransmitters firing in our brain and the countless chemical reactions taking place in the trillions of cells in our body. Everything that moves creates energy. There is a field of energy around us that is created by us. Some people project positive energy, others project negative energy.

Every time you meet a person there is a communion of energy between you and that person. And positive energy from another person has such healing effect on our life. Now, would you like to receive positive energy from just a few people in your group, your religion, or your country, or have the energy that comes from wider connections? Imagine receiving positive energy from all the people around the globe? It is like receiving 6 billion blessings a day.

That is why I like to think of myself first as a human being, before I identify myself with any specific group or religion. I want the positive energy from six billion human beings on this planet and when I have that, I bask in the glory of peace, contentment and unity. It is a feeling of being in heaven on earth, of restoring the Garden of Eden, of attaining enlightenment.

**By becoming human, Jesus showed that human beings are important, that human experiences are worthy of our attention and that we should look beyond barriers and divisions and embrace all people as our brothers and sisters.**

Jesus always looked beyond what he saw. For example, when the people looked at Levi, they saw a sinful tax collector; but Jesus saw him as a future disciple. When his disciples saw the woman at the well as a hated Samaritan, Jesus saw her as a possible candidate for the Kingdom. For ordinary eyes, the woman kneading flour in the kitchen is just a woman doing her cooking, but for Jesus, she is engaged in matters of the Kingdom of God. As far as the crowd is concerned, the man hanging on the cross at the side of Jesus is a thief, but Jesus sees him as a candidate for paradise.

In today's gospel story, Jesus heals a man born blind, but the Pharisees are furious that Jesus healed on Sabbath. They could not see beyond the Law which prohibits doing work on Sabbath. They were unable to see the good that was done, because they were spiritually blind. Compared to the blind man, the Pharisees claimed to have eye sight, but Jesus said: "For judgment I have come into this world, so that the blind will see and those who see will become blind." Jesus was referring to the blindness that refuses to see the goodness in front of them.

Jesus invites us today, to remove whatever blinders we may have and look at the world with the eyes of compassion and love and when we do that, we will see the world differently. As Wayne Dyer said, "when you change the way you look at things, the things you look at change."

Years ago, when Neale Donald Walsch was at a book signing ceremony, he wrote these words for a fan: "I see who you are and I like what I see." He was referring to seeing the image of God in the person standing in front of him. He was seeing the soul of that person with the eyes of his soul.

**Today, Jesus invites us to see the world and the people in it, through a third eye that penetrates through the externals and see the mystery, the beauty and the divinity of everything and everyone we behold.**

# 24. Blessings Through the 'Least Among Us'

Mathew 25: 31-41

*I was hungry and you gave me to eat, I was thirsty and you gave me to drink, I was a stranger and you invited me in. I needed clothes and you clothed me, I was sick and you looked after me, I was in prison and you came to visit me...whatever you did for one the least of these brothers of mine, you did for me."*

Senator Ted Kennedy died last week. There was endless media coverage about his life and legacy. Two words that were repeatedly used by almost all the commentators were 'tragedy' and 'redemption.'

I counted 14 tragedies in his life that the public is aware of. I am sure there are private tragedies too. Human tendency is to keep tragedies private, especially if they are embarrassing. But Kennedy had no such luck. He was a public figure and so his tragedies were dissected, explored, examined and analyzed in the media.

The first tragedy was the death of his oldest brother, Joe, who died in a plane crash during World War II. Then came the assassinations of both of his remaining brothers. Teddy responded to those tragedies by making sure that his brothers' dream of equality for all was achieved by passing the historic Civil Rights Act of 1964.

After that senate vote on June 19, 1964, Kennedy boarded a private plane that would take him to the Democratic Party Convention in Springfield, Mass. But as the plane descended into Springfield airport, it struck a row of trees and somersaulted across the field. The pilot died at the scene. An aide died few hours later. Kennedy suffered a broken back and a collapsed lung. He spent five months in hospital recovering but the back pain from that accident continued throughout his life.

Again on July 18, 1969, a huge personal tragedy occurred. He had hosted a reunion party for six women who had worked for his brother's presidential campaign. The gathering took place in a rented cottage on Chappaquiddick Island. At 11.15 PM, that night, he got into his car with Mary Jo Kopechne, an aide to his brother, to drive her to her hotel.

According to the testimony, he took a wrong turn onto an unlit dirt road and onto an unrailed wooden bridge. His car flipped and landed upside down in the water. Kennedy managed to escape. The woman did not. At the inquest he testified that after escaping from the car, he dived back into the water seven or eight times in a vain attempt to free the woman. Then he walked a mile back to the cottage to get some help.

Can you imagine that happening to you? You are driving with a friend and the car goes into a canal, you escape and your friend dies! The guilt coming out that experience is enough to sink a life. In Kennedy's case it was not just guilt, but plenty of shame too. Where was he going in the middle of the night with a young woman in the car?

There were too many unanswered questions about Chappaquiddick, and it stayed as a cloud over his head all his life. That is why he did not run for president in 1972 or 1976.

In 1971, his oldest son, Teddy Jr. was diagnosed with bone cancer. He was just 11 years old. His right leg was amputated. I have two sons, and I cannot imagine how I would deal with such a diagnosis. Years later, his daughter Kara was diagnosed with inoperable lung cancer and she was given one year to live. He found a doctor to operate on her, and she is now clear of cancer for five years. His youngest son, Patrick Kennedy had a non-cancerous tumor on his spine which was also operated.

How are parents to deal with such pain? Ted and Jean had also suffered three miscarriages. The stress from all these may have contributed to their eventual divorce which is a tragedy in itself.

In March 1991, while visiting the family compound in Palm Beach Florida, Kennedy took his son Patrick and his nephew William Kennedy Smith for drinks at a local bar. Smith returned that night with a girl who would later accuse him of raping her. His trial was on television and Kennedy was called as a witness. It was yet another embarrassing tragedy for an elderly senator.

Then came the tragic death of his nephew, John Kennedy Jr. and his wife in a plane accident in July 1999. Witnessing the funeral of his young nephew, whose father was assassinated, must have been a very painful experience for Ted Kennedy.

And last but not least, was his own diagnosis with brain cancer that took his life.

Seventy seven years of life, fourteen huge tragedies that must have brought excruciating emotional pain and agony. How did he deal with them without breaking and falling apart? How did he become one of most effective legislators in American history? Where did he find the strength to deal with his own pain and to ease the pain that was all around him?

He functioned effectively as a senator; he served the needs of his constituents; he attended all the family functions bringing support and comfort in times of need. He went sailing almost every week. How did he function with all that tragedy and pain in his life?

**My theory is that he was blessed by God; not by a God somewhere in the sky, but by the God present in the people he loved. He was strengthened by the God-energy of the people.** Let me explain:

Despite all his flaws, there was one conviction that was the bed rock of Kennedy's life: **His deep and abiding concern for the "least among us."** He was the greatest champion for causes that affected the poor, the marginalized, and the disadvantaged in society. His favorite Bible passage was Mathew Chapter 25, verses 31-45, where Jesus talks about the sheep and the goat at the last judgment. Kennedy chose that passage to be read at his funeral mass.

When people from all nations are gathered in front of the Son of man for the final judgment, he will separate them into two groups, as a shepherd separates sheep from goats. He will place the sheep on his right side and the goats on the left side. To the ones on his right, the King will say: "Come, you have my father's blessing. Inherit the kingdom prepared for you from the creation of the world:

*"For, I was hungry, and you gave me to food. I was thirsty and you gave me drink. I was a stranger and you welcomed, naked and you clothed me. I was ill and you comforted me, in prison and you came to visit me."*

Examine closely and you will find that there is no mention about worshipping or praising God. Nothing is mentioned about what faith they practiced, what country they belonged to, how much money they made, or how many medals and honors they achieved during their life time. It does not say anything about the schools they attended or the degrees they earned. There is no mention about any of the things that we usually consider important in life, such as name, fame, status, money, or possessions.

**Your entrance into eternal life is based on just ONE single criterion. How you treated the people around you, especially the weak and the vulnerable, the hungry, the poor and the stranger.**

Kennedy really understood the meaning of that passage and consistently put it into practice. You can see the impact of that bible passage in his legislative passion. For example, take the phrase: “I was hungry you gave me food, I was thirsty, and you gave me drink.” His relentless fight for increasing the minimum wage was born of the conviction that the poor workers should have a decent wage to put food on the table for their families. It was his persistence that passed the bill raising minimum wage to $7, last year.

Another phrase from Mt. 25 is: “I was a stranger and you welcomed me.” Kennedy had a special affection for immigrants and strangers. He worked hard to increase immigration quotas to allow more arrivals from nations outside northern Europe.

Another line from Mt. 25 that Kennedy took to heart was this: “I was ill and you comforted me.” For 40 long years, he fought tirelessly for universal health care. He repeatedly said that health care is not a privilege for those who can afford it but a right for all those who live here. There are 47 million people in this country without health insurance. These people are one serious sickness away from bankruptcy.

That does not seem to bother a lot of people. But it bothered Ted Kennedy and he tried so hard to make health insurance available and affordable to all.

**For Kennedy, the “least among us” were his passion, comfort and redemption.**

Mathew 25: 31-45 is one of my favorite passages too. I try to shape my spiritual life around the message of that passage.

It sums up what Christian life is all about. If you can live the message of Mathew 25: 31- 45, you will experience peace and joy now, despite all the painful things that may be going on around you and eternal life` hereafter.

Everything in our life is all about energy. We are energy, and we are surrounded by energy. There is an energy flow between you and other human beings and everything around you such as plants, animals and the entire universe.

In human interactions, whether it is a direct contact with a person in front of you or an indirect connection with someone on the other side of the globe, there is an exchange of energy. When I think about my mom in India and say a prayer for her, my thoughts and prayers generate energy that travels half way around the globe to reach my mom as a healing balm. Referring to this energy flow, someone said: "When a butterfly flaps its wings in San Francisco, weather changes in Singapore."

So, when you stand in front of a person, there is an invisible, yet real, energy movement between the two of you. Your lungs are moving, your heart is beating, and you have thoughts and feelings about that person. All these movements create energy.

If your thoughts and feelings are loving, kind and compassionate, you receive positive energy from that person. If your thoughts and feelings towards that person are tinged with prejudice, malice and anger, you receive negative energy from that person. If you generate positive energy; you receive positive energy in return. On the other hand, if you emanate negative energy, you will receive negative energy.

I believe that due to his love for the "least among us," Kennedy received positive energy from millions of them, which help erase the stigma of his weaknesses, eased the pain of his tragedies and gave him the strength to live.

Do you want blessings from God? Despite the problems that life brings, would you like to have a peaceful life now and eternal life hereafter? Start loving more people regardless of their status in life. Be compassionate towards the least among us. God will bless you through them.

**Blessings come to you, not from an imaginary connection to an invisible God, but through the real bonding with the human being right in front of you**. That is where the rubber meets the road. It is easy to sing praises to an invisible God, but hard to love your neighbor next door.

But that is the best way to love and serve God. Jesus clearly says: "Whatever you did to the least of my brothers, you did it to me."

**God's blessings are not favors from the sky, which are dropped on you when you say some prayers. They come to you as energy from the people you love and care about. The larger your circle of concern, the larger your share of blessings.**

# 25. The Isness of Life

Luke: 12: 22-31

*Then Jesus said to his disciples: "Therefore I tell you, do not worry about our life, what you will eat; or about your body, what you will wear. Life is more than food, and the body more than clothes. Consider the ravens: They do not sow or reap, they have no storeroom or barn; yet God feeds them. And how much more valuable you are than birds! Who of you by worrying can add a single hour to his life? Since you cannot do this very little thing, why do you worry about the rest?.. But seek his kingdom, and these things will be given to you as well."*

Let us do a sentence completion exercise this morning starting with the word, "Life."

According to Shakespeare, "Life is a tale told by an idiot, full of sound and fury, signifying nothing." One of my patients in a Nursing Home said: "Life is a terminal disease." Ouch! "Life is a journey, not a destination". "Life is not about the number of breaths you take; it is about the moments that take your breath away." My view of life is close to John Lennon's: "Life is what happens when we make other plans," but that is not my definition.

My definition of life is that it is not a definition. Because when you define something, you limit it. You enclose it within the confines of words which are always imperfect. Alan Watts echoes this sentiment when he writes: "It has been said that to define is to kill, and if the wind were to stop for one second for us to catch hold of it, it would cease to be wind. The same is true of life."

Besides, you cannot define something that is so vast and limitless. Now, what do I mean by that? Everything in life has opposites, but life itself has no opposites. For example, we have night and day, darkness and light, up and down, black and white, hills and valleys, joy and sadness, long and short.

We cannot understand one concept in the absence of the other. For example, we cannot speak of up without down, we cannot speak of night without day, we will not be able to understand it. These are relational realities. That is why Carl Jung said: "**There is no reality without polarity**." Neale Donald Walsch, author of *Conversations with God*, said it even more profoundly when he wrote: **"You cannot experience that which is, in the absence of that which is not."**

So what is the opposite of life? Death? Ninety nine percent of people say death. We have been saying it for centuries that we don't even think about it. But the fact of the matter is that life has no opposite. Life is the only thing in life that does not have an opposite. The opposite of death is birth. ***It is not life and death, it is birth and death***.

Since life has no opposites, this is how I would complete the sentence beginning with the word Life: **Life IS.** Period. I don't put another word or phrase after that. Because, when you put another word or phrase after it, you are defining life, and as I said, when you define something you are limiting it or containing it. For example, if you say life is not fair, you are likely to compare your life to that of others and get depressed; Or if you say, "life is hard," you are likely to live out that definition, like a self-fulfilling prophesy. So I don't define life, because it limits life.

Life is what you think it is; life is what you make of it today, because it makes no guarantees about tomorrow.

So life just IS, and it means that you have to **live in the present** to make most of life. To make your life happy, joyful and fulfilling is to follow the advice of Jesus who asks us to live in the present: without regretting the past and not being anxious about the future.

Ninety percent of the people live 12 hours of their day regretting the past and the remaining 12 hours of their day, worrying about the tomorrows. It may be an exaggeration, but you get the point. I meet such people every day in my work as a hospice chaplain. It is when a dear one dies, that they think about all the things they should have done, or should not have done when they were alive.

**Surveys have shown that the most predominant emotion at funerals is not sadness, but guilt.**

Last week a young woman and her mother in law came to my bereavement support group. Both women were crying throughout the session. The young woman's husband had died in a car accident. They have three year old twins. The woman talked tearfully about not telling her husband that she loved her.

"We had plans to take our children to Disney world, we wanted to move to North Carolina, I wanted to go to nursing school, we wanted to travel the world, we imagined getting old together, becoming grandparents," etc. etc. All that ended for him when a train hit his car on Tuesday, June $19^{th}$ at 10 PM. Everything ended for her, four hours later, when a Broward Sheriff's Officer woke her up at 2 in the morning and told her that her husband had died in a car accident.

Life is so fragile, it has no guarantees, it makes no promises about the future and that is why Jesus told us to live in the present. Yesterday is history, tomorrow is mystery and today is the only thing you have. That is why I strongly believe that life just IS. The past of IS is WAS, and its future is WILL. You don't want to spent your life in the WAS or the WILL.

I came to the realization that life IS, about 15 years ago. Before that, I was a worrier. I used to get depressed, every other day. Between

1989 and 1991, for a period of about two years, I was clinically depressed. It was just after I got married.

Getting married is supposed to be the happiest event for any normal person, but for me it was just the opposite, because, I was a priest and I was not supposed to get married. I got married against the wishes of my family, friends and my Church. I did not tell my parents that I was married for six months.

When they found out that I had left the priesthood and gotten married, they were extremely upset and the letters that followed from family and friends in India were not friendly to say the least. "How could you do this to us?" You have brought shame on the family." "You have disappointed us; we thought you were going to become a bishop in the Church." My aunt who is a nun wrote to me that I had betrayed Christ and that she did not want to see me as a married man.

Things were not better here in Florida either. My wife's family wouldn't talk to me. Nobody attended our wedding except two people who were witnesses. The total expense for our wedding was $35 for a lunch; yes we saved a lot of money, money we did not have anyway.

We had no support, no friends, and I had no job either. I was still a visitor to the country married to an American citizen.

Imagine, a medical doctor, waking up in the morning and finding out that he has lost his practice, and his hospital privileges; his colleagues don't talk to him and he will never see his patients again; Not only that, he had to start work in McDonalds's. My experience was very similar to that.

I went into a deep depression. Every day, I will sit around and ask the question: "What is life? What is life? It was my depression looking for answers.

I asked that question, because, I was living in the past. I was heartbroken about all the things I had lost as a result of getting married: Thirteen years of priesthood, hundreds of friends, thousands of people I had met and served in different churches, position in the church, and respect in the community. I could not bring myself to appreciate or enjoy anything in my present life.

Things began to change after our first child was born. That event brought me right into the present. Ever since the birth of our son, I have not asked the question about life, because I found meaning in having a son; his presence in flesh and blood, right before me, brought me to the reality of life **now.**

It was a concrete reminder that the celibate priesthood was over forever: I am now, a parent. When I cut the umbilical cord of my son, I was simultaneously cutting the umbilical cord to my past as a clerical priest. *Rev. Father Paul had become, just* ***father.***

Two years after he was born, I had to face another challenge in life: we found out that our son was autistic. But that diagnosis did not drag me into another bout of depression. By that time, I had learned to accept life as IS, and live in the present. The serenity prayer has been of tremendous help in my spirituality.

It says, "God, give me the serenity to accept the things I cannot change, the courage to change the things I can, and the wisdom to know the difference." It is an invitation to accept life as it is...

A great advantage of accepting life as IS, is that we will stop asking the "Why?" questions. I am sure all of us have asked many "Why" questions especially at difficult times.

Why did the Tsunami hit the poor people in Indonesia and not the rich people in Beverly Hills?

Why my son does have to be autistic and attending a special school, while my neighbor's son is an honor student heading to a prestigious

University? But then again, why does my other neighbor's son have Down Syndrome and he is on a wheel chair, but my son can at least walk? Then again, why did my new neighbor's son die in a car accident at age 18 while his great grandmother, is still alive at age 107? Why?

**Why Paris Hilton is on Magazine covers but a Maid in the Hilton Hotel is changing pillow covers? Why is Bill Gates so rich but Bill Smith is at the gate begging for a handout?" Why? I don't have answers to any of these questions, except to say that Life just IS.....**

If anyone claims to have answers to these questions, I suggest that you run fast and far, because no one does. In this instance, it may be good to remember the Zen Master's advise to his disciple: "If you meet the Buddha on the road, kill him."

I have chosen not to delve into the mysterious "Why Questions" of life, which is an exercise in futility. I have made a conscious decision to accept and embrace the Isness of life which is peace.

There is another very important reason why I believe that Life just, IS: Look at the scene in the book of Exodus where Moses wanted to find out the name of God. What did God say? I AM who AM: He did not say, "I was who I was or I will be who I will be," but, I AM. God is only in the present, she is not in the past or in the future; He is here with us now, in the **Isness of life.** And if God is with us, everything is bearable, all things are possible.

Also, I invite you to focus on the last verse of the last chapter of Mathew's gospel, 28:20. When Jesus bids farewell to his disciples, he says, "Go and preach the good news, I AM with you till the end of times." He does not say, I was with you, he does not say, I will be with you, but I AM with you.

Wayne Dyer said it beautifully when he wrote: "You will only come to truly know God when you give up the past and the future in your mind and merge totally into the Now because God is always here now."

**So start believing in the Isness of life,** and embrace the God and the God-made man Jesus, both of whom are, I AM present with you every moment, and your lives will be transformed beyond your imagination!

# 26. Inconvenient Truths

Mark 8: 31-37

*He then began to teach them that the Son of Man must suffer many things and be rejected by the elders, chief priests and teachers of the law, and that he must be killed and after three days rise again. He spoke plainly about this, and Peter took him aside and began to rebuke him. But when Jesus turned and looked at his disciples, he rebuked Peter. "Get behind me, Satan!" he said. "You do not have in mind the things of God, but the things of men.*

In the movie *A Few Good Men*, an angry Tom Cruise asks Jack Nicholson to tell the truth. But an angrier Jack Nicholson tells him: "You can't handle the truth." Whether we like it or not, that statement is very true in our daily lives. We don't like to hear the bitter truths of life. And so we have come up with ways to delay, deny or distort truths.

The billion dollar hair color industry is proof that we don't want to face the truth about aging. Women usually don't reveal their age, for fear of admitting that they may be getting old. That is why we come up with roundabout ways of answering questions regarding age. The other day, I asked an elderly woman who was celebrating her 79th birthday, how old she was and she said: "This is the 50th anniversary of my 29th birthday."

We have come up with a smart way to soften the blow of hard truths with the clever use of the "good news bad news" scenario to break bad news. Like this one for example: A criminal lawyer told his client: "I have good news and bad news for you." "The bad news is that the blood found on the crime scene is yours; the good news is that your cholesterol level is only 130."

The pastor to his congregation: "The good news is that we have enough money to pay for the new building program; the bad news is that it is still in your pocket."

We like to massage the truth and mask reality to avoid hurting or to make it hurt less. We do it nationally and personally. A good example of the national massaging of the truth is the prohibition by the Bush Administration not to show pictures of coffins of dead soldiers arriving from Iraq at the Dover Air force base in Delaware.

Again, it is hard to hear the word 'torture' and still approve of it, and so we call it "enhanced interrogation techniques."

More than 4000 soldiers have died in Iraq, but how many flag draped coffins have you seen? None, because that is the bitter truth and the government feels that the bitter truth will be hard for us to swallow; If we face the hard truth, there will be less support for the war and so they hide it from us.

Our aversion to the truth of Global Warming and the damage it does to our environment was beautifully portrayed in a documentary called the *Inconvenient Truth.* There are many people who are still in denial about the reality of global warming. They like to ignore that scientific truth or refuse to face it, because that would require them to change their attitude and behaviors regarding industrial pollution, auto manufacturing etc. which would affect their bottom line.

On Saturday, September 15, 2001 I was officiating a wedding. During the ceremony, I happened to mention the horrible tragedy that had happened four days earlier–the events of 9/11--just to remember and pray for the victims. It was a terrible national tragedy and I thought we should pray about it. After the service, the mother of the bride came up to me and said: "You spoiled my daughter's wedding."

Thinking about the sadness of 9/11 apparently spoiled the joy of the wedding.

Since then, I have made it a practice to ask prospective couples about mentioning inconvenient truths during the wedding service such as remembering a loved one. For example, a bride would say, "My brother is walking me down the aisle because my dad died ten years ago." I would ask her: "Would you like me to mention your dad at the beginning of the ceremony, in such words: "Jen's dad is not with us today to witness this beautiful moment, but he is watching over her from heaven and blessing her at this moment." Some couples would say: "that is beautiful...please say that."

But there are others who have told me not to mention death. They cannot integrate that inconvenient truth into their life.

In my hospice work, I have found out this to be very true. Many people are afraid of talking about death, even in the hospice setting where death is the front and center issue. There is no other reality in our life that is more definite, more certain, unavoidable and inevitable than death, but people don't want to talk about it.

I have patients who are in their 90s who don't want to talk about it. I can understand a 20 year old avoiding the topic, but at 90? When I ask them, if they are afraid to die, they would say: "I don't want to talk about it." They think that if they don't mention it, it would just go away.

I have grown children of hospice patients who refuse to address the issue and fail to make funeral arrangements. They would take me aside and say: "Don't tell my mom you are from hospice; just tell them you are from an insurance company or Medicaid office." I have a hard time pretending to be an insurance agent, but sometimes I play along because that is the only way I can get an appointment to make the first visit.

I have elderly patients who don't want to face the realities of aging such as loss of sight and hearing. A 90 year old woman who was losing her eye sight asked: "Why is this happening to me? (I wanted to ask her why it shouldn't happen, but I didn't). She wanted me to take her to Rand Eye Institute to have an eye surgery to get her sight back. I wanted to tell her regardless of what she did, she was not going to get her sight back. That is reality; that is truth.

This refusal to face reality or massaging the bitter truth starts at an early age. Chicago tribune had an article about telling the truth to kids. How many times did you tell your five year old on the first day of school: "School is fun. You will like school; you will play games and make friends, and on your birthday, your mama will bake cup cakes and you will have a big party with all your friends."

Why don't we have the guts to tell them: "Learning is hard work; some day you could die from boredom and sleep from the repetition, but it is necessary. Teachers are not there to entertain you; School is not like watching TV. It is one of the hardest phases of your life."

While preparing this sermon, I came across this book: *Horseradish: Bitter truths you can't Avoid.* On its jacket are these words: "Life is a turbulent journey fraught with confusion, heartbreak, and inconvenience. This book will not help." It is a humorous look at how people try to deny and delay truths and avoid the bitter realities of life.

In today's gospel, Jesus gives us a horseradish treatment. He tells his disciples an inconvenient truth. Jesus is a straight talker, a teller of truth. He told them. "The Son of Man had to suffer much, be rejected by the elders, the chief priests, and the scribes, be put to death, and rise three days later." He laid it out right in front of them, no gimmicks, no massaging the truth to soften the blow, or to ease the shock. No euphemisms, no good news bad news scenario.

**Three very difficult words: suffering, rejection, death. We don't want to think about them. They are difficult truths.**

We are not alone; the first disciples did not want to hear it either. Mark Says: "He spoke plainly about this." That is why Peter took Jesus aside and "began to remonstrate with him." Now, that is not a word we use in usual conversation. Remonstrate means to plead, protest, object, complain, etc. So, Peter told Jesus not to talk about suffering, rejection, and death: that is no fun.

Peter was so upset that he rebuked Jesus and Jesus rebuked him back, calling him Satan. "Get behind me Satan," Jesus told him pretty harsh words. Every time we deny reality, or hide from truth or avoid inconvenient truths, Jesus is not pleased with us. When we do that, Jesus says; "You do not have in mind, the things of God, but the things of men."

Then he goes further. Until this time, Jesus was talking to his disciples. V. 34 says, "Then he called the crowd to him along with his disciples and said; "If anyone would come after me, he must deny himself, and take up his cross and follow me; For whoever, wants to save his life will lose it but whoever loses his life for me and for the gospel, will save it."

Again, three more difficult phrases: "deny yourself, take up your cross, and lose your life." It is very hard to face the bitter truths contained in these phrases and that is why many people who heard these, left Jesus. They could not handle the truth. What do you want to do? Leave Jesus or stay with him? I am sure that you want to stay. Then be prepared to accept suffering, self-denial and cross as part of life.

**Why is it called the "good news?" At the outset, the whole thing sounds like bad news: suffering, rejection, death, self denial, taking up cross, losing life: there is no glimpse of apparent good news in any of this.**

So how does this apparent bad news become good news? That is the irony of life. For example, take a mango seed or any seed for that matter. You keep it in a nice container and leave it in a safe place in your house. It will stay that way for a while, and then dry up; crack and turn into dust, becoming totally useless. On the other hand, put that seed on the ground. It will be surrounded by suffocating dirt, its outer shell will burst open with pressure from inside, its soft crust will disintegrate and disappear, but a beautiful little mango plant will sprout up, and in a few years it will become a tree, and hundreds of beautiful plum mangoes will hang from its branches. That is the irony and mystery of dying and rising: losing and finding.

Jesus is not asking us to attract suffering, rejection and death into our life. Don't go out looking for suffering and rejection and untimely death. But, denying them is not going to make them disappear; ignoring them is not going to make them dissipate, avoiding them is not going to eliminate them.

Basically, what Jesus is saying is this: Don't argue with reality; when you try to follow in his footsteps, as a disciple, suffering and pain are inevitable. Pain is also unavoidable because we live in a sinful world; everybody is not a disciple of Jesus and you are going to be hurt by some people.

Suffering and pain, struggling and dying are part of life; accept them, acknowledge them, face them and deal with them. And he showed us how to face them calmly and peacefully, by the way he suffered, carried the cross, died on the cross and by rising again. That is the blueprint for our life; that is the path of discipleship.

# 27. Living in a Dreadful and Wonderful World

2Cor: 1: 1-7

*For just as the sufferings of Christ flow over into our lives, so also through Christ our comfort overflows... And our hope for you is firm, because we know that just as you share in our sufferings, so also you share in our comfort.*

An elderly couple was getting ready for bed one night, the wife turned to her husband and said: "I am just so hungry for ice cream and there isn't any in the house." "I will get you some," the husband offered.

"You are so sweet, dear. Vanilla with chocolate sauce; write it down, you will forget."

"I won't forget," he said."

"With whipped cream on top."

"Vanilla with chocolate sauce and whipped cream on top," he repeated.

"And a cherry" she said; "And a cherry on the top."

"Please write it down; I know you will forget."

"I won't forget," he insisted. "Vanilla with chocolate sauce, whipped cream, and a cherry on top."

The husband left the house and returned after a while with a paper bag. He handed the bag to his wife in bed. She opened the bag and pulled out a ham sandwich.

She yelled at him:

"I told you to write it down; you forgot the mustard!"

Forgetting is a common experience; we all forget things. Scientists say that we forget 90% of what we learn. Most of the things we know are not at the forefront of our consciousness.

But there are certain undeniable realities of life we should never forget. One such reality is that we live in a dreadful and wonderful world; that our life can be both dreadful and wonderful at the same time. We want the world around us to be always wonderful. The fact of the matter is that it is mostly wonderful, but we don't see it that way, because the dreadful part takes center stage and we forget the wonderful part. What we see on TV is the dreadful part; the wonderful part rarely makes it to the 6 p.m. newscast.

Let me give you a few examples. During the last few weeks we have been exposed to two murder trials: The beating death of the homeless man in a Broward County court room, and the trial of Michael Hernandez in an Orlando court room.

On the night of January 12, 2006, two teenagers from Plantation, Brian Hooks and Thomas Dougherty, went to Esplanade Park in Fort Lauderdale, with base ball bats in hand. They wanted to beat up some homeless people for fun. A homeless man, named Norris Gaynor, 45, was sound asleep on a bench. The boys dragged him out of a sound sleep and beat his head repeatedly and he was killed. Gaynor's head caved in. You must have seen those chilling video tapes.

The prosecutor in his closing arguments said this: "Instead of being used for the fun and joy of playing baseball, the bats were used for the perverted fun and despicable joy of bashing the skulls of other human beings."

Hundreds of people reacted to this story by posting comments on the internet and some of the words used to describe this crime are: "reprehensible, horrible, brutal, unconscionable, grotesque, despicable, heartless and gut wrenching." So, that is a scene from the dreadful world.

Let me now take you to a scene in the Salvation Army homeless shelter, also in Fort Lauderdale just two miles north of the park where Norris Gaynor was brutally beaten to death. In that shelter, hundreds of homeless people wake up every morning, and they stand in line for their breakfast.

And you will see a group of men and women volunteers, some of them teenagers, who do it for extra credits, serving bacon, scrambled eggs and coffee to the homeless people with so much love and compassion in their hearts. So, that is a scene from the wonderful world.

Let me take you to a court room in Orlando where the trial of 18 year of Michael Hernandez took place.

On the morning of February 3rd, 2004, 14 year old Jaime Gough went to school like any other teenager. On that same, day, another 14 year old boy, Michael Hernandez, also went to school, but he had a knife in his bag. He apparently wanted to be a serial killer when he grew up. Michael asked Jamie, his friend, to go the bath room stalls with him. When they got there, according to Michael's testimony, he put his hand over Jaime's mouth, lifted his face up, and slit his throat.

According to Police, Jaime was slashed and stabbed more than 40 times. Michael left him there and went to his first period class. The victim was found lying in a pool of blood, his jacket, saturated in blood. Prosecutors said, "Michael killed Jaime in cold blood, without provocation and without mercy."

No normal human being can watch this trial without being profoundly affected by it. It is yet another incident from the dreadful world we live in. But there is a wonderful side to that same world: Every day, millions of young boys and girls go to school, they learn, they forge friendships, and they graduate and grow up to be productive citizens.

Let me give you one more example, the events of September, 11, 2001. We all know what happened that day. When 19 men flew air planes into the World Trade Center and when the towers were falling, which is the dreadful part, we also saw, hundreds of dedicated fire fighters, climbing the stairs of the burning building to save the lives of other human beings, which is the wonderful side of that dreadful event.

The dreadful and the wonderful always come as a package. They never come alone. All experiences in life are in pairs. Love and hate, joy and sorrow, night and day, good and bad are experienced in pairs. If you want to be happy and peaceful in life, you have to come to grips with that undeniable reality of life; there is no other way. It is called the law of polarity. "There is no reality without polarity."

Our human tendency is to be caught up in one, and forget the other; it does not work that way. To be emotionally free, you have to embrace both. Deepak Chopra says: "When a person quietly reconciles himself to all the contradictions that life offers, and can comfortably ride out the flow between the banks of birth and death, experiencing both, but getting stuck in neither, then he has attained freedom."

Jesus is a great example of this. Jesus lived in a dreadful world too. His time was not any different from ours. There was poverty and cruelty, injustice and murder during his time. The difference is that he faced those situations calmly and peacefully. Let us take a couple of examples.

When the Pharisees brought the woman caught in adultery in front of Jesus, it was a very dreadful situation. They were standing around this poor woman with stones in their hands, calling for bloody murder. What does Jesus do? In the midst of this noisy and angry crowd, where he could witness the cruel death of a woman right before him, Jesus sits on the ground and writes on the sand. Now how cool is that? They were so angry that they could have thrown those stones at Jesus himself, but Jesus is calm.

Let me take you to another scene, where a man is deathly ill. It is a very dreadful experience for the family of Lazarus. His sisters, Mary and Martha were hysterical that their brother was sick. So they send word to Jesus. What does Jesus do? John says: "Jesus loved Martha and her sister, and Lazarus very much. Yet after hearing that Lazarus was sick, he stayed on where he was for two more days."

Imagine hearing that your best friend is sick. You will begin to panic, stop what you are doing, and rush there, and while you drive there, your mind will be going in all directions, "Oh my God, what will happen if he dies; how is his family going to cope; I wonder if he has enough life insurance; his wife is going to be devastated." In dreadful situations, our heart and mind and soul are so wrapped with uncontrollable emotions that we are barely able to function.

What does Jesus do, he takes extra time, he is calm and cool and collected and peaceful. Jesus had this calmness and peacefulness not just when dreadful things happened around him. It was also true when the most dreadful thing happened **to** him.

Think of the arrest, and trial and crucifixion of Jesus. Look at his attitude and demeanor facing the most cruel and dreadful events in his life. Jesus does not get mad at his accusers, he does not curse out the soldiers who spat on his face, he prayed: "Lord, forgive them, for they don't know that they are doing." He prayed again: "Father, into your hands I commend my spirit."

Now, how did Jesus do that? Jesus was a very reflective person. His inner depth came from his prayerfulness. So many times in the gospels, the authors say, "and then Jesus went to pray." They don't say what he prayed for or how he prayed. I think most of his prayer was just meditation. Sitting quietly in a place and pondering on the mysteries of life. Spending time alone, away from the crowds and chatter, Jesus experienced God inside his heart.

**We are disciples of a man in whom the dreadful and the wonderful aspects of life blended beautifully: the crucifixion and the resurrection. The dreadful part did not destroy him; it elevated him to a new level of being, to a wonderful and glorious resurrection.**

That is our model: to be unflappable, steadfast and peaceful in the midst of the dreadful whether it happens to us or around us. To find that place inside us, that is unaffected by the turmoil of the world. It is like the bottom of the ocean. Although the top of the ocean is disturbed by wind and storm and debris, the bottom is calm, serene and peaceful. We reach that level of peace when we meditate on a regular basis.

Saint Paul guarantees that, as disciples, the dreadful and the wonderful will merge in our lives too through the sufferings and comfort that come from Jesus. "For just as the sufferings of Christ flow over into our lives, so also through Christ, our comfort overflows."

Notice that Paul uses "suffering and comfort" in the same sentence, as part of one package deal. As long as we live in this imperfect world, we cannot avoid suffering; but the comfort is knowing that Jesus is with us always and all ways.

**Never forget that we live in a Good Friday world, but we are an Easter people!**

# 28. God Can Only Do for You, What God Can Do Through You

Luke 9: 10-17

*Late in the afternoon, the Twelve came to him and said, "Send the crowds away so they can go to the surrounding villages and countryside and find food and lodging, because we are in a remote place here." He replied, "You give them something to eat.*

An old lady who was well known for her faith, loved to shout every day, "Praise the Lord" at the top of her voice. This particularly irritated her next door neighbor who was a confirmed atheist. He would tell the old lady: "There isn't any Lord."

The old lady struggled to make ends meet with her meager pension, and with no food in the pantry, she decided to pray to God for help.

"Praise the Lord," she exclaimed from her front porch, "God I need food; please send me some groceries."

The next morning, she found a large bag of groceries on her front porch. She shouted: "Praise the Lord: God has delivered for me."

"Aha," said the neighbor, emerging from behind a bush: "That is where you are wrong; I bought those groceries, not God. Like I keep telling you there is no Lord!"

The old lady threw her hands in the air in delight, "Praise the Lord! He not only sent me groceries, but he made the devil pay for it."

Apart from its hilariousness, there is a larger meaning to this story and that is where I want to focus this morning. And that is the title of today's sermon: "God can only do for you, what God can do through you." When you hear that, you might raise your eye brows in disbelief. You might say: "That is not true; God can do anything he wants; God is God, and man is man; this is blasphemy."

When I say, "God can only do for you what God can do through you," it is not a statement about God's weakness, but rather, it is an affirmation of man's strength and our vocation to be co-creators with God.

Over the centuries, we have been beaten down as wretched sinners and unworthy souls who helplessly toil in the valley of tears; we have been labeled as weaklings, born with original sin, that unless we do certain specific things, we are destined for hell. Our spirituality was centered on a God "up there" and us "down here," and there is a chasm separating us. God will smite us, if we dare to touch him, and punish us if we disobey him. These ideas were handed down to us, over the centuries, and are based on the Old Testament and the thinking of theologians like Augustine and Aquinas.

They are great thinkers and pillars of the church, but we do not have to uncritically believe everything everyone says, even if they are the greatest thinkers of times past. We are allowed to think and figure out for ourselves and that is what faith- seeking understanding is all about. We need to consciously unlearn what we have unconsciously learned. According to psychologist James Hollis, "**Any spirituality that keeps people in bondage to fear, to tradition, to anything other than that which is validated by their personal experience, is doing violence to the soul.**"

It doesn't matter who said it, or how profound the statement is, if it does not apply to you, it won't work for you. For example, Jesus said, "Love your enemies, do good to those who hate you." It is a great teaching, given by the greatest teacher of all times, Jesus Christ, son of

God himself, but if you don't practice that teaching, it means nothing. It doesn't build up the kingdom that Jesus wanted to establish on earth.

In other words, God cannot force you to love everybody; God does not just make things happen without our willingness to align with the will of God. So we have a responsibility and a vocation to be instruments of God in this world. That is what being co-creators mean.

Let us look at the miracle of Jesus feeding five thousand people with five loaves of bread and two fishes. According to the story, there was a crowd listening to Jesus one day. It got late in the evening, and the disciples became concerned. They wanted Jesus to dismiss the crowd so that they could go home and eat.

But people were hungry. The disciples were kind of lazy and they had no imagination. Instead of trying to address the needs of the people, they wanted to take the easy way; send the people home. But Jesus wouldn't do that. He wanted to give them some food. Jesus called everyone together and tells them to sit down. They sat on the grass, and Jesus takes the five loaves of bread and two fish and somehow everyone was satisfied.

Mathew's account clarifies the number. He makes it explicit that it was 5000 men "besides women and children." That means the number could be as high as 20,000 to 30,000 people. In those days, women and children didn't count; they didn't matter.

What do you think really happened? Some preachers say that when Jesus prayed, the heavens opened and the loaves of bread and fish fell from heaven into the hands of people, like a rain of bread and fish. Or maybe like the magician, David Copperfield, who makes things appear with the sleight of his hand. I do not think that is what happened. I don't think Jesus was a magician.

What happened that day was definitely a miracle. **The miracle was not bread and fish falling from the sky, but the miracle**

**of transformation that happened in the hearts of people:** the transformation that Jesus caused with his presence and his power. Now, what do I mean by that?

In those days with no television or radio, people went out to listen to teachers. Since there were no McDonalds of Burger King or any restaurant for that matter, people packed food with them when they went for public events. Instead of each one eating his own food alone and separate from the other, Jesus must have invited them and encouraged them to sit as a group and share their food.

**Jesus transformed a group of selfish individual eaters to a community of sharers**. That is the miracle: changing them from a "group" to a "community," from meeting their needs as separate individuals to meeting the needs of the community. That is the miracle that happened on that hillside.

When each one shared what he had, there was plenty for everyone, and 12 baskets of leftovers. This was the first potluck dinner in the bible! Anybody who has been to potluck dinners knows that there is always plenty of food.

It was not so much that the people didn't have anything, but they had not realized what they had. They also realized their willingness to share; they also found out that when things are shared, there is plenty to go around. That's the real miracle. That's where the power lies; when people realize their own abilities to help someone else.

Statistics show that there is enough food in the world to feed every one if we find a way to equitably make it happen. As Billy Graham used to say, "There is enough for every man's need, not for every man's greed." Jesus had the power to make ordinary people do extraordinary things. The question is whether we will let Jesus enter our hearts and transform us.

When we pool our resources, miracles will happen.

We have to get over this notion that God will take care of it, or that a supernatural miracle will solve all our personal and national problems. When was the last time you saw manna falling from heaven to take care of poverty in the world? When was the last time you saw a war stop because God came down and stopped it?

Poverty will end when people realize that hoarding of food and wealth is a sin against God's people and open their hearts and wallets. Wars will end when people realize that killing people for one's selfish gain is wrong.

You may have seen the movie, *Bruce Almighty*. The movie is about Jim Carey getting all the powers of God for a week. When he gets so frustrated by the problems of the world, he goes to God, played by Morgan Freeman, and complains. When God walks up the ladder, a helpless Bruce asks God, looking up: "Are you leaving me, I need help" and God replies: "You are looking up, Bruce. That is your problem; that is everybody's problem."

Always remember, God can only do for you what he can do through you. When our hearts are transformed by the power of Christ, then the world will be transformed. Francis of Assisi understood this so well, and that is why he prayed:

*Lord, make me an instrument of your peace,*
*Where there is hatred, let me sow love;*
*Where there is injury, pardon;*
*Where there is doubt, faith;*
*Where there is despair, hope;*
*Where there is darkness, light;*
*Where there is sadness, joy;*

*O Divine Master, grant that I may not so much seek*
*To be consoled as to console;*
*To be understood as to understand;*
*To be loved as to love.*

*For it is in giving that we receive;*
*It is in pardoning that we are pardoned;*
*And it is in dying that we are born to eternal life.*

Let us make that prayer, our daily prayer.

# 29. Change Is Inevitable

Rom: 8: 28-31, 37-39

*For I am convinced that neither death nor life, neither angels nor demons, neither the present nor the future, nor any powers, neither height nor depth, nor anything else in all creation, will be able to separate us from the love of god that is in Christ Jesus our Lord.*

I just returned from a trip to India a few days ago. I went to visit my mom who suddenly became ill and is now bedridden. It was a draining experience both physically and emotionally. Physically, because I traveled for 32 hours taking 3 separate flights, one lasting 14 hours non-stop, and went through three different time zones, throwing my body clock off the balance.

It was emotionally draining because I was going to see my mom, bedridden for the first time in 86 years of her life. I walked into the house at 6 a.m. Thursday morning three weeks ago, totally exhausted and saw my mom in bed, barely able to speak. She motioned with her hands, acknowledging my presence, but that was all she was able to do. And I began to cry. Then, she began to cry. And then my brother, sister-in-law, nephew and his wife, who all live in the same house, also began to cry. For about ten minutes, no one spoke a word.

My tears were the result of the thoughts going through my mind at that time, because it is our thoughts that generate emotions. I was processing a huge change of reality in my life. To understand this, you have to know my mom and the dynamics of our relationship.

She is a very devout Catholic and in her younger days, she used to go to church three days a week; on Fridays in honor of The Sacred Heart of Jesus, on Saturdays in honor of Mary, and on Sundays for mass. She went walking two miles each way on dusty roads, and offered the strains of walking as a sacrifice to God.

During my 11 visits to India in the last 20 years, there was one thing that was constant: My mom standing in the portico of the house, waiting for my car to turn the corner. As soon as my journey begins, she starts saying special prayers for my safe trip. She knows I am taking three separate flights and traveling 10,000 miles, and she is worried about safety. A few hours before I am supposed to arrive, she would start pacing through the house with her rosary in hand, nervously praying and anxiously waiting.

Once I arrive, she makes sure that I shower and change, and eat a sumptuous Indian breakfast and rest for a few hours. She would make sure that the small children in the house, my nephew's kids, don't make too much noise to disturb me; she would tell the neighbors dropping in to see me to come another time. It is pure, protective maternal love.

All that was missing this time, and it was a huge change for me. Knowing that my mom will not be the same again, ever, was too much to bear, and that explains the flood of tears.

But one thing that helped me process that experience and to cope with its pain, was this book which was part of my reading material for the trip. It is called *When Everything Changes, Change_Everything: In a Time of Turmoil, a Pathway to Peace*, by one of my favorite authors, Neale Donald Walsh.

In this book, he talks about 9 changes that can change everything. But the one that got my attention was the chapter called. "Change your ideas about why change occurs." And at the end of the chapter in capital letters he states: ALL CHANGE IS FOR THE

BETTER; THERE IS NO SUCH THING AS A CHANGE FOR THE WORSE.

My first reaction was disagreement with that statement. How can being laid off, or losing a house, or the end of a relationship, or the death of a loved one, be changes for the better? How can my mother's illness and anticipated death, be a change for the better for me? I have never heard anyone say that so forcefully and argue it so convincingly. You have to read the entire book to grasp all the ramifications of his argument, but the gist of it is this:

Life is about change. Change starts at the moment of our conception. We change from a zygote with two cells to an embryo and a fetus in a matter of weeks, and to a full grown baby in nine months. The process of birth is a huge change: from the comforts of our mother's womb to the calamities of a crazy world. There is blood and muck and pain. The mother is screaming, the baby is crying but nobody in their right mind wants to stop any of it, because with the change of environment for the baby, something beautiful is happening.

The baby changes from an innocent infant to a terrible toddler to a precocious child to an awkward adolescent to a confused teenager; and then to young adulthood to adulthood, to middle age, old age and then ultimately death. There is no way to stop any of these changes. Actually, nobody wants to stop them.

Imagine a one year old baby never growing and developing. He is now five years old, but still lies in the crib, wears diapers, does not walk or talk or eat by himself. Nothing has changed from the day he was one year old. You won't like that; in fact you will be extremely sad and angry about the changes not happening.

Change happens in our bodies all the time. All the cells in our body are replaced every 7 years; our skin is replaced every 30 days; the inner linings of our digestive system are replaced every 36 hours. If those changes did not happen, we will not be alive.

Change happens in our personal lives: end of relationships, moving from one place to another, losing a job or a home, losing dear ones to death, etc.

Change is happening nationally and globally, too. Change was the one word that helped Barack Obama rise to the presidency of the United States in a historic election last year.

Look at what happened last month. General Motors filed for bankruptcy; an American icon that lasted for 101 years, changing its face and its fate. Nobody thought that would happen.

Change is happening much faster than before. Our ability to communicate globally about everything within seconds is what has changed the way we experience change. The speed of our communications is catching up with the speed of our changes.

**So *change is what is, and there is no way to change that.*** What can be changed are the way we deal with change, and the way we are changed by change.

Some of us deny that change ever took place, or we cope with it by ignoring it. We just don't want to face that something is different for us; we retreat into silence, into an attitude of "business as usual." There's a cost, though, for change is here, whether we like it or not.

Others of us do not deny the presence of change. We fight against its uncertainty. Anger is often our first response. We resent having to accommodate to anything different. We fear what we might lose. We can't imagine that change could bring about an improvement; therefore we conclude that it will always be for the worse. Sometimes we become depressed. Change brings us great grief.

Another way to resist change is with an excessive idealization of the past and the way things were. We say things like: "We can't do that, we've never done it that way before," "Remember the good old days?" "Why can't we just stay the way we are?"

I do not know anyone who is able to take change completely in stride. There are so many complex feelings associated with change. It is unsettling; it pulls us out of our security zone, and presents us with something different. It takes away the notion that we can predict the future; it takes away our illusion of control.

It means we lose that which we have known. Whether we hated the status quo or loved it, whether we were comfortable with it or not, change is often deeply frightening and always anxiety producing. So how in the world are we supposed to cope with it?

The best way to cope with change is to realize that change is synonymous with LIFE, because if nothing changes, that means we are dead. And LIFE is synonymous with GOD, who is the source of all life.

God is not a detached observer of the changes in our lives, but an active participant. God is right in the middle of everything that we go through in life. God is the animating force behind everything that happens in the universe. "Animating" comes from the word "anima" which means "spirit", and "Spirit" is another word for God.

So when changes happen in our lives, we don't have to pray to a far away God to help us cope. All we have to do is realize that GOD IS CHANGE, because as St. Paul said: "He is not far from us; in him we live, move and have our being." Nothing happens, apart from God, away from God, aside from God.

That is why the Psalmist asks: "Where can I go from your Spirit? Where can I go from your presence? If I go up to the heavens you are there. If I make my bed in the depths, you are there."

And then comes my most favorite line from psalm 139: V .13

"For you created my inmost being; you knit me together in my mother's womb."

As I sat at my mother's bedside, I remembered those words: I was knit together by a loving God, in the womb of this woman who is now coming to the conclusion of her life. God is right in the midst of the changes that are happening in my mom's life. **She is now very fragile; God is in that fragility; I am now very sad; God is in that sadness; God is the witness and the strength of everything I m going through.**

Regardless of what we go through in our lives, these words of Apostle Paul should comfort us:

"I am convinced that neither death nor life, neither angels nor demons, neither the present, nor the future, nor any powers, neither height nor depth, nor anything else in all creation, will be able to separate us from the love of God that is in Christ Jesus Our Lord."

# 30. Apply Directly to Your Heart

John 13: 34-35

*A new command I give you: Love one another. As I have loved you, so you must love one another. By this all men will know that you are my disciples, if you love one another.*

In the last two sermons, we were reflecting on the nature of love, and today I am going to talk about how to practice that love, because love is the central message of the gospels. Love is at the core of Christian life. In today's reading Jesus says that it is love that makes us disciples.

Jesus says: **"I give you a new commandment."** That means there must have been an **old** commandment. What was the old commandment? Actually there are ten of them, given through Moses on Mount Sinai. These are the ones we learn first in religion classes. These are the ones that Judge Moore in Alabama wanted displayed in front of his court house.

Only two of the Ten Commandments are stated in a positive language: about keeping Sabbath holy and honoring parents. The other eight are cast in a negative language.

Thou shall not have another God except me, Thou shall not take God's name in vain, thou shall not kill, thou shall not steal, thou shall not commit adultery, thou shall not bear false witness, thou shalt not covet your neighbor's house, and thou shalt not covet your neighbor's wife or animals or property.

Notice that wife and animals and property are bunched into one, because women had no value or equality in those days.

A Sunday school teacher was once discussing commandments with 5th graders. After explaining the commandment to "honor thy father and mother," she asked the class: "Is there a commandment that teaches how to treat our brothers and sisters?" Without missing a beat, one little boy answered: "Thou shall not kill."

By using negative language, the old commandments prohibit bad behavior rather than promote good behavior. Many Christians observe Lent like this. You are familiar with the question: "What are you giving up for lent?" And people would say, "I am giving up chocolate or meat." The emphasis is on avoiding wrong rather than doing good.

Jesus changes the negative tone of the old commandments. The new commandment is not just to refrain from doing wrong things, but practice doing the right thing. "I give you a new commandment; love one another as I have loved you."

In the second line Jesus makes it very clear how we should practice love. It is not just any kind of love; there is a benchmark for this love: **"**You must love one another, **just as I have loved you."**

We usually love those who love us; we love people of the same group, or people who think like us, or look like us. We don't make great effort to go out of our way to love people who are outside our circle.

When was the last time you invited somebody you dislike to your house for dinner? Have you heard anyone say: "I love Bin Laden," or "I love bad drivers," or "I love that neighbor who always parks his huge car in the street right in front of my house?" No, we don't hear that because we don't extend our love to such people.

Jesus lays down a very clear, unambiguous criterion for our love: We must love as Jesus loved. And how did he love us? There are three main characteristics of Jesus' love. **It is forgiving love, it is sacrificial love and it is an inclusive love.**

First, it is forgiving love. If Jesus were to love only those who loved him back, he should have loved Mary Magdalene and a few other women.

Mary Magdalene is the only person mentioned by name in the gospels who stood by Jesus till the end. Read sections of the gospels about "the death of Jesus." Mt: 5:45 says: "When he was crucified, many women were present looking from a distance. Among them were Mary Magdalene and the mother of Zebedee's sons." Mk: 16:33, says the same thing. Luke 24: 44 repeats it and John: 19:25 mentions the names of both Mary, mother of Jesus, and Mary Magdalene.

There were just a handful of people who stood by him till the end. Everyone else including his disciples abandoned him and ran away. Not just mere abandonment, but betrayal and denial, not once, but three times by Peter who is supposed to be the leader of the pack.

The members of the religious establishment did not love Jesus. They hated him enough to kill him. The political establishment, headed by the Romans, wanted to eliminate him because he was a threat to them. People did not like his message, because it was a difficult message to follow.

But he forgave them all: the disciples who ran away, the authorities who condemned him, the soldiers who slapped him, and the crowd that mocked him: "Father forgives them, for they don't know what they are doing." Jesus practiced forgiving love till the end.

The second characteristic of Jesus' love is that it was sacrificial love. He said: "There is no greater love than to lay down one's life for the other", and he did exactly that.

It is very important to notice that this new commandment to love appears in the 13th chapter of John's gospel. If you look at that chapter, it begins with Jesus washing the feet of his disciples. It was the most humbling thing to do, to kneel in front of his disciples and wash their dirty feet. After doing that act of humility, service and sacrifice, he told his disciples: "I give you a new commandment, love one another just as I have loved you." It s a direct command, set in the context of a powerful imagery of service and sacrifice.

The third characteristic of Jesus' love is that it is all inclusive. In other words, his circle of love was large enough to include everyone: the sinners, the tax collectors, the prostitutes, the Samaritan woman, the leper whom no one even would look at, the soldiers who slapped him, the thief who ridiculed him, and the disciples who betrayed him. **Jesus did not keep anybody outside the circle of his love.**

When you hear this, you must be saying to yourself: "It is very hard; nobody is practicing this kind of love." You are right; very few people are practicing it. The majority of Christians are not, and that is why the world is in the shape it is today. That is why there is so much hatred, prejudice, terrorism and wars, because majority of the followers of Jesus have not taken his advice to love others, seriously. They talk the talk, but they don't walk the walk.

You must have seen Christian preachers like Pat Robertson, Jerry Falwell, Ted Haggard, John Haggee, et.al. on your television screens. All of them preach partisan love, not Christian love. After events of 9/11, I heard Jerry Falwell say, "Let us go over to the Middle East and nuke all the Muslim terrorists, in the name of the Lord."

Loving like Jesus is the only thing that will change the world. Imagine Jesus cursing out the soldiers, or asking his disciples to take sword and fight the injustice that was done to him? Imagine a Jesus who hated his tormentors? Had he done that, he would have ended up as just another forgotten criminal.

Had he not loved his enemies, there would have been no Jesus Christ. There would have been no Christianity, and we would not be sitting here worshiping him as our Lord and Savior. So, loving your enemies is a good thing, it is what changes the world, it is what brings joy in our hearts and peace in the world; it is what makes us disciples.

When I think about this difficult commandment, I am reminded of a commercial that was on TV. I am sure you have seen it a hundred times. The announcer says: *"Head on, apply directly to your head..." and then this girl comes on and says with such disdain: "Head on apply directly to your head, head on apply directly to your head....I hate your commercial, but your product is amazing."*

**Loving others as Jesus loved, forgiving, sacrificial, inclusive love is an unpleasant message, but it is good for you if you practice i**t. You might hate the commercial, but the byproduct is very good. Let me share with you a recent experience.

A few months ago, my car was damaged by landscapers. The car was parked on my drive way. This guy was mowing the grass on his motorized lawnmower, and accidentally scraped the side of my car. So I called the lawn company. One of the managers came out, examined the car, and asked the employee if he had hit my car. He denied it, and the manager concluded that his company was not responsible for the damage. He even alleged that I might have caused the damage myself, but didn't know about it.

I was obviously upset. I called the owner of the company and complained about the decision of the on-site manager, but to no avail. In the meantime, I am walking around feeling angry in my heart. Every time I saw their vehicles in the neighborhood, I had revengeful feelings; every time I looked at the scrape on the side of my car, I felt angry towards those people.

It went on for a few days, and I did not like it. I am a disciple of Jesus who is supposed to love others as Jesus loved; I am supposed to love my enemies. So one day, I sat down and prayed: "*Lord, I don't like these negative feelings in my heart. Please help me to forgive them, please help me to love them even though they don't deserve it.*"

After that prayer, my anger began to subside, my heart began to clear up and I felt a sense of wholeness and peace again. It was a good feeling and I liked it much better than walking around with a dark, heavy, and unloving heart. Then, an idea popped up in my mind: Write a letter to the owner of the lawn company.

That evening, I wrote a letter explaining the situation. I mailed the letter on a Monday, and that Friday, I got a call from the owner: "I received your letter; I still don't believe that my employee caused the damage to your car, but as a courtesy, I am going to send you a check for $500. I want my customers to be happy."

The estimate for the repairs of my car was $509! I believe that my forgiveness and positive energy affected the attitude of the owner towards me.

I want you know that loving those who do you wrong and forgiving those who hurt you will always produce positive results. Hating others never works for the good. As Gandhi said, "An eye for an eye makes the whole world blind."

**So if you claim that you have Jesus in your heart, you have to practice forgiving, sacrificial and inclusive love. You have no other choice.**

That is the only way others are going to find out that you are his disciples. "Apply Jesus directly to your heart."

# 31. `Prayer As Energy

Mt 7: 7-11

*Ask and it will be given to you; seek and you will find; knock and the door will be opened to you. For everyone who asks receives; he who seeks finds; and to him who knocks, the door will be opened.*

Prayer is a very complicated thing. Nobody knows how it works. For example in today's reading Jesus tells his disciples: "Ask and you shall receive; for everyone who asks, receives and everyone who knocks enters." But we know from our experience that everything we ask for, we don't get.

When we don't get what we pray for, we come up with explanations and excuses. We say things like: "It may not be God's will," "God sees the future and it may not be good for me at this time," "Man proposes, God disposes." "God is in charge," etc.

Most people think that God is separate from us, something like a celestial vending machine; when we say a prayer, it is like pushing a button and God answers them. If that idea helps you, keep it.

I like to share with you a new way of understanding prayer: Prayer as energy:

For example, what happens when I pray for Dolores here is that my prayerful thoughts and feelings towards Dolores travel through space as energy waves and reaches Dolores, and they act as healing balm for her. It is different from praying to a God "up there" who hands out a favor, which is a vertical understanding of prayer. What I am talking about is more of a horizontal understanding.

I found a great example of prayer as energy in the book, *Eat Pray Love*.

This book came out a couple of years ago; I used to see it in bookstores, but never picked up, because there is a picture of spaghetti on the cover, and it is my least favorite food; Besides, someone had told me that it was a 'chic book.' But the secretary at my church suggested that I read it, and she assured me that I would like it. Even though it is a chic book, she said, anyone with a feminine side would like it. I have a strong feminine side, so I really enjoyed reading it.

The heroine of the book is the author herself, Elizabeth Gilbert, who is 34 years old. She was going through a contentious divorce, a volatile rebound romance, and a severe bout of depression. She had everything a modern American woman would want: a husband, an apartment in New York, a house in Connecticut, a successful career as a writer, and plenty of money But instead of feeling happy and fulfilled, she felt consumed by panic and confusion. More than once, she was at risk of suicide.

So she decided to leave everything behind: her marriage, her home, her boyfriend, and her job, and decided to devote 12 months of her life to a journey of introspection and self-discovery. She decided to do this by spending time in three countries, Italy, India and Indonesia. Four months each in each country.

In Italy, she would explore the aspects of pleasure: eating, drinking, dancing, visiting places, but no sexual pleasures. She had taken a vow of celibacy. In India, she would spend four months in an Ashram praying and meditating. And in Indonesia she would find true love.

She thought that all these countries begin with the letter I, a fairly auspicious sign of a voyage of self-discovery.

This is a good book for anyone who is really struggling in life or having a hard time in relationships, a crisis of faith, lack of meaning, or just terribly depressed, confused or at the brink of suicide. The author's life epitomizes all that. And she talks about it openly and plainly, and shows how she came out of it through her inner journey.

It is a memoir, a travel guide, self-help and philosophy all in one, and a real page turner. I enjoyed this book for its insights about God, spirituality and prayer.

She writes: "Faith is walking face first and full speed into the dark." **"To know God, you need only to renounce one thing: your sense of division from God."**

But the main reason I chose to share this book with you is to show how prayer can be understood as energy.

As I said, the author was going through a bitter divorce. Her husband did not want a divorce; so he gave her a hard time. He refused to sign the divorce papers and she was extremely frustrated. She would call her lawyer ten times a day and ask him if her husband had signed the papers and after each call she would get angry and frustrated, because the husband had again refused to sign the papers.

She would curse her husband, cuss at her lawyer, throw the phone against the wall, pound the table in anger and frustration, and drink too much to mask the pain. But she never prayed. It never occurred to her that she could pray about it.

So, one day, while driving through Kansas, her best friend Iva told her that she should pray to God about her divorce.

She was not sure if she should ask God for specific things. Iva convinced her that she should petition the Universe for whatever she needed. "You are part of this universe, Liz, you are a constituent and you have every right to participate in the actions of the universe and to let your feelings known. So put your opinion out there. Make your case."

If you were to write a petition to God, right now, what would it say? So, she pulled out a notebook and wrote this petition:

*Dear God: Please intervene and help end this divorce. My husband and I have failed at our marriage and now we are failing at our divorce. This poisonous process is bringing suffering to us and to everyone who cares about us.*

*I recognize that you are busy with wars and tragedies and much larger conflicts than the ongoing dispute of one dysfunctional couple. But it is my understanding that the health of the planet is affected by the health of every individual on it. As long as even two souls are locked in conflict, the whole world is contaminated by it; Similarly, if even one or two souls can be free from discord, this will increase the general health of the whole world, the way few healthy cells in a body can increase the general health of that body.*

*It is my most humble request , then, that you help us end this conflict, so that two more people can have the chance to become free and healthy, and so there will be just a little bit less animosity and bitterness in a world that is already far too troubled by suffering.*

*I thank you for your kind attention.*

Respectfully, Elizabeth M. Gilbert.

She read it to her friend Iva, who she said she would sign that petition to God. So she gave it to her to sign it, but her friend was driving, so she said: "Let us say, I just signed it in my heart."

And she asked who else would sign it; her father, mother and sister. OK, they just did, consider their names added. Who else would sign it? Start naming names:

So she started naming names of all the people who she thought would sign that petition. She named all her close friends, more family members, the people she worked with. She closed her eyes and waited for more names to come to her mind. "I think Bill and Hillary Clinton just signed it."

Iva said to her that anybody can sign that petition. "Call on anyone living or dead and start collecting signatures."

"Abraham Lincoln just signed it; And Gandhi, and Mandela and all the peacemakers. Eleanor Roosevelt, Mother Teresa, Bono, Jimmy Carter, Mohammad Ali, Jackie Robinson, and the Dalia Lama. My Italian teacher, my therapist, and my agent, Martin Luther King and Katherine Hepburn, Joan of Arc, Ms. Carpenter, my $4^{th}$ grade teacher and Jim Henson.

The names just spilled from her and they did not stop for almost an hour as they drove through Kansas. And she became filled with a grand sense of protection, surrounded by the collective good will of so many people.

The list finally wound down and her anxiety wound down with it. She was sleepy and Iva told her to take a nap. She closed her eyes and slept for about ten minutes and when she woke up, her friend was still driving.

And then the cell phone rang. "I looked at that crazy little phone vibrating with excitement in the ash tray of the rental car. I felt disoriented, kind of stoned from my nap, suddenly unable to remember how the telephone works."

"Go ahead, answer the thing" Iva said. I picked up the phone and whispered "hello."

"Great news", my lawyer announced from distant New York City. **"He just signed it."**

Her husband had signed the divorce papers.

For me it is great story about how communal prayer works; how the positive energy from all the people around us work in our favor, because everything is energy. When we think loving thoughts about someone or say a prayer for somebody, we are sending positive energy towards that person. Imagine having hundreds of people to send that energy to you.

But this energy is not separate from God. It is actually God's energy, coming through God's people, who are created in the image and likeness of God. God lives in each one of them. So when people pray for us, they are sharing the God within them with us. When we pray for someone else, we are sharing our God energy with them.

So the more people you have in your circle of concern, the more blessings you receive.

So if you want your prayers to be answered, love everybody in the world. If you can love 6 billion people without prejudice and judgmental attitude, you will get 6 billion pieces of divine energy.

Every time you ask, you will receive; every time you seek, you will find; every time you knock, it will be opened to you.

**So, if your prayers are not answered, check your heart to see how many people are outside your circle of love.**

Look at Mathew Chapter 7. The section on the "Power of Prayer," verses 7 through 11, is sand witched between two other teachings. Verses 1 through 6 ask us to "Avoid judging people." Jesus says: "Stop passing judgment; why look at the speck in your brother's eye when you miss the plank in your own?"

Then verse 12 is the Golden Rule: "Treat others the way you would have them treat you: this sums up the law and the prophets."

So the message here is that, if you can stop judging people and start loving everyone, all your prayers will be answered.

**Every unanswered prayer has the love component missing!**

# 32. Implications of 'Our Father'

Luke: 11:1-5

*One day Jesus was praying in a certain place .When he finished, one of his disciples said to him, "Lord, teach us to pray, just as John taught his disciples to pray. He said to them: "When you pray, say, Father, hallowed be your name, your kingdom come. Give us this day our daily bread, forgive us our sins, for we also forgive everyone who sins against us and lead us not into temptation, but deliver us from evil.*

We all have experience with voice mails. Imagine God having a voice mail?

"Thank you for calling heaven. I am sorry, all of our angels are busy helping other sinners; however, your prayer is important to us and we will answer it in the order it was received. If you would like to speak to God. Press 1, Jesus press 2, Holy Spirit, press 3. To find a loved one who has been assigned to heaven, enter his or her date of baptism followed by the pound sign. If you get a negative response, please hang up and call area code 666. For reservations in heaven, please enter John 3: 16. For answers to nagging questions about dinosaurs, the age of the earth, and evolution, wait until you arrive. If you are calling after hours and need emergency assistance, please contact your local pastor."

Pastors and churches are symbols of the presence of God. We call our pastor when we have a spiritual need. We come to this church every week, because we want to get something that nourishes our soul. We come here because it is a special place; we come here because it is God's house. But who is God? What is God's name?

About 3000 years ago, this question was asked by Moses on Mount Sinai. We read about that in the book of Genesis. Moses was told by God to go to the people but before he did that, Moses wanted to know God's name. So he asked, "What shall I say your name is when people ask me." And God said: I AM.

Now imagine going to a party and introducing yourself: "Hi, I am who am" and people will look at you funny. We always say I am Paul, or Jim, or Tom, etc. When we place a name after I am, we define and limit ourselves. If I am Paul, that means I am not Jim, or Joe, or Tom.

Why did God stop with I AM? Because God is limitless, infinite, incomprehensible, eternal, immutable, invisible, omniscient, omnipotent, and omnipresent, the alpha and the omega, the beginning and end of everything.

But man could not deal with God being so far and high, with all these qualities that his small mind could not fathom. So ever since the beginning of time, humans have tried to complete the sentence, "I AM", with names like Allah, Krishna, Rama, Vishnu, Jahveh, and started separate religions. According to Kabalah, God has 72 names!

Many wars have been fought in the name of God. The 19 hijackers who flew planes into the World Trade Center were doing it in the name of Allah. Our president who is waging war in Iraq is doing it after consulting with a 'higher power." A few months ago, Army General Boykin said: "Our God is bigger than their god."

Today, I like to reflect on the name of God that Jesus revealed to us. The most revolutionary teaching of Jesus was that he taught us to call God, father. The Hebrew word "abba" literally means "daddy." In the parable of the prodigal son, Luke 15, God is portrayed as a father: kind, generous, forgiving and unconditionally loving. Some authors have said that it should be called the story of the 'prodigal father,' who lavishes his love limitlessly.

Compare this with the God of Moses who is distant, vengeful and cruel. Moses was afraid to look at that God. This is a God who strikes you dead if you dare to touch him.

Read the story in the 2nd book of Samuel chapter six when the Ark of the Covenant was being carried to the town. Sons of a man named Abinabad was walking on the side of the cart that was carrying the Ark. When they came to the threshing floor of Nordan, the oxen that were carrying the cart went towards the hay and the cart began to tip, and Uzzah reached out his hand to the Ark of God and steadied it, and guess what happened to Uzzah? Chapter 6, v. 7 says: "And the Lord was angry with Uzzah; God struck him on that spot and he died there before the Lord."

King David himself was frightened by this experience that he sent the Ark to the house of a guy named Obeddedom.

It is unfortunate that majority of people today still believe that God is somewhere up there, outside of us, a separate entity away from us, someone who will reward us if we do good and punish us if we behave badly. People still talk about the 'wrath of God' and the 'fear of God.' It is almost like people don't want to believe what Jesus said about God: our **father.**

By teaching us to call God "our father," Jesus lays down once and for all that the relationship between God and man is that of a father and child. Not master and slave, not lord and servant, but parent and child.

We know that, men and women, despite all their imperfections, always try to be the best parents for their children. Now there are exceptions; there are fathers who don't provide for their children, who don't pay child support, who abuse or abandon their children.

But by and large, a father loves, takes care of, and protects his child. At least, that is the ideal of fatherhood.

I have to say that my experience of God as father is directly related to my own father. I grew up in a village in India. My father was a farmer and we had a paddy field in front of our house that became a lake during the monsoon. My school was across the lake and we had no canoe or boat. On school days, my father would carry me on his shoulders across the lake walking through four feet of water. I would sit on his shoulders, clutching his head, feeling safe and secure on my dad's shoulders.......and my relationship with God originated in that relationship with my father.

If God is my father, and I am his son or daughter, it follows that I share in the nature of God. From genetics and biology, we know that the child shares genes with his parent. Do you believe that we have "divine genes" in us? And since God is divine spirit, man must essentially be divine spirit also. That is why a famous author said: "We are primarily spiritual beings with a human experiences, rather than just human beings with spiritual experiences." That is the meaning of the statement that "we are created in the image and likeness of God."

**So prayer is not just repetition of certain formulas, but experiencing the power of the divinity within us. It is an invitation to be co-creators with God, to make the world a better place; it is about taking responsibility for the welfare of our neighbors who are also children of the same God.**

It is about finding solutions to the problems we mostly create, rather than complaining and saying: "Why God doesn't care?" "Or, why is God punishing us?" It is more about changing ourselves, rather than asking God to change the world.

Another important point is that Jesus did not tell us to call God "**my** father," but "**our** father," and this indicates beyond any doubt, that every other human being is my brother or my sister. By teaching us to call God, our father, Jesus is ending people's false thinking about a "chosen race," or about the spiritual superiority of any one group of humans over any other group. **He removes the illusion that the members of any nation, or race or territory, or group or class, or color, are in the sight of God superior to any other group.**

St. Peter said it so beautifully when he proclaimed in Acts 10: 34: "God has no favorites; anyone who does his will is acceptable to God."

Look at the world around us. Problems such as prejudice, racism, hatred, terrorism, and wars come from the false thinking that we are separate from each other; that we are better than the other, that we are in competition with each other; the false thinking that other people are our enemies, that we have to diminish, dominate or destroy them to ensure our safety and survival.

So if you want to be a truly prayerful person, you have to be willing to accept others as your brothers and sisters, and embrace them in love. **Until we do that, praying the Lord's Prayer will be just empty sounds coming from tongues that are disconnected from the soul.**

My entire spiritual life is contained in the first two words of the Lord's Prayer: **Our Father**. I take each word very seriously. I take the word "father" seriously and firmly believe that God is my loving father. Regardless of what happens in my life, good or bad, blessings or tragedies, He is always with me, loving me, protecting me, and giving me the strength to deal with life as it unfolds.

I take the word "our" extremely seriously. If God is the father of every human being on the face of this planet, that makes every person my brother or sister.

**For me, the cord that connects me with God, does not go from my heart towards God directly, but it weaves through the heart of**

**every human being on this earth, and reaches God, as a long and colorful string, binding us all together in a cosmic fellowship.**

Having a prayer life means experiencing that connection and living in the awareness of that relationship.

# 33. What Is Heaven's Zip Code?

Luke: 17:20-22

*Once having been asked by the Pharisees when the kingdom of God would come, Jesus replied, "The Kingdom of God does not come with your careful observation, nor will people say, "here it is or "there it is," because the Kingdom of God is within you!*

During our Vacation Bible School a few weeks ago, I had the honor of teaching the adult class. There were about 10 people in the class and we had some very interesting discussions. And the topic of heaven came up. "Where is heaven? "Who gets there?" "What is it like?"

Let me start with a story. It is called *Mother Theresa's Heavenly Experience*. She went to heaven. God met her at the pearly gates and asked her if she was hungry. "I could eat," she said. So God reached for a can of tuna and rye bread, and they began to eat. While sharing this humble meal, Mother Theresa looked down and saw inhabitants of hell eating steaks, lobsters and pastries.

Curious but deeply trusting, she remained silent. Next day, God invited her for dinner, and they again had tuna sandwich on a rye bread. She saw what the people in hell were eating, but still said nothing. On the third day, when God opened the tuna can, she could not contain herself.

"Lord, I am grateful to be in heaven for this humble life. But here all I get to eat is tuna sandwiches, and in the other place, they are having a feast. I just don't understand." God sighed: "Let's be honest Terry," He said: "For just two people, it doesn't pay to cook."

Let me ask you a question. How many of you want to go to heaven? When I asked this question in another church, one nice lady looked at me in disbelief, and asked me a question of her own: "Why do you ask such a silly question? Of course I want to go to heaven, don't you?" And I said, "No," and she was flabbergasted. She could not believe I didn't want to go to the number one final destination of all believers. She was very concerned but also curious.

I told her that I did not want to "go to" heaven, because, I am already there. She gave me this, "you must be kidding" look. "If you think that living a miserable life in this lousy world is being in heaven, I have a bridge in Brooklyn I want to sell you," she said.

A philosopher once said that human life is like a book that's first and last chapters are missing. No one knows exactly where we came from or where we go after death.

So, every religion has made up its own theories, based on faith. Hindus believe in re-incarnation. Muslims believe in heaven and hell. Christians in general, believe in heaven and hell, but for Catholics, there is another stop in between, purgatory, for those who are not eligible for heaven at the time of death. Catholics also had a place called 'limbo' for children who died before being baptized. But the current pope eliminated limbo few months ago.

So the idea of heaven is pervasive in all religions, and it is considered as a reward we receive from God at the end, after death.

A teacher asked a question to her class; "If I sold my house and my car, and gave the money to the poor, would I go to heaven?" The children said: "No." "If I attended church every week, helped out in the church, led a moral life, would I go to heaven?" Again, they answered "No." "Well then, if I joined a monastery, and lived a holy life, would I go to heaven?" she asked again and the children said "No."

She was frustrated, "well then, how can I get into heaven?" A five year old boy shouted from the back of the class: "You got to be dead first."

**If we have to wait until our death to experience heaven, we are such spiritual losers and the incarnation of Jesus is such a waste.** If heaven is only after death, there was no reason for Jesus to come down to earth. He could have just stayed there, waited for us to struggle through this life and somehow make it there.

But Jesus came down to us and said: "I came that you may have life and have it abundantly." And he is referring primarily to the life now. The Greek word for life is *Zoë*, and it means, divine life. Jesus came that we will have divine life, heavenly life now, not later.

That is why in the Lord's Prayer, Jesus taught us to pray: "Thy kingdom come, thy will be done on earth as it is in heaven." Whatever is up there, the heavenly experience, Jesus wants us to have it right here, right now.

**Another misconception about heaven is that it is a location with a zip code, somewhere up there with pearly gates, golden pavements, and singing angels.** These are very popular images that are indelible in our minds. If those images help you, by all means hold on to them. But I just want to share some of my personal reflections today.

Where did that idea come from? Three thousand years ago, when the Bible was written, people thought about the universe as a three tier system, with earth being flat. So here is earth, heaven is up there and hell down under. The Bible writers thought that earth stood still and the sun moved around the earth.

There are many references in the Bible about heaven as the dwelling place of God. Ps. 108 says that heaven is high above the earth. Isaiah speaks about the “son of man coming down from the clouds.” We have images of Jesus ascending into heaven.

In 1453, a polish astronomer named Copernicus discovered that earth is not flat, but round and it revolves around the sun. This went against the teachings of the Bible and so Copernicus was condemned by the Church. His disciple, Galileo was also condemned and imprisoned by the Church and 350 years later, in 1991, Pope John Paul apologized to Galileo.

Today, nobody, including those who take the Bible literally believes that earth is flat. It is round. And if the earth is round, there is no real ‘up’ or ‘down.’ Today’s up is tomorrow’s down.

Then you might argue that Jesus said in John 14 : “There are many mansions in my father’s house, I am going to prepare a place for you”. But Jesus also said, “Don’t’ say the Kingdom of God is here or there; the Kingdom of heaven is within you.” Jesus also said: “I am the vine and you are the branches.” That does not mean that Jesus is a tree and we are branches with leaves. Jesus also said: “I am the bread from heaven.” That doesn’t mean he is a loaf of bread either.

Jesus was speaking in symbols and images. He was trying to express the inexpressible using words. So we have to be very careful when we say it is in the Bible and the case is closed.

The Bible is a collection of 72 books (for Catholics) and 66 (for Protestants), because six book including 1&2 Maccabees are not recognized as part of the cannon. It is a collection of books composed from oral tradition, by at least 40 authors, mostly anonymous, during a period of 1500 years, 2000 years ago. It is written in a dead language, Aramaic, with a world view and level of consciousness, totally foreign to us.

It is interesting that the Catholic Church, which used to teach that heaven was a place, in its new Catechism of the Catholic Church, states "that heaven is a state or dimension, not necessarily a place."

Bishop NT Wright, a prominent Anglican bishop, has just written a new book called *Surprised by Hop*e. It is a modern day discussion of heaven. He writes: "Heaven is not the longed for destination of dying people, but the realm of God that intersects our universe in such a way, as to transform the way we live." **So, every time, our lives intersect with God, there is heaven.**

So don't ask: "How to go to heaven?" which implies, traveling somewhere else. Don't ask: "Are you in heaven?" which implies that you have to enter into something that is outside of you. **The right question is: "Is heaven in you?**

It is a dimension within you, that is calm and peaceful, serene and joyful, a dimension that permeates your entire being, something that you experience where ever you are, and take it with you, where ever you go. You will not wait for it; you will not be looking for it somewhere else, but feeling it inside. That is why Jesus said: "The kingdom of heaven is within you."

Heaven is always with us. It flows like a river through our lives, always reminding us that there is magic and power beyond what our eyes can see. At times we catch its subtle beauty, like during chance meetings, and insights that seem to come from nowhere. Heaven exists in all situations, in every moment, yet all too often we may overlook its presence.

Imagine how it would feel to live an entire day in heaven, to fully appreciate that your day is unfolding in absolute perfection. Whereas usually you might miss the magic in ordinary events and interactions, on this day you would recognize them all as little miracles. Perhaps you could begin with your first deep breaths in the morning, becoming aware that there is an abundant supply of air for you to breathe.

Your lungs know just how to carry oxygen to your blood, and your blood knows where to carry it from there. This is heaven at work. You might appreciate the brilliant sunshine, the warm summertime rain, or the possibilities for learning that greet you at every turn. You might notice the ease with which you do your job or laugh with a close friend. These things are also heaven. Even laying your head down at the end of this day and resting in the stillness of night is heaven.

Every time you enjoy that benevolence, you may discover a deeper peace. Your faith may strengthen and your heart may open. You might begin to wonder if struggle is really all that necessary after all. By living this one day in heaven, you might open the door to many more.

You remember the nice lady who told me that heaven cannot be here because we live in lousy world leading miserable lives. Perception is everything. Perception generates thinking, thinking causes feeling and feelings lead to behavior. So if we think that the world is lousy, and life is miserable, we are going to feel lousy and miserable.

**The world that God created and described as 'good' cannot be lousy. The life that God gave to us as a gift, our life that Jesus found worthy to embrace, should not be called miserable.** So start thinking differently. Instead of thinking that heaven is up there, something to wait for after death, start thinking:

Heaven is not a place to go to, but knowing that you are already there. The key word is "knowing." Repeat that sentence a few times a day, for the next thirty days. Look around, enjoy the beauty of God in creation; look for the face of Jesus around you with the mindset of a child and you will start experiencing heaven now.

# 34. God's Glory Is Man's Wholeness

Mt: 25: 14-30

*Again, it will be like a man going on a journey, who called his servants and entrusted his property to them. To one he gave five talents of money, to another two talents and to another one talent, each according to his ability. Then he went on his journey. The man who had received the five talents went at once and put his money to work and gained five more. So also, the one with the two talents gained two more. But the man who had received the one talent went off, dug a hole in the ground and hid is master's money.*

Today I like to continue my series of sermons on the Lord's Prayer. In the past weeks, we reflected on the first two phrases, "Our Father" and "Who art in Heaven." Today let us reflect on the phrase "Hallowed be Thy Name." We say it every time we say the Lord's Prayer, but what does that mean?

Before we get into that, I like to tell you a story. This is the story of Forest Gump going to heaven. Peter stopped him at the gates and said that he had to answer three questions. 1) Name two days of the week that begins with the letter 'T' 2) How many seconds are in a year 3) What is God's first name?

Gump thought for a moment and said: "The two days of the week that begins with T are Today and Tomorrow." Peter said: "That was not the answer I was expecting, but will take it. "How many seconds are in a year?" Gump: "12; January 2nd, Feb 2nd etc. "OK, OK, what about God's first name? Gump said "God has two first names: 'Andy' and 'Harold,' from the song: "Andy walks with me,

Andy talks to me, Andy holds me, Andy is almighty," and 'Harold,' from the Lord's Prayer: "Harold be thy Name."

We have said "Hallowed be thy name" 1000s of time, but what does that mean? I looked in the dictionary and it means "make holy," or "glorify" or "honor." Now how do we humans glorify Almighty God?

But before we can glorify God's name, we have to know God's name first. What is God's name?

The name given to Moses on Mount Sinai, "I am Who Am" does not explain much. It is a mysterious name or shall I say, "Non-name."

As disciples, we have to go with the name that Jesus revealed to us about God. The fact of the matter is that Jesus did not give a name to God; He did not bother to complete the sentence "I am" with a name, because Jesus knew that he could never contain Almighty God in one name.

So what did Jesus do? Instead of defining God with a name, he described God and the best description, of God is that he is a father. The Hebrew word 'Abba' literally means, 'daddy'. In the parable of the prodigal son, in Luke 15, God is portrayed as kind, generous, forgiving and unconditionally loving.

So if God is our father, how do we hallow or glorify or honor God?

I asked this question to a friend: He said: "Sing praises to the Lord; Sing holy, holy, holy Lord, during worship, attend church on Sundays, ask God for guidance," etc. Does my singing "glory to God, or repeating "holy, holy, holy" make any difference in God's glory or holiness?

Then I began to think. I have two sons, Johnny and Tommy. Johnny has autism; for the purposes of this sermon, I like to talk about

Tommy. As a father, what is the best thing my son can do to honor me or glorify me?

After he turns 21, if he still sits at home all day, and tells me how great I am, or how much I have done for him, or asks my opinion before he does anything, I will be very upset. I want him to grow up, I want him to make a life for himself, and marry a beautiful girl. I want him to make decisions for himself; I want him to excel in all areas of life.

If he fails in school, gets involved in drugs, and sleeps under a bridge, I will be devastated. On the other hand, if he becomes the valedictorian in his school, goes to Harvard and becomes a famous surgeon, I will be very happy, glorified and honored.

Tommy went to a Christian summer camp this year. He is ten years old, and has never been away from home. He was in Ocala, about 50 miles away. His very protective mother, my wife, was anxious. She accompanied him to the camp, the only parent to do so. After saying goodbye to him, she went into the bathroom and cried. She mailed three letters to him, all from Ocala so that he would receive them before the camp ended.

When he came home, Judy asked him: "Did you miss me?"

And Tommy said: "Not really because I was so busy having fun." My wife was happy that he had fun, but she was little disappointed that he did not miss her. And I told her that she should be so proud that we raised a child who is not a mommy's boy, but who can hold his own, act responsibly, and function independently.

**God is glorified when we grow up. God is glorified when we develop all our gifts and reach our full potential. God is glorified when we take charge of our lives and that of this earth, because in the creation story, we are given "dominion over all the earth."**

God is glorified when our energies are directed not towards God, but **towards** others to become the most loving, compassionate human being we possibly can become; God is glorified when we love other human beings who are children of the same God. That is the message in today's reading.

There was a master who called his three servants and gave them talents: The servant who had five talents doubled them due to his effort and diligence. The servant who had two talents did the same; but the servant, who had one, was afraid, lazy, and he did not do anything with the gift the master gave him. The master called him a worthless lazy lout, who had no confidence in the master who entrusted him with the gifts. The scripture says that he was thrown out into the darkness where there was weeping and gnashing of teeth.

The story says that after giving the money, the master went away; he did not stay with them to hold their hands, to answer their questions or to guide them step by step. As a matter of fact, he gave them no instructions as to what to do with the money. The servants had to do it alone, and two of them did an excellent job and honored the trust the master had in them, and made him proud, while the third dishonored the master by worrying about what kind of a master he was, and buried his talents.

Referring to this parable, St. Ireneus, a great saint of the Church said: "*Homo vivens, dei Gloria*," which means "The glory of God is man fully alive."

I want to end with a story: A very religious man lived next door to an atheist. While the religious man prayed day in and day out, the atheist never bothered to pray or attend church. However, the atheist seemed to have a good life; he had a great job, a beautiful wife, well behaved children, good health, etc. whereas the pious man's job was tedious, his wife was getting sick every day and his kids had issues.

The pious man asked God: "Oh Lord, I honor you every day; I ask your advice for every problem and confess my sins daily and ask your forgiveness; I praise and worship you three times a day and attend church every week; Yet my neighbor, who doesn't even believe in you, let alone praise you and certainly don't pray to you, seems blessed with every happiness, while I suffer every indignity: why is that?"

And a great voice was heard from above: "Because he doesn't bother me all the time."

**God is our loving father. The best way for us his children to glorify him, is to grow up spiritually.** When we walk around with sullen faces, feeling like victims and unworthy sinners, God is not glorified; when we refuse to take charge of our lives and use the gifts that God has given us, God is not glorified; when we fight wars and kill each other, God is not glorified.

When we are fully alive in the spirit, joyful in His presence, grateful for the gift of life, and loving towards other people, God is glorified.

In this sense, prayer becomes life, not just repeating formulas at set times or places. We will glorify His name always, not just when we say the Lord's Prayer.

Always remember: HUMAN BEING FULLY ALIVE IS THE GLORY OF GOD. And that is what Jesus promised us: "I came that you may have life and have it abundantly."

# 35. Thy Kingdom Come/ My Kingdom Go

Luke: 4:16-20

*The Spirit of the Lord is on me, because he has anointed me to preach good news to the poor. He has sent me to proclaim freedom for the prisoners and recovery of sight for the blind, to release the oppressed, to proclaim the year of the Lord's favor. Then he rolled up the scroll, gave it back to the attendant and sat down. The eyes of everyone in the synagogue were fastened on him, and he began by saying to him, "Today this scripture is fulfilled in your hearing."*

In our series of sermons on the Lord's Prayer, today, let us reflect on the meaning of the phrase, "Thy Kingdom Come." If someone asks you to summarize the entire teachings of Jesus in two words, you could say, "Kingdom of God." All his parables, teachings and miracles were centered on that theme.

According to the gospels of Matthew and Mark, the first words out of the mouth of Jesus as he begins his public ministry is: "Reform your lives, the Kingdom of God is at hand."

However, in Luke, Jesus does not use this phrase to inaugurate his ministry. He actually explains what 'Kingdom' means through the first public speech he gave. It is in the fourth chapter of Luke. Jesus goes into a synagogue; He picks up the book of Isaiah and reads from the 60th chapter. "The Spirit of the Lord is upon me; therefore he has anointed me; He has sent me to bring good news to the poor, to proclaim liberty to captives, recovery of sight to the blind and release to prisoners and to announce the Year of the Lord."

Jesus is saying that when the good news is preached, the captives are free, when the blind see, the prisoners are free and the 'Year of the Lord' is proclaimed, God's Kingdom will be established on earth.

We know what freedom for captives and sight for the blind means. But what did he mean when he said that he had come "to proclaim the 'Year of the Lord?' In order to understand the meaning of the "Year of the Lord," we have to go to chapter 25 of the book of Leviticus.

It speaks about the Jubilee Year, the Israelites were supposed to observe. They were asked to count forty nine years, and on the tenth day of the seventh month of the 49th year, they had to announce to the community, by using a trumpet, that the 50th year was going to be a Jubilee Year. Remember that they had no TV, radio, newspaper or internet to make this announcement.

They had to make the 50th year sacred by proclaiming liberty in the land for all its inhabitants. This is relevant because during that period, slavery was rampant. In the 50th year they had to let slaves go free; they should not sow, nor reap the after growth or pick the grapes from the untrimmed vines; they were supposed to leave them for the poor people.

When they sold land to a neighbor, they should not deal unfairly; the land will yield its fruits and they will have food in abundance so that they could live there without worry.

When one of your fellow countrymen is reduced to poverty, extend to him the privilege of an alien or a tenant so that he may continue to live with you. Do not exact interest from them either in money or in kind, but out of fear of God, let them live with you.

In short, the Jubilee year is a year of jubilation, freedom, generosity, kindness and all the qualities of the Kingdom of God.

So Jesus confronts that culture with the bold vision of prophetic proclamation. He denounced the oppression, challenged the hypocritical religious leaders of his time and inaugurated a whole new scheme of relationships.

In the new mode of relating to each other in the Kingdom of God, the key quality is inclusiveness; everybody, at all times and in all situations must be included and not excluded. The disciples could not handle that idea. They thought they were the privileged few who would inherit the Kingdom; the Pharisees thought that they were better than the lepers and the prostitutes. Jesus deflated their sense of superiority by eating with the so called sinners and talking to a woman at the well, thus breaking the barriers of exclusivism.

When the disciples asked Jesus as to who would enter the Kingdom of God, he said: "People will come from east and west, from north and south and enter the Kingdom of God." Jesus was saying that the Kingdom has no boundaries. There is no privileged seating in the Kingdom of God for any special group of people. Everyone who does the will of God is welcome, regardless of their religious, cultural or ethnic backgrounds.

Even today, there are millions of Christians who think that they are the only ones who are going to inherit the Kingdom. There are denominations that teach this dogma. Until recently, the Catholic Church used to teach: "*extra ecelsiam nulla salus,*" which means "outside the Church no salvation." In 1962, during the 2nd Vatican council, they removed that phrase from the documents. Still there are Christians, who believe that they are the privileged ones, but in the Kingdom of Jesus, no one has special privilege; all are included.

Equality is another characteristic of the Kingdom of God, there is no status or class distinctions in the Kingdom, where all are paid equally whether they arrive at the first hour or the eleventh. There is a powerful parable illustrating this point in the 20th chapter of Mathew's gospel. It is the story of the laborers in the vineyard. It starts by saying: "The Kingdom of God is like the case of the owner of an estate who went out at dawn to hire workmen for his vineyard." The owner of the vineyard hired different groups of men at different times of the day.

He hired one group early in the morning. Another group in mid morning, another group at noon, another group at mid afternoon, and finally another group of men late in the evening. Some men worked full 8 hours, others did 4 hours and some worked only 1 hour. When it was time for them to get paid, the first group thought, they would get a higher pay; but when they received the same pay as the last group of men, they were upset and outraged.

But the master told them; "Didn't you agree on the usual wage and did I not give it you, so why are you angry, why are you arguing with me, take your money and go home."

Jesus said: "The first shall be last and the last shall be first; this is how the rules of the kingdom work; it has very little comparison to our worldly ways of thinking. Just because, we are Christians and we believe in Jesus and attend church, we may think that we have a privileged or better status in God's kingdom. Jesus says no; and it might come as a shock to us just as it was a shock to the laborers in the vineyard.

If we really open our eyes and understand the meaning and message of the Kingdom of God, there should not be any reason for surprises.

The Kingdom that Jesus proclaimed is essentially about transformation; that is why, he said:"The Kingdom of God is at hand, reform your lives and that is a fitting message for the first Sunday of Lent.

The next few weeks are about reforming our lives so that we can experience the richness of God's Kingdom in our lives. The church proposes three ways to do it: prayer, fasting and almsgiving.

Try to devote some special time each day for personal prayer and reflection; try to fast at least once a week; fasting does not mean just skipping a meal. Use the material or the money that you would have spent on that meal to buy food for someone without food that day. Almsgiving means giving more than you usually give in time, talents, and tithing, for the benefit of others.

If we do all that, we will experience the Kingdom in our lives. So, remember that Christian life in general and the period of Lent in particular is about praying for the coming of God's Kingdom. It is about letting go of my kingdom, where I am the boss, with my priorities, my possessions, my money, my life, my ideas, my way of thinking, my prejudices, mine, mine, mine. **God's Kingdom will become a reality in our lives only when our little kingdoms disappear.**

When we pray the Lord's Prayer, we should silently add another phrase: **Thy Kingdom come, my kingdom go.**

# 36. Surrendering With a Smile

Luke: 1: 26-38

*"I am the Lord's servant," Mary answered. "May it be to me as you have said." Then the angel left her.*

In our series of sermons on the Lord's Prayer, today we reflect on the phrase "Thy will be done on earth as it is in heaven." How do we find out what is God's will for us?

A few weeks ago, there was a question in our paper, *Sun-sentinel* under the feature: *Ask Pastor Bob,* from 'JB Fort Lauderdale'

"There were ten of us in our family. My mother and one brother died of heart attacks; my father and a sister died of cerebral thrombosis; a sister drowned; one brother died of cancer; one brother died of pneumonia; I know what my fate is? Is this the will of God?"

When we experience unexplainable tragedies, personally or nationally, we usually explain it as the will of God. I have heard people say that 9/11 was the will of God; that hurricane Katrina was the will of God; that the Tsunami was the will of God.

In my line of work as a hospice chaplain, I hear a lot of it. When someone has a terminal illness or when they die, friends and neighbors will say to the grieving family: "Don't worry; it is the will of God." I cringe when I hear people say that, because they don't know what they are talking about. It is funny that people have this urge to comfort the grieving by dishing out platitudes. It is very hard for many to be quiet or handle the silence. It is OK not to say anything; just stay with the person.

How do we humans know God's will? **My definition of will of God is "pious people's alibi for unexplainable events."** I don't think anybody knows the will of God. If anyone claims to know the will of God, I will run far away from that person. As the Buddhists say: "He who knows does not talk, and he who talks, does not know."

Every time we say the Lord's Prayer we say: "Thy will be done on earth as it is in heaven." What does it mean to pray for God's will to be done in your life? Does it mean throwing up your arms and resigning yourself to an uncertain fate? Or is there a deeper promise you can hold on to when you pray for His will?

I don't think it is the will of God that the tsunami hit the poor people of Indonesia. I don't think it is the will of God that a hurricane should hit the United States or a young person should die in a car accident. I don't think God is a deity up there who capriciously imposes his will on his creation. That may be the God of the Old Testament, but that is definitely not the God of Jesus, God our loving Father.

So therefore, the will of God is not about an outsider God imposing His will on humanity. It is about our acceptance and surrender to life as it unfolds before us on a daily basis. It is about saying yes to God on a continuous basis, without complaining, without whining, without being angry and frustrated. It means asking God to take over our lives entirely, with all its ramifications the good, the bad and the ugly.

According to William Barclay "Thy will be done" can be prayed with at least three meanings:

**Resentment**, **Resignation** or **Trust**: Resentment is the attitude of a person who knows that there is no escape and there is no other way. There are many people who know quite well that they must accept life as it is, but they spent their life in bitter resentment about the events in their lives.

There are Christians who go through life praying the Lord's Prayer all the while bitterly resenting the fact that God's will did not align with their plan: the death of a spouse, or a child, collapse of a business, an unfulfilled dream, all these can cause resentment.

I had a patient who lost her husband when he was 55 years old. It happened 40 years ago, and at 95, she is still resentful. "Why did God have to take my husband; he was such a nice, productive man. There were so many drug addicts and prostitutes who are useless people; why couldn't God take them?" she asked.

Secondly, this prayer can be prayed with **resignation.** It is acceptance of the will of God, but it is utterly joyless; it is tired, and weary and defeated, not content. There are many who live with a grim acceptance of their lives. Phrases like: "You have to play with the card you are dealt; "you have to roll with the punches," "that is the way it is" "there is nothing you can do about it," are examples of surrendering to the will of God with a sense of helpless resignation.

Thirdly, this prayer can be said in a tone of serenity, trust, and peace. There is neither resentment nor defeat, but determination never to doubt the purposes of God. Jesus' prayer in Gethsemane is a good example. "My father, if it is possible, let this cup pass me by, but if it cannot pass me by without my drinking it, let your will be done." His sorrow and distress were real; so was his confidence in his father's love and the desire to obey his will. Again, on the cross, right before taking his last breath, Jesus surrendered to God by saying: "Father into your hands I commend my spirit."

Or look at Mary's response at the annunciation: "Be it done to me according to thy will." She was a young girl; she was chosen by God to be the mother of the messiah; she was not married; she was not educated; she was not from a famous family; she was so innocent and helpless to understand the deep mysteries of God and to ask probing questions about how all this was going to take place.

So what does Mary do? Mary surrenders; she makes herself available to God, placing her life completely in the hands of God. She said: "Be it done to me according to thy will."

From that moment on, we know what happened in Mary's life; it was definitely not an easy ride. Things became difficult from that point on; she had to deal with misunderstanding, confusion, doubt, and ultimately had to face the most painful sight a mother could ever face: the crucifixion of her son and having to hold his lifeless body in her lap.

All this happened after she said 'yes' to the will God; but the beauty of that surrender is God's eternal promise to stand by us all the way, even when we go through the hardest and most painful experiences of our lives. Mary's life proves it; Jesus' life proves it.

Saying 'yes' to the will of God is about letting go; it is about giving up that insatiable desire to find out, to figure out, or to control the events of our life; it is about not being upset when things don't go as planned or in our favor. It is about total surrender to a God, knowing that God is fully in charge and that nothing is impossible to God.

Surrender happens when you no longer ask "Why is this happening to me?" There are situations in life where all answers and explanations fail. Life does not make sense anymore; when you fully accept the fact that you don't have all the answers, that is when God works through you

**Sometimes surrender means giving up trying to understand and becoming comfortable with not knowing.**

Surrender is the inner transition from resistance to acceptance, from 'no' to 'yes," fully, completely and totally, and thus living with the freedom of the children of God. That is how we can meaningfully pray: "Thy will be done on earth as it is in heaven."

# 37. Live Simply So That Others May Simply Live

Exodus: 15:1-20

*Moses said to them, "It is the bread the Lord has given you to eat. This is what the Lord has commanded: 'Each one is to gather as much as he needs. Take an omer for each person you have in your tent... no one is to keep any of it until morning."*

A priest was preparing a man for his journey into the great beyond. Whispering firmly into his ear, the priest said: "Denounce the devil and let him know of his evil ways." The dying man said nothing; the priest repeated his order; still the man said nothing; the priest asked: "Why do you refuse to denounce the devil?" The dying man said: "Until I know where I am heading, I don't want to aggravate anybody."

I hope my sermon today does not aggravate or disturb you, because the topic is a very difficult and disturbing one for those of us privileged to live in this country. As part of our series of sermons on the Lord's Prayer, we are going to reflect on the deeper meaning of "Give us this day our daily bread."

Understand that with this petition, we have turned a major corner in the Lord's Prayer; the first part of the prayer is related to matters of God: 'Hallowed be Thy Name,' 'Thy Kingdom Come,' 'Thy Will be done.'

In the second part we are told to pray for provision, pardon and protection, which pertain to present, past and future. Provision for today as bread, pardon for past as forgiveness and protection for tomorrow from temptations.

To grasp the deeper meaning of this petition, "give us this day our daily bread," you have to understand its connection to the story of *Manna* in the 16th chapter of Exodus. A few days after the Israelites were led out of slavery in Egypt, they began complaining to Moses and Aaron because they were hungry. They wished they could have stayed in slavery, because at least they had food. So Moses and Aaron prayed to God and they are provided with food from heaven called *Manna*.

*Manna* means, "What is this" because when they saw it they asked: "What is this?" Look at the regulations regarding *manna*: They were to gather an *omer,* which is an ancient measurement, let us say, gather one pound each of *manna* per person. They were not supposed to gather more than needed or hoard it in the tent.

Moses specifically told them, "Let no one keep any of it until tomorrow morning." They were supposed to pick up what was necessary for the day and eat it; no hoarding, no keeping in freezers or refrigerators. (Of course they had no such storage facilities). Obviously some of them did not listen to Moses and they hoarded some *manna*, and look what happened to them. "When some kept part of it till morning, it rotted and became filled with worms; and Moses was displeased with them."

The Bible says, "Morning after morning they gathered it, till each had enough to eat, but when the sun grew hot, the *manna* melted away." There was plenty of *manna* lying around, and they could have gathered more than they needed; but they were not supposed to. They had to trust in the providence of God that they would be fed each day. The Lord kept his promise, because God provided them with *manna* for 40 years!

When Jesus taught his disciples to pray for daily bread, he was alluding to the daily bread of the *manna* of the chosen people. Notice that Jesus did not want them to pray for "bread for days to come." **It does not say give us bread for every day anticipating future needs; just daily bread, just enough for today**!

Now fast forward, 2006, United States of America: Nobody, including myself, can say this prayer with a straight face or a sincere heart today.

None of us are worried about our daily bread; our bread is guaranteed not just for the day, but for every day of the future. Not just bread, but steak, pasta, rice, vegetables, potatoes and all kinds of food. Is there anyone here today who worries that he won't have food to eat next day, the next week, the next month or even the next year? I don't think so; I don't have that worry.

Our refrigerators are full. In some cases, we have an extra freezer to stock up for days. If we don't feel like cooking what we have at home, there are always restaurants where we can sit for hours and enjoy a great meal; now if we don't want to sit for hours, we have the fast food places; McDonalds, Burger King, Wendy's, Checkers, Arby's. You name them, we have them. And if we are too tired or lazy to go out to eat, we can always pick up the phone and place an order for our favorite food, and it will be brought to our door: Chinese, Italian, Mexican or anything else we want.

We have no shortage of our daily bread. As a matter of fact, we waste tons of food every day from restaurants and grocery stores.

**Also notice that we are praying for our daily bread, not out daily steak. Jesus wants us to pray for our needs, not our greeds.**

Are you content or are you always wanting more? Millions of people are killing themselves for more: more choices, more money, more stuff. We are bombarded everyday with the message that more will eventually lead to happiness. Messages that tell us that we are just one purchase away from happiness.

There was a Peanut cartoon on Thanksgiving Day. Snoopy is sitting on top of his doghouse. He is bitter because Charlie Brown and his family are having this huge feast inside the house; but Snoopy is stuck in the doghouse with only dog food. And he is angry about it. Then a thought occurs to him and he says to himself: “It could be worse; I could have been born a turkey.”

Now remember that; when you leave this church today and get into your vehicle you may be tempted to say: “If I just had another car, a nicer car, a new car a more expensive car, I would be content; or when you get home, you may be tempted to say, “if only I had a bigger house, a better house, a house in a gated community, a house with an ocean view, I would be happier.”

But today you are not going to think that; Instead today, you are going to say, “It could be worse.” It is worse for a lot of people, for almost half of humanity. About three billion people have no real houses to live in, no cars to drive, no daily bread, no health care, no running water, no electricity, and the list of depravations goes on and on.

Which brings me to another important aspect of this prayer: It says “give **us** this day our daily bread;” It does not say, give **me.** Every time you pray this prayer, you are not just encouraged but commanded to pray with and for your brothers and sisters.

If you are just praying for your own needs without concern for the needs of others, you are not praying. You missed the whole point of prayer. **God is ‘our’ father, and we cannot approach the father, if we leave our siblings behind.**

Jesus is teaching us that Christian life is an “us thing” not a “me thing.” This is a revolutionary prayer for us who live in a self-centered and affluent culture.

Once Tony Compallo, a famous Evangelical preacher, was giving a sermon on poverty: “Tonight in Africa alone, 6000 children will die of poverty, and nobody cares a shit about it." About half of his congregation walked out because they were offended by his use of the word shit inside the church. As they were walking out, he challenged them and asked: "You seem to be offended that I used a bad word; aren't you offended that 6000 children will die tonight because they have no food?"

We need to examine our hearts and see what really offends us. Is it just peripheral issues or the real issues? Every time we pray, "Give us this day, our daily bread," we have to stop and ask: "Does everybody in the world have food?" We cannot say, "It is not our responsibility to make sure that the people in Africa, of India or other poor countries have enough food." It **is** our responsibility, if we want to say this prayer meaningfully.

As you know well, there is not going to be any miraculous showering of *manna* from heaven. When was the last time anybody saw God sending *manna* down to Africa? God created us and gave us intelligence to realize that there is so much poverty in the world. There is enough food for all God's people on this earth, if only it was equitably distributed. When some people hoard more than they need, and refuse to share, others are deprived.

If we really mean the words of the prayer, "give us this day our daily bread," our pantries and our bank accounts must open up to share our resources with those who are in need. Until our hearts are transformed to make that happen, this prayer will just remain an empty formula.

Notice that Jesus' primary audience was the peasant class. The powerful and the wealthy elites mostly lived in the cities. The peasants lived in rural areas. Jesus avoided cities, except when he went to Jerusalem temple. He spoke in small towns, villages and countryside; the wealthy people heard of him, but few of them were attracted to him because if they followed him, they had so much to lose and they were not willing to give up their possessions and comforts.

In this context, the Lord's Prayer is about experiences of peasants' life; finding enough food for the day was a big concern for those poor people. Jesus is connecting the issue of having enough food with the presence of the Kingdom. **The kingdom of God is about having enough food.**

If you want to be in the Kingdom of God, make every effort that everyone, all our brothers and sisters who are near and far, have enough food. Saying this prayer meaningfully is about living simply so that others may simply live.

# 38. A Contractual Prayer

Mathew: 18:21-35

*Then Peter came to Jesus and asked, "Lord, how many times shall I forgive my brother when he sins against me? 'Up to seven times?' Jesus answered, "I tell you, not seven times, but seventy times seven."*

A preacher asked his congregation: "How many of you have forgiven your enemies?" About half held up their hands. He repeated the question: About 80% held up their hands. He repeated the question again: "How many of you have forgiven your enemies?" All but one old lady held up their hands.

"Mrs. Jones, are you not willing to forgive your enemies?" asked the Pastor. "I don't have any," she replied. "Mrs. Jones, that is very unusual; how old are you?" "93" she replied. Mrs. Jones please come up and tell the congregation how you can live such long years, and have no enemies in the world. The little sweetheart of a lady, tottered down the aisle, stood in front of the congregation and said: "It is easy, I just outlived the bitches."

Forgiveness is at the heart of Christianity; it is the hallmark of a follower of Jesus. That is why Jesus said: "Love your enemies; pray for those who persecute you; if someone strikes you on the right cheek, show him the other cheek." These are extremely difficult things to do; and that is why Peter had to ask: "How many times we have to forgive others?"

In the rabbinical tradition, it was enough to forgive three times; Peter thought he was being generous, when he doubled it and added one more and asked, "is it enough to forgive seven times?" And Jesus deflated Peter's generous ego by saying that he had to forgive seven times seventy, which is mathematically, 490 times, but what Jesus meant was that he had to forgive all the time, without counting.

I want you to take a few minutes to think about some of the times you have been hurt in life, all the instances you had to forgive somebody. It may be a parent who abused you, a spouse who betrayed you, or a drunk driver who killed someone dear to you; or a neighbor who gossiped about you, and an employer who fired you or did not give you a promotion you thought you deserved.

I was hurt three times in my life, instances that I needed to forgive. That is a low number for all these years of living. There are two reasons why I don't have a lot of forgiving to do. First, I don't get hurt or offended easily; it will take a lot for someone to hurt me. Secondly, I try not to place myself in hurtful situations.

The last time I was hurt was about ten years ago, when my boss did not give me the promotion I thought I deserved. It was given to another person on my team, who had less education, and experience than me, and I was furious. I did not say anything to the boss or to the person who received the promotion. But I was angry and hurt and my relationship to both of them changed even as I continued to work with the same team. Every time I saw the person that was promoted, I was angry and jealous. Every time I had to deal with my boss, I felt slighted and upset.

It took a long time to forgive them and it was very hard. It took a long time because I did not know any better; I was immature and did not have the spiritual insights I have today. **Now I realize that forgiving others is in my best interests. Keeping grudges is like carrying a garbage bag on my back.**

All of us are familiar with the garbage at home. On Tuesdays and Fridays, I leave the garbage in front of my house for pick up. The bag is filled with coffee filters, tea bags, chicken bones, pizza crumbs, and all other nasty stuff you can imagine. It is filthy and smelly and it has to be disposed of. Now imagine carrying that bag around, in your car, into the office and you will say that is such a stupid, horrible and unhealthy thing to do.

Yes it is; but every time you carry the pain and hurt in your heart, you are carrying garbage with you. The person who hurt you has moved on; he may not even realize that he hurt you. You are paying a heavy price when you refuse to forgive, because it continues to hurt you physically, emotionally and spiritually.

**So forgiveness is not a favor towards the person who wronged you: forgiveness is an act of kindness toward yourself.** It is not about what your offender needs; it is about what you deserve, and to forgive is to rid yourself of anger, fear, hurt and obsession. Imagine the relief of not feeling these emotions; imagine the energy you will have for other things; imagine the positive thoughts you could entertain, if you did not have to have angry thoughts.

It is all too easy to recall how we have been hurt and feel anger towards those who inflicted the pain. How many times have we said the words: "I may forgive, but I can't forget." I tell you this and, I want you to understand this clearly--it is the beginning of a nasty process that makes the heart grow cold as a stone. If you say you forgive, then forgive; if you are willing to forgive, but unwilling to forget, you have not fully forgiven. Forgiveness is letting go, completely letting go, totally letting go, holding nothing back, just letting go; anything less is not forgiveness.

"But I don't want to forget" you might say. There are two reasons why we don't want to forget. First, we think that if we remember the hurt, it will somehow be a way of "making them pay" for what they did. Second, if we remember what has been done to us, we can erect a wall around us that will insulate us from future hurt. Both these reasons are illusions. You are damaging yourself by constantly remembering the misdeed. And remembering does not build a wall of protection; it reopens an old wound only to bleed again.

Nelson Mandela is a great example of forgiveness in recent memory. He was imprisoned in South Africa for 27 years. A friend told him: "As you were marching across the courtyard of the prison, the camera zeroed in on your face and I will never forget your face. It was full of anger and hatred and animosity. I had never seen so much anger and hatred written on a man's face. That is not the Mandela I know today."

Mandela said: "When I left the prison block and marched across the courtyard, I thought to myself: they took away everything that was important to me; my life, my house, my family. My friends have been put to death; everything and everyone that means anything to me, they have taken away. It is all gone and I hated them for it.

Then I remembered what Jesus said about forgiveness and God spoke to me and said: "**Nelson, for 27 years you were their prisoner; don't let them turn you into a free man only to make you into a prisoner of hate. And I realized the importance of forgiveness."**

There was a time in my life when I said the Lord's Prayer; I fell silent during the second half of the prayer. After I said, "Give us this day our daily bread," I could not say the next line: "Forgive us our sins as we forgive those who sin against us." This is the only line in the Lord's Prayer, with a condition attached to it, which shows almost a contractual agreement between our ability to forgive others and God's willingness to forgive us.

We are saying to God: "Lord, forgive me, only when I forgive others." We say this prayer all the time, without understanding the huge implications for our spiritual life.

Are you aware of what you are saying to God? "Forgive me ONLY to the extent that I forgive others." What you are saying is that God's forgiveness is contingent upon you forgiving others.

When we withhold forgiveness from others, we are acting like the servant in today's gospel, who refused to forgive a small debt, while he was forgiven a huge debt by his own master.

Jesus does not ask us to do anything that he has not done himself first. Jesus, who wants us to forgive seven times seventy, forgave his enemies. While hanging on the cross in extreme agony, he prayed: "Father, forgive them, for they do not know what they are doing." He forgave those who had betrayed him, condemned him unjustly, mocked and derided him, and inflicted upon him the most excruciating pain that killed him.

I can assure you that any injury we may have endured in our lives, pale in comparison to what Jesus had to suffer. And if Jesus could forgive those who did great harm to him, we too must, if we want to call ourselves disciples of Christ.

# 39. Lead Us Not Into Temptation

Luke: 4: 1-13

*Jesus, full of the Holy Spirit, returned from the Jordan and was led by the Spirit in the desert, where for forty days he was tempted by the evil...When the devil had finished all this tempting, he left him until an opportune time.*

This is the 8th in a series of sermons on the Lord's Prayer. Today we reflect on the meaning of the phrase: "Lead us not into temptation," but before that, I like to tell you a story.

A pastor was struggling to make ends meet. He was livid when he found out that his wife had spent $300 for a dress. He asked: "How could you do this?" She said: "I was outside this store looking at the dress through the window, and then I found myself trying it on; it was like Satan was whispering in my ears; 'You look fabulous in that dress; buy it." "Well," the pastor replied: "You know how I deal with that kind of temptation? I say "Get behind me, Satan." "I did," replied the wife; "but then he said: "It looks fabulous from the back too."

You all know what temptation is and I am sure we all have succumbed sometimes to some temptations. Temptations are opportunities that either strengthen us or corrupt us. A preacher has classified them as the fearsome foursome: temptation to sensuality, food, possessions, and false speech. There is not a human being alive who does not face sensual temptations.

Even Jimmy Carter admitted that he has lusted in his heart. Many people battle temptations regarding overeating and gluttony, and we see them on Dr. Phil or Oprah. All are tempted to want more, to believe the lie that position, success, and stuff will bring happiness. And we are all tempted to respond to our spouse, child or parent, a neighbor, a fellow worker or a driver on the road with an acerbic tongue or an unfriendly gesture.

Where do temptations come from? St. James tells us that they do not come from God: "Let no one say when he is tempted, 'I am being tempted by God,' for God does not tempt anyone." Though God does not cause temptations, He does, however, allow them.

God allowed his son Jesus to be tempted. According to the gospels, Jesus had three temptations: The first was to turn the stone into bread. The devil knew that he will be really hungry after 40 days of fasting and so he thought that Jesus would easily succumb. But he did not.

So he tried again by tempting him to use his divine powers and act like a magician, to jump from high and show how his angels would protect him. Jesus did not fall for that either; and so the third time the devil tried to lure Jesus into owning the whole world, and Jesus did not fall for that either.

The three temptations of Jesus can be categorized under three major headings: temptation to indulge in food and bodily pleasures, temptation to wield power over other people and temptation to possess material things.

**There are three major misunderstandings about temptation: First, that temptation itself is sin.** It is interesting to note that the same Greek word, translated as 'temptation' in Luke is translated in other New Testament passages as 'trial' or 'fiery ordeal.' For example in his first epistle, Peter says: "do not be surprised, beloved, that a trial by fire is occurring in your midst. It is a test for you but it should not catch you off guard."

We need to understand that circumstances are never the cause of sin. They are best at exposing some of our hidden tendencies, showing us our spiritual state, manifesting some carefully hidden selfish affections that lurk in our hearts, affections, we normally would not own up to or, gloss over with excuses

**The second misunderstanding about temptation is that, when we are tempted, God is disappointed or displeased with us**: far from it. God in fact allows the trial to see how faithful we are to Him. It is a clear test of our maturity as a Christian. St. Paul assures us in his letter to Corinthians: "No test has been sent you that do not come to all men; besides, God keeps his promise. He will not let you be tested beyond your strength.

Along with the test, God will give you a way out of it so that you may be able to endure it. A minister once said: "If the devil is still after you, it means that he hasn't gotten you; the devil tempts only those who are living right; he doesn't need to tempt those who are already living for him."

**The third misconception about temptation is that when I am spiritually mature, there will be no more temptations**. During seminary training, our spiritual director told us that temptations will be with us fifteen minutes after we are buried, underscoring the point that, we will never stop having them.

Many people think that Jesus had only three temptations during his 33 years of life. I am sure Jesus had many more of them. For example, look at the last verse of today's gospel. It says, "The devil left him temporarily." The Pharisees tempted him by asking for a sign from heaven to prove that he was the son of God. On the way to Jerusalem, the disciples tempted him: they tried to stop him from going there because, they knew he would be killed; but Jesus still went to Jerusalem.

As a matter of fact there was a movie that came out in 1988, called The *Last Temptation of Christ* by Martin Scorsese. According to that movie, the last temptation happened when Jesus was hanging on the cross; the temptation was to come down from the cross, marry Mary Magdalene, and live happily ever after.

No one can say for sure, if Jesus was tempted to do that, because nobody knows. It is quite possible, but the important thing is that Jesus did not succumb.

How did Jesus overcome his temptations? Today's reading gives us the answer. He overcame them by remembering and quoting from the Scriptures. He defeated each temptation by quoting a scripture passage: Against the temptation for food and gluttony, Jesus said: "Man does not live by bread alone."

Against the temptation to wield power, he said: "You shall not put your Lord your God to test." Against the temptation to amass wealth, Jesus said: "You shall do homage to the Lord your God; him alone shall you adore."

Most Christians would not want to jump into sin, yet we cannot resist falling into it because, very often, our flesh is not strong enough to resist. Jesus has an excellent advise: "If your right eye is your trouble, gouge it out and throw it away; better to lose part of your body than to have it all cast into hell." We don't take that literally, and gouging out the eye is a drastic measure, but Jesus is teaching us that if necessary, drastic measures should be taken to avoid sin.

Always remember that nothing can come into human experience that does not come as a thought. A thought or idea becomes real only if we pay attention to it. The more we dwell on an idea, the stronger it becomes. Let me explain with an example.

I have a patient, who is 90. He had a gambling addiction. He lost all his money to gambling. One night after losing five thousand dollars, he was leaving Hard Rock Casino in Hollywood. He was disoriented, drove erratically, got into an accident and killed an innocent driver in another car. Now he is on hospice and during my visits, all he talks about is his desire to go back to the casino. He wants me to take him there. Every waking moment, he thinks about going to the casino.

We call that an addiction. But, what is an addiction? **An addiction is a solidified temptation.** When you repeatedly succumb to a temptation, be it gambling, pornography, over eating, they become addictions. The key is that as soon as a negative or evil thought originates in our mind, we have to turn away from it.

Let me use an imagery to explain how temptation works. We are all familiar with hurricanes. A hurricane just does not happen suddenly. For example, there is not going to be a hurricane today, tomorrow, or the day after. It takes about two weeks for a hurricane to come ashore to the mainland.

First, it forms as a tropical depression near Africa, thousands of miles away. A few days later it becomes a tropical storm, and as it travels over warm waters, it gathers speed and strength, and finally becomes a hurricane and you know the huge destruction it can cause. Think Katrina and New Orleans.

A hurricane does not necessarily have to attack the mainland and cause destruction. If a mass of cold air from the mainland pushes down at the appropriate time, the hurricane will turn back toward the ocean.

Temptations are very much like that. First, it originates in our mind as a thought: To go into a casino, or to a bar, or to do anything that is sinful or immoral, and if we don't check it at the thought level and abandon it, it leads into a behavior. If the massive cold air of prayer or a scripture verse comes into our mind, the tempting thought will return to the ocean of nothingness.

A recent survey of Discipleship Journal readers ranked areas of greatest spiritual challenge to them. They were materialism, pride, self centeredness, laziness, anger, sexual lust, envy, gluttony and lying. 81% of respondents said that temptations were more potent when they neglected time with God. In other words, people with no prayer life, easily succumb to temptations. The same survey noted that 84 % of respondents said that resisting temptations was accomplished by prayer and scripture reading.

So, how do we resist temptations? Let me answer that using the words of Jesus: "Be on guard and pray that you may not enter into temptation; the spirit is willing but the flesh is weak."

# 40. Eight Words That Could Change Your Life

John 1: 14

*The Word became flesh and dwelt among us.*

I would like to talk to you today about eight words that could change your lives, and it depends on how you celebrate Christmas this year.

There are three ways of celebrating Christmas. **The first one is based on the shopping mall**. Most of the western world mainly follows this pattern. Its focus is to buy the right stuff for yourself, and to find the ideal gift for your loved ones. It is centered on black Friday and Cyber Monday. You put all this stuff under the Christmas tree, open them on Christmas morning, have a great Christmas dinner with family and friends, and the day after Christmas is just like any other day. I owe, I owe, so off to work I go.

The second way of celebrating Christmas is **based on the gospel of Luke**. Now what do I mean by that? Only Luke writes about the baby Jesus being born in a manger; only Luke talks about the angels announcing the birth of Jesus to the shepherds: "Glory to God in the highest; and peace to men of good will." Christmas songs like "Silent Night, Holy Night,' "Joy to the World," "Hark! The Herald Angels Sing," "What Child Is This?", "O little Town of Bethlehem," "We Three Kings of Orient Are," "Away in a Manger," and "O Come All Ye Faithful" would not exist without the gospel of Luke.

We would not have any of the external trappings of Christmas without the gospel of Luke. For the majority of Christians, their Christmas is centered on the events described in the gospel of Luke.

Most of the third world which is economically poor celebrates Christmas the Lukan way. When I was growing up in India, we celebrated it that way. I made a small manger at home and the characters of the nativity scene such as Mary, Joseph, Baby Jesus, the shepherds, and the sheep were laid out. I made a star with transparent color paper and lit a candle in it. We had no electricity. We had no Black Friday shopping spree, because we had no Thanksgiving weekend. We had no cyber Monday shopping because we had no computers. It was very basic.

There is a third way of celebrating Christmas which is very rarely done and I like to draw your attention to that. If you celebrate Christmas that way, it will change your life forever, not just on Christmas day, but for the entire year, for the rest of your life. It is a celebration based on the gospel of John, actually **based on just eight words in the gospel of John.**

The gospel of John which does not mention the manger or the angels, the shepherds or the wise men from the east, the holy family or baby Jesus, describes Christmas in just eight words: **The word became flesh and dwelt among us**. The implications of these eight words are enormous.

To grasp the implications of this, we have to understand what *Logos* means in Greek. *Logos* means Word, which is God. *Logos* is the omnipotent, omnipresent, and omniscient God, who is the creator of everything. John starts the gospel with these words: “In the beginning was the Word and the Word was with God and the Word was God.”

We see the same expression in the first verse of the first chapter of the book of Genesis; ‘In the beginning God created heaven and earth.” By using the same language to talk about Jesus, John is saying that

Jesus is God, he is the Word. He was with God in the beginning of creation.

But then he makes a startling statement: This all powerful God, this Logos, this Word became flesh, and dwelt among us; he pitched his tent among humans! St. Paul talks about this self-emptying of God in these words: "Though he was in the form of God, he did not deem equality with God something to be grasped at; rather, he emptied himself, and took the form a salve, being born in the likeness of man." That is Christmas for Paul.

So what are the implications of the Word, who is Almighty God, becoming flesh and living among us?

First of all, it means that God is no longer a distant deity living somewhere up in the heavens, someone to be feared and worshiped, but someone who is deeply immersed in the affairs of man.

This is a huge shift from the God of the Old Testament who appears in a burning bush, a God who smites and kills those who don't fear him, a God who punishes you if you don't obey his Commandments. On Christmas day, the God who refuses to give his name to Moses becomes "Emmanuel" which means "God with us."

If God is with us who can be against us? **Thus Christmas gives us such a sense of security and safety, a safety that comes from having a God who walks with us, behind us, beside us and in front of us, loving us and protecting us.**

Secondly it means that God understands how a human being thinks, feels and behaves with all his flaws, follies and frivolities because, on Christmas day, God became one of us so that he can understand us from within.

Thirdly, it means that despite our perceived sense of weakness, human beings have the innate capacity to rise to the level of godliness with the strength that we receive by accepting Jesus into our lives. John says it so beautifully: "Anyone who accepts him, he **empowered** them to become children of God." So, stop defining yourself as sinners.

Fourthly, the first Christmas or the mystery of incarnation, means that God embraces the entire humanity. Look at the words of John. He does not say, "God became an American, or an Indian, or a Christian or a Hindu," but God became "human." In that sense, every human being, on the face of this planet, whether they are black, white or yellow, male, female, gay or straight, every human is the person of Jesus, the image of God.

**By becoming human, God embraced every human being and we should not refuse to embrace someone whom God embraced first!**

It may be hard for us to admit that, but if you really want to understand the real meaning of Christmas and experience the peace and joy that comes with it, we need to admit that.

Do you know why we don't feel like Christmas always, because we don't see Jesus in others always. December 25$^{th}$ becomes such a manufactured day, with song and dance, Santa Claus and all other external paraphernalia. Some people celebrate Christmas without even talking to their siblings; others harbor grudges or prejudices in their hearts and they wonder why the peace of Christmas has eluded them.

When we discover the face of Jesus on the myriad faces that we see everywhere, we are truly celebrating Christmas.

**Being Jesus for others and seeing Jesus in others is the best Christmas present given and received.**

In this sense, the message of Christmas is a message of unity, love and peace among human beings of all races, religions and nationalities.

And this feeling of love and unity does not have to be limited to one day of the year, December 25th.

The birth of Jesus is such a grace filled event that it has the power to make every day of our lives feel like Christmas. It is a spiritual tragedy not to expect to feel that peace every day. So why do we feel it only one day or a few days in December?

This story explains why:

It was Christmas day in a monastery consisting of students from different religions. The master glanced at the calendar, saw it was Monday and said: "I wish you a happy Monday." This offended the Christians in the monastery. So the master explained: "Millions will enjoy not today, but Christmas, but their joy is short-lived; however, for those who have learned to enjoy today, every day is Christmas."

These are the same people who are offended if the store clerk at Macy's says "Happy Holidays" instead of "Happy Christmas." If your heart is filled with Jesus, words from others won't really matter.

For us disciples of Christ, every day should be Christmas because John tells us that "God became man and dwelt among us." Feeling His presence among us and seeing His face around us is the real celebration of Christmas.

# 41. Ego-Stripping in the New Year

Luke 2: 22-25

*On the eighth day, when it was time to circumcise him, he was named Jesus, the name the angel had given him before he had been conceived. When the time of their purification according to the Law of Moses had been completed, Joseph and Mary took him to Jerusalem to present him to the Lord and to offer a sacrifice in keeping with what is said in the law of the Lord: "a pair of doves or two young pigeons."*

A southern Baptist minister was finishing a sermon on the evils of drinking. With great emphasis he said: "If I had all the beer in the world, I'd take it and pour it into the river; with even greater force, he said; "If I had all the wine in the world, I would pour it into the river. Finally, shaking his fist in the air, he said: "If I had all the whiskey in the world, I would pour it into the river."

Sermon completed, he sat down. The music director stood up, and announced with a smile: "For our closing song, let us sing hymn #701 'Shall We Gather at the River.'

I hope we don't gather at the river too much on this New Year's Eve.

On this last day of the year, my most predominant emotion is a feeling of gratitude. I m sure you feel the same. We are grateful that we had no hurricanes this year. We are blessed because we reached the end of the year to start a New Year tomorrow. Millions of people who started their life journeys with us on January 1, 2006, were not able to complete it.

Did you know that every seven seconds someone dies in this country? By the time we finish this worship service, 600 people will die in America and by the end of this day, 8000 people will die. Since I work in hospice, I am fascinated by these facts.

I witnessed the death of 198 of my patients this year that is about four patients a week. The Lord kept us healthy and alive this year and brought us together again today to finish the year. It is not a right that we are entitled to, but a gift that is given, and we are grateful to God.

The Lord is going to give us a new lease on life, tomorrow. And how are we going to use the new lease? One of the things that people usually do is making New Year resolutions. I went on Google yesterday and found out that the Top Ten New Year resolutions are: 1) Spend more time with family and friends; 2) Exercise daily; 3) Lose weight; 4) Quit smoking; 5) Enjoy life more; 6) Quit drinking; 7) Get out of debt; 8) Learn something new; 9) Help others; 10) Get organized.

My advice to you is: don't make any resolutions because surveys show that 90% of the people break 90% of their resolutions within 90 days.

The reason why people are unable to keep their resolutions is because it is like stitching a new piece of cloth to an old garment or as Jesus said: "It is like pouring new wine into old wineskins." The garment will tear apart and the wineskin will burst.

Let me give you an analogy: You wake up in the morning and while getting dressed, come to realize that the buttons on your shirt are not aligned. You find out only when you try the neck button. Now how will you correct that? You cannot do it by playing with the neck button or even the one or two beneath that. You have to unbutton all of them, and start all over again. If the first one is aligned, the rest will fall into place.

So what you should do in the New Year is, overhaul your entire life, not just some aspects of it. Resolutions address only some aspects. Woody Allen once said that making resolutions is like putting lipstick on a pig. It will look pretty for a while, but by the end of the day, the pig will still be a pig.

If you overhaul your entire life in the New Year, you won't need separate resolutions, because your life will flow like one unified river. It is about raising to a higher level of consciousness in the New Year, a whole new you, not just new in some parts of your life.

Most people think that creating themselves new is very difficult; it becomes a struggle. So they will just make some changes, and after a few days, they fall into the old ways. The happiness that was wished and received at the beginning of the New Year, turns into misery in yet another soon to be old year.

So the first step in overhauling your life and making a new you is realizing that there are two aspects to our personality: Your Ego and your Spirit. The ego is about competing, getting ahead, fighting and winning. It is focused on the externals and worried about material possessions. The spirit is focused on the internal and it is more about giving in, forgiving, loving and surrendering. Our goal is to break the ego and let the spirit take charge of our life. **It is about changing the direction of our life from "ego-driven" to "spirit driven."**

There is a famous Franciscan priest named Richard Rhor. He has a center for spirituality in Albuquerque, New Mexico, where he invites men for a five day retreat called *Men's Rite of Passage.* The goal of the retreat is to transform these men to new human beings. During the first session he initiates the men to a practice called **"ego-stripping",** using five essential truths. They are: 1) Life is hard, 2) You are not that important, 3) You are not in control, 4) Your life is not about you, and 5) You are going to die.

Now if you can keep these five truths always in your consciousness, your lives will be very different in the New Year. Let us reflect on each one of them.

**Life is hard:** If we can consciously accept the fact that life is hard, then we will stop complaining, which is one of the most important reasons for unhappiness in our life. When we accept that life is hard, we develop a mind-set that is able to deal with anything that comes our way. If you expect life to be easy, then every little thing will bother you. It is a matter of consciousness. As Wayne Dyer says, "When you change the way you look at things, the things you look at change."

The second truth is: **You are not that important.** Understanding that statement is the ultimate blow to the ego, which always wants to feel important and dominate. If we really grasp the meaning of that truth, it will help us deal with all the pain and suffering that we feel in our interpersonal relationships. Because the root of all the problems, at home, in church, in nations and the world is the feeling "I am right and you are wrong!"

The third truth is: **You are not in control**. The ego wants to control people and events in our life. The fact of the matter is that we have very little control over anything. Trying to control people and events can make us very miserable. When I say this I am thinking of some of my patients. I have this 97 year old man.

He said to me: "I am not ready to die, I need at least four more years, and I have some business to take care of." He used to belong to the union in Chicago and was a big shot in his younger days. Every time I visit him, he is in an angry mood, throws up his hands in the air and asks: 'Why is this happening to me?"

Instead of thanking God for the 97 years he had, he is griping about the problems that old age inevitably brings. Instead of surrendering his life to God in gratitude, he wants to control his destiny. No wonder he is angry and miserable; he is still under the grip of the ego.

According to Eckhart Tolle, author of *The Power of Now,* "No other life form on the planet knows the negativity of the ego." He asks: "Have you ever seen an unhappy flower or a stressed out tree? Have you come across a depressed dolphin, a frog that has a self esteem problem, a cow that cannot relax or a bird that carries hatred and resentment? The only animals that may occasionally experience something akin to negativity or show signs of neurotic behavior are those that live in close contact with humans, and so link into the human mind and its insanity."

The fourth truth is: **Your life is not about you.** It is about God; it is about the community around you and that includes your family, your church, your city, your nation. As Jesus said, "Unless the grain of wheat falls to the ground and dies, it produces nothing." When you are tempted to make ego-based decisions in life, you must always ask how it affects others.

We live in a consumer society. When we think about doing something or going somewhere or joining a group, the first question in our mind usually is, "What can I get out it?" That is a consumer-focused question; it is an ego based question. Instead of asking, "What can I get out of it", we should ask: "What can I give in this situation?" As Christians, we are called to be givers, not consumers, and church is one place we should never approach as a consumer, because we are here to worship someone who gave himself up for us. **Church is one place we enter, leaving the ego at the door.**

The fifth truth about ego stripping is: **You are going to die**. Death is the final blow to the ego. That is the moment when the spirit is free of the material world. Meditating on our death can be a very useful exercise in the New Year to keep our ego in check and live spirit-driven lives.

**So when you become conscious of the fact that life is hard, that you are not that important, you are not in control, your life is not about you and you are going to die, you will completely**

**surrender your life to God.** Mary and Jesus are prime examples of that surrender.

Think of Mary, a young girl, under 20 years old, and she is told by an angel that she is going to be the mother of the Messiah. She is not even married. The scripture says that Mary was troubled by the words of the angel. You can only imagine the array of emotions Mary must have felt: anxiety, fear, not knowing what her family is going to think, not knowing what the future will be. Her entire life was going to be completely overturned. So what does Mary do?

Instead of trying to find answers to all her questions, Mary surrenders completely to God. She said: "Behold the handmaid of the Lord, be it done to me according to thy word." And the same Mary stands in the temple eight days after she gave birth, which is tomorrow, offering her son Jesus to God.

Tomorrow is the feast of the presentation of Jesus in the temple where Mary and Joseph came with baby Jesus and with two pigeons as it was the custom and offered Jesus to God. And we know, Jesus lived his life as an offering to God, led by the Spirit, always surrendering to the will of God.

There is no incident in the four gospels where we find Jesus acting out of his ego. His words and actions are always spirit-driven. He always taught about turning your other cheek, going the extra mile, loving your enemies, forgiving those who offend you: all of them ego-breaking behaviors.

**If Jesus had an ego, when Judas betrayed him with a kiss, he could have paralyzed him; If Jesus had an ego, when Peter denied him three time, he could have denounced him; If Jesus had an ego, when the soldiers slapped him, he could have destroyed their whole battalion.**

He always behaved out of his spirit, and surrendered his life to God, right before his death on the cross: "Father, into your hands I commend my spirit."

So in the New Year, instead of becoming angry, depressed and anxious, or struggling and fighting, or stressed out, all of which are ego-driven emotions and behaviors, try to focus on the spirit inside and surrender your life to God. As soon as an emotion or a decision originates inside your consciousness, ask a simple question: "Is this emotion or decision ego driven or spirit driven?" "Is this coming from my ego, or this coming from my spirit?"

There is no promise that your life will be easy in the New Year, but there is a guarantee that Jesus will be with you every moment, keeping his promise, "I am with you always." And when we become constantly aware of the presence of Jesus in our life, the ego breaks down, and all the negativity that comes with it, disappears, and life becomes joyful, and peaceful every day of the New Year.

# 42. Have a Mind That Is Open to Everything

Mathew: 2: 1-12

*After Jesus was born in Bethlehem in Judea, during the time of King Herod, Magi from the east came to Jerusalem and asked, "Where is the one who has been born king of Jews?" We saw his star in the east and have come to worship him."*

After the busy time of Christmas and New Year, the Church celebrates today, the feast of the Epiphany. Now, what does the word, *Epiphany* mean? It is a Greek word and it means 'manifestation' or 'showing.'

So, epiphany means the manifestation of Jesus to the outside world. Jesus was born in a small, obscure town called Bethlehem; he was born of unknown parents, Joseph and Mary, and he was born in a manger, not a palace. But Jesus is not meant to be confined to a small village, Jesus is not just the savior of a small group of people, but he is the way, the truth and the life for the whole world, the entire humanity, and that is the meaning of the feast of Epiphany.

And the story of this manifestation of Jesus to the whole world is told through the story of the astrologers visiting baby Jesus. It is also called the story of the *Magi* or the 'Three wise men.' The Bible tells very little about this story. As a matter of fact, it is found only in the gospel of Matthew, not in Mark, Luke or John.

When the Bible says very little about an event, what happens is that tradition develops around it, and this is a good example of a story that developed in tradition. Tradition says that they were kings, and that is how we got the hymn: *The Three Kings* but the text says nothing about them being kings.

Tradition gives names to the visitors: Balthazar, king of Arabia, Melchior, king of Persia and Gasper, king of India, but we don't find such names in the gospel.

Tradition says, they were riding on camels, but the Bible does not say anything about their mode of transportation.

Tradition says there were three of them, but the Bible does not say how many. The number three probably comes from the three gifts, gold, incense and myrrh.

Now why would they take gold, incense and myrrh as gifts for a baby? What is a two week old baby to do with a gold bar, incense and myrrh? Can you imagine taking that to a child these days? Someone said if the three visitors were women, they would have asked for directions, arrived on time to help deliver the baby, clean up the stable, made a casserole and given practical gifts.

What is the meaning and message of epiphany for us today? I would like to draw your attention to two main messages. First, what the three wise men saw was not impressive at all. A baby wrapped in swaddling clothes. There is nothing majestic or miraculous about that; it is something very simple and ordinary; **the message is that they saw God in the simple and the ordinary, they saw God in a helpless infant.**

They had the courage to leave their familiar land and let go off their comfortable settings and look for God elsewhere, to be open to finding the holy in unholy and unfamiliar places. We may have this preconceived notion that God is in church, or God is always associated with our idea of holiness and goodness.

But we have to open our mind to the possibility that God is everywhere and in all circumstances which brings me to the second message of epiphany: **that we must continue to search and learn and grow in our spiritual life.**

The three wise men were obviously seekers. They could have said to themselves: "We know enough, we are already wise, why look for more?" But they were on a journey to find out more about life. A truly wise person does not think he or she has all the answers. It is the ignorant person who thinks that he knows it all.

Socrates, one of the wisest of men said: "One thing I know is that I don't know."

The fact of the matter is that the ocean of knowledge is so vast that we know very little, we may have taken in a drop from that ocean, but there is so much out there that we don't know, and this applies to all areas of knowledge including our knowledge of God, Jesus and spirituality.

That is why along with Wayne Dyer, I feel that we should **have a mind that is open to everything and attached to nothing.** To be open to everything is so hard, because we humans are conditioned creatures. We are conditioned by geography, the religious beliefs of our ancestors, the color of our skin, our gender, etc. All these factors play a huge role in who we are and how we think and behave in life.

**It is very difficult to go through the hard drive of our lives, to delete old files and add new ones. So, most of us just stay in our comfort zones.**

But we have to remember that no one knows enough to be a pessimist. Resist being a pessimist, because we hardly know anything at all in comparison to what there is to know. Can you imagine what a pessimist who lived two hundred years ago would think about the world today? Airplanes, automobiles, electricity, TV, internet, fax, cell phones; all these happened because of a spark of open mindedness.

What about the future and all our tomorrows? Nobody knows for sure: So, have a miracle mind set and an insatiable curiosity. Open your minds to all possibilities; that is what the three wise men did when they set out on a journey to an unknown land.

Or at least if you are not able to entertain such openness and curiosity, don't snub those who have it. If someone tells you something that sounds outrageous or impossible, listen anyway. Just because your mind is not open enough to grasp it, does not mean something is an impossibility.

There is a cartoon called, *Baby Blues.* It is the story of two children and their parents. One day, the father and his six year old daughter are lying on the beach, looking up the sky. She asked her father: "Dad, how many stars are in the sky? The father: "I don't know; how many do you think there are? After a pause, the girl said: "Twenty-six." "Why 26?" asked the father and the girl replied: "I can count only up to 26."

**Just because our small minds can understand or contain only certain amount of information, or certain limited data, does not mean, that is all there is.** That is why it is so important to have a mind that is open to everything and attached to nothing.

Now, this "attached to nothing" attitude is very important. We can be so stuck in our positions that we won't budge regardless of the evidence to the contrary. It is called the fanaticism of close mindedness. It can be so destructive to our spiritual growth and over all well being.

In religion, that kind of attitude is called the "bumper sticker theology," the belief that everything about God, Jesus, and faith are fully understood and there is no need for further study or reflection.

You have seen the bumper sticker that says: "God said it, I believe it, and that settles it." People who believe in such bumper stickers can be so narrow-minded that they will even hate those who don't believe what they believe.

I have a patient whose daughter is an engineer. She developed the part for an instrument that is used in the space shuttle Discovery. She was honored last June during the launch of the Shuttle Discovery with a reception and a front row seat near the launch pad. This engineer daughter made an album of her pictures and gave to her mother, who proudly showed me the album. Among the many pictures, one attracted my special attention and had an inscription which read:

***The exciting thing is that we don't know what lies beyond and the unopened door...and each door will open to many more doors.... each answer leading to many more questions...that is discovery.***

It is exciting to be living in such a world with an open mind and generosity of spirit. That is what the three wise men did, when they left their familiar surroundings, and set out on a journey, focusing their gaze on a star and they found Jesus.

On this epiphany, Jesus invites us to leave our close mindedness behind, gaze beyond the false security of the familiar, enjoy our faith journeys, and be open to new discoveries and understandings about God, Jesus and life itself.

# 43. Are You a Barren Tree in the Garden of God?

Luke: 13: 6-9

*Then he told this parable: 'A man had a fig tree, planted in his vineyard, and he went to look for fruit on it, but did not find any. So he said, to the man who took care of the vineyard. 'For three years I've been coming to look for fruit on this fig tree and haven't found any. Cut it down! Why should it use up the soil?"*

*'Sir', the man replied, 'leave it alone for one more year, and I'll dig around it and fertilize it. If it bears fruit next year, fine! If not, then cut it down.'*

I love mangoes. Back home in India, we had three mango trees on our property. And during the season, the first thing I did when I woke up in the morning was to look under the tree, to see how many fruits had fallen during the night. I really enjoyed eating juicy, tasty mangoes.

In Florida, we can buy them in Publix, but they are expensive. Some people have mango trees in their back yard. So a few years ago, I went to Margate Swap Shop and bought a mango plant, about two feet high, and planted it in my back yard. Then I went to Home Depot, got the right fertilizer for it and did everything by the book, and it began to grow. Three years after I planted it, it had fruits for the first time. In the first year, I had about three mangoes. In the second year, there were about seventy five mangoes; in the third year, more than two hundred.

But last year, there were no mangoes and there was a reason for it. Hurricane Wilma uprooted my mango tree. It fell sideways, and rested on my neighbor's concrete fence. Its roots were shaken. By the way, that was the only damage I had from hurricane Wilma. I trimmed all the big branches, and with help from neighbors, propped it up and staked it. It seems to be thriving. I am hoping that this year, it will have some fruits.

When I read the Scripture for today, I was thinking of my mango tree. According to the gospel story, a man had a fig tree in the middle of his vineyard and he came looking for fruit. The story says that he had been looking for fruits, not just once or twice but for three years and there weren't any. It was a barren tree. So he asked the vine dresser to cut down the tree, because it was just using space. But the vine dresser pleaded with the owner and said: "Leave it for another year and let me fertilize it some more, and may be next year there will be fruits."

The story of this fig tree is the story of each one of us, especially during this season of Lent. Each one of us is like a tree planted by God in His garden, which is the world. God expects us to bear fruits. What are the fruits that God expects from us?

To find answer, I have to take you to Galatians chapter five, where St. Paul talks about the fruits of the Spirit. He talks about two kinds of fruits that we can produce. One set of fruits proceeds from the flesh: they are lewd conduct, impurity, licentiousness, idolatry, sorcery, hostilities, bickering, jealousy, outbursts of rage, selfish rivalries, dissensions, factions, envy, drunkenness, orgies and the like. He says, "I warn you, and I have warned you before: those who do such things will not inherit the kingdom of God."

In contrast, then Paul talks about the fruits that proceed from the Spirit. They are love, peace, joy, patience, kindness, goodness, faithfulness, gentleness, and generosity. Throughout his letters, St. Paul talks about two aspects of our personality: the flesh and the spirit, and the constant battles between desires of the flesh and desires of the spirit.

When we look at ourselves or others, what we see first is the body. Even though what we see first is the external package, ultimately, we are spiritual beings. For example, when someone feels sick in the morning and calls his boss, what does he say? He does not say, "My body cannot come to work today? We say, "I can't come to work today. This "I" is more than the body, more than the flesh.

The fact of the matter is that we are not from here. We are not from this world. Our body is not our primary identity. We are aliens, not in a science fiction way, but in a spiritual way, and that is why Jesus said, "You are in this world, but not of this world." You have been taught that you are a body made up of atoms and molecules, bones, tissues, oxygen, hydrogen and nitrogen. You identify with your job, possessions and achievements.

You also have some other information stored away in your brain. If you are lucky, you will get old and die and at the end of this entire struggle called life, you will go to heaven. I always hear people say, **"I can't wait to see God after I die." How about seeing God while you are still alive?** If you are a spiritual being, you should be able to see God, because God is Spirit.

**I don't want you to believe that you are only this collection of bones and tissues, destined to be annihilated after death.**

We are primarily spiritual beings and human beings second. I want you to seriously think about it; yes, we are spiritual beings with human experiences rather than human beings with a few spiritual experiences. Our spirit or soul which is part of God, existed first, and on the day we were born, what people described as a baby, was actually a piece of God, wrapped around in a body. A temporal body was placed around the eternal soul.

That is why Isaiah says; "before I formed you in your mother's womb, I knew you." "Your names are written in the palm of my hands."

When someone dies, we usually say: "The soul left the body." We should reverse that and say, "the body left the soul," because the soul is still alive and present, but body is not. Let me explain this with an example.

Take for example a TV show. It is transmitted from New York, and it comes on your TV. In the middle of the show, you get tired, and you turn the TV off. What happens to the program? The program does not stop existing, just because your TV is off. It is in the air as electromagnetic waves. Just like the program existed before it was on your TV, and will continue to exist after you shut off the TV, your soul which existed before it was in your body, will continue to exist after you die; but we easily forget this fact.

The drama of Anna Nicole Smith played out in our county court room is a clear example of this blind focus on the body. The whole fight was about where to bury her body which was stored in a morgue for three weeks. Her mother, who was described as her "estranged mother" who never had a positive relationship with her while she was alive, wanted to bury her in Texas.

Her boyfriend wanted to bury her in the Bahamas and we witnessed the "hostilities, bickering, and jealousy, outbursts of rage, selfish rivalries, dissensions, and factions (all world of St. Paul) that went on in the courtroom.

If the focus was on the soul, this drama would not have played out for three weeks, and Larry King would not have devoted ten hours of programming for this, and three hundred reporters from around the world would not have hung around the medical examiner's office waiting to take a picture of a casket.

This is happening because people are obsessed with the body. Think about it: Most of our attention and majority of our efforts on a daily basis are related to matters of the body; our house, our cars, our job, the clothes, the food, the bank accounts. People will spend $5000 for a plastic surgery to make the body look beautiful, but won't spend $50 to attend a retreat to refresh the soul.

Many people have no problem spending an hour in the gym, working out or lifting weights, and getting a tan. One million Americans step into a tanning booth every day, but they will not step into a church. On a Sunday morning, people will pack up their cars and go to the beach, and spend all day there, but won't take the time to attend a worship service.

You get the point: I would say 99% of our time, resources, and efforts are focused on matters pertaining to the body. How much time do we devote to matters of the spirit like prayer, meditation, spiritual reading on a daily basis? Except for an hour on a Sunday, what else do we do to attend to the needs of our soul?

During this Lent, Jesus the Gardner wants us to think about all this and produce fruits of the Spirit. As I mentioned earlier, St. Paul lists nine fruits of the Spirit, and they are love, peace, joy, patience, kindness, goodness, faithfulness, gentleness and generosity.

We use the plural, "fruits" but if you look at that passage, you will see that St. Paul does not say fruits. He does not use the plural; he uses the singular, the FRUIT of the spirit. Because there is only one big fruit and that is LOVE, and every other fruit is a byproduct of love. If you have love, you will be kind, and patient, and gentle, and faithful and generous and joyful.

So, the one fruit that Jesus wants us to produce in our lives is love, and he is giving us another chance during this Lent to do that.

My mango tree did not produce mangoes last year, because it was uprooted from the ground. Similarly, if our lives are not connected to God who is the source of our lives, we too will remain barren like my mango tree or the fig tree in today's gospel story.

During this Lent, let us re-establish those connections through prayer, scripture reading and church attendance so that we can produce the fruit of LOVE.

# 44. Why Hosanna, Why Not Cheers?

Mark: 11:7-10; 15-18

*When they brought the colt to Jesus and threw their cloaks over it, he sat on it. Many people spread their cloaks on the road, while others spread branches they had cut in the fields. Those who went ahead and those who followed shouted, "Hosanna! Blessed is he who comes in the name of the Lord; Hosanna in the highest!*

A man bought a donkey from a preacher. The donkey was trained in a unique way. When you say "Alleluia" he starts to run. And when you say the word "Amen," he stops. The man pays the preacher, mounts the donkey and said: "Alleluia" and the donkey began to run. He rode for a long time, through mountains and valleys, forests and fields, and wanted to rest, but had forgotten the word to stop the donkey. "Stop" he yelled, but the donkey kept going, he started saying words like, "Bible," "Prayer," "Church," "Jesus," "Messiah," "God," but no luck; it kept going.

He was fast approaching a cliff and knew that the donkey would jump off the cliff and he would die. So he began a prayer: "Lord Jesus, son of the living God, have mercy on me, for you are God forever and ever... Amen!" And the donkey came to a sudden stop at the edge of the cliff; he was so relieved and shouted: "Alleluia."

The one word that is on the lips of millions of Christians all over the world today is not "Alleluia" or "Amen," it is "Hosanna." About 3 billion Christians in different parts of the world will hold palms in their hands and say that word. What does it mean? It is a Hebrew word that means: "Save, we pray."

There is a reason why they use this word, because the Jewish people were waiting for a messiah, a savior. They thought that Jesus would be that savior. The Jewish people understood salvation very differently than what we understand today. For us, salvation is life after death, on the other side of the grave, life in a future heaven. For them, salvation meant freedom from captivity, slavery and foreign rule.

The history of the Jewish people was a history of slavery, captivity and foreign rule. From 450 to 1400 BC, they were slaves in Egypt. Then they wandered for 40 years in the desert. From 734 to 722 BC, they were in captivity in Assyria. From 608 to 581 BC, they were in Babylonian captivity. From 400 to 330, the Persian captivity; From 330 to 166 was the captivity in Greece; From 166 to 63 BC was the Hasmonean period of captivity, and from 63 BC to 37 AD was the Roman period. So, when Jesus was born, the Israelites were under rule of Rome and Pontius Pilate was the governor.

You can understand the longings of a people who have suffered so much slavery and captivity to be free. They wanted freedom so badly, and they thought Jesus would make it happen for them by throwing the Romans out, and establishing a kingdom where he would rule as a temporal king. They expected him to save them from political domination.

But the people were totally mistaken about the kind of salvation that Jesus was about to bring about and they did not like it. That is why the same crowd that shouted "Hosanna" on Palm Sunday, cried out "crucify him," five days later. When Jesus failed to deliver on their expectations, they turned against him.

Jesus never misled the people regarding what he was about. He had told them that his kingdom was not of this world; but they did not want to believe it.

There were signs all around even during his entry into Jerusalem. He arrives on a donkey, which is the poor man's transportation in that part of the world. He does not arrive on a horse. He does not get a red carpet welcome from the political or religious authorities. He got a green leaves welcome from the common man. Look at what he does first when he enters the temple. He does not go and worship in the temple or pay homage to anyone.

Jesus goes to the temple to overturn the tables of money changers and stalls of those selling doves. Now this is a very misunderstood and misinterpreted event in the gospels. Many people use this event to justify their anger. "Even Jesus got angry in the temple, so I can get angry sometimes." People have used this to justify war: "Jesus threw out bad people from the temple, so we can fight and destroy bad people in the world." This is a good example of misusing and misquoting the bible to find scriptural basis for any feeling or behavior we want to justify. We have to be very careful about using the bible to validate our ideas.

I am reminded of a story. There was this pastor who was new in town. In an effort to get to know the members of his congregation, he began visiting. He stopped at a house. There was a car in the drive way and light inside, but no one answered the door when he knocked and he knocked several times. So he took out his business card, wrote Rev. 3.20 on it and tucked it on the door. (*Behold, I stand at the door and knock; if any man hears my voice and opens the door, I will come in and dine with him)*

The following Sunday, the pastor found his business card in the collection plate, with another bible verse written under his and that was Gen: 3:10 (*And he said: I heard thy voice in the garden and I was afraid, because I was naked)*.

Always remember that the bible is a collection of 66 different books for Protestants and 72 books for Catholics. There are also books called Gospel of Thomas, Gospel of Judas, and Gospel of Philip which are not even included in any official cannon. They were written in Middle Eastern culture most of us know nothing about, and in a language we don't read, speak or understand. Books of the

the Old and New Testaments were written by about forty different authors, mostly anonymous, during a period of about 1500 years, two thousand years ago.

The world view and level of consciousness of the biblical authors were totally different from ours. So we have to be very careful, and extremely humble when using the bible to argue about current social or cultural issues or to justify our emotions or behaviors.

First of all this passage does not say Jesus got angry. It says: "He overturned the tables of money changers and benches of those selling doves." "My house shall be called a house of prayer but you are turning it into a den of thieves."

The Webster's dictionary defines anger as "feeling of displeasure resulting from injury; feelings of resentful, revengeful displeasure." We know from the gospels that Jesus was not a revengeful person. If anything, he was just the opposite. What we see in this incident is moral indignation rather than anger. Indignation: righteous anger aroused by what seems unjust or unrighteous. That is exactly what is happening here, and I will tell you why.

Do you know why Jesus overturned the tables of money changers? Money changers were obviously changing money. Why did they have to change money in the temple? And why would Jesus be upset about that? It was not an issue of location, but a moral issue. Let me explain:

During Passover, Jews from all over the world came to Jerusalem temple. They came with money from whatever region they came, and the money had images of local kings or rulers on them. The priests at the temple insisted that foreign money cannot be deposited in the temple box. So they had to change it into local money and in that exchange the priests exploited the people.

Another regulation was that the doves offered in the temple should be purchased from the priests in the temple. During Passover, the temple priesthood used to hatch thousands of doves and they insisted that only those doves should be used for sacrifice. What people brought from their homes were declared "unclean" or "blemished." This monopoly caused exploitation and it was done in the name of God and that is what infuriated Jesus. The priests were using God and religious rules to exploit people, and Jesus was indignant about that.

**Jesus is also using this incident to teach us that God does not need our money or our ritual sacrifices. Jesus is all about internal transformation and change of heart.**

Which brings me to the title of the sermon: "Why hosanna, and why not cheers? Like in regular parades, the people could have shouted: "Long live Jesus," or "Cheers" to Jesus but they did not; they chose, "Hosanna." Why? Because **"Cheers" is an applause, "Hosanna" is an invitation. Applause originates from the tongue; Invitation originates in the heart. "Cheers" is a slogan; "Hosanna" is a prayer.**

We can applaud somebody without inviting them into our house or our lives. Jesus does not want us just to applaud him and keep him at bay. About applauders, Jesus said: "These people honor me with their lips, but their hearts are far from me."

When we say, "Hosanna," we are saying: "Save us Lord" and Jesus can save us only if he enters into the temple of our hearts. If he comes in, he might have to turn over a few tables, or expel a few things from our hearts. We may have to agree for a spring cleaning: to cleanse our hearts of fear, anger, lust, greed, narrow mindedness, rigidity, jealousy, holier than thou attitude, sense of superiority, etc.

**Before we can experience the power of the Resurrection, cleansing of the heart is imperative and that is why Passion Sunday precedes Easter Sunday.**

If we hold palms in our hands today and say "Hosanna," we should be willing to open our hearts to Jesus so that he can cleanse our hearts and save us from within.

# 45. If Jesus Is in Your Heart, Notify Your Face

John: 20: 1-18

*Jesus said, "Do not hold on to me, for I have not yet returned to the Father. Go instead to my brothers and tell them, 'I am returning to my Father and your Father, to my God and your God.' Mary Magdalene went to the disciples with the news: "I have seen the Lord!" and she told them that he had said these things to her.*

First of all I want to wish you a very happy Easter. I have heard pastors say that it is hard to preach on Easter, because people already know the message. If you ask any Christian she would say that Easter means that Jesus rose from the dead. But if you ask a deeper question, but what does it really mean or how does it affect your daily life, we often do not get a clear answer.

Let me tell you a story. Once upon a time, there was a pastor who always started his service with these words: 'The Lord is with you." Every Sunday, every service, these are the words that will inevitably come from his lips. People got so used to him, they would automatically respond: "And also with you."

One Sunday when he began service, he realized that there was something wrong with the sound system. He began fiddling with his microphone, and instead of the usual greeting, "The Lord is with you," he said: "There is something wrong with this mike." And the people automatically responded: "And also with you."

Life can be so automatic, so robotic, that we go through the motions without really thinking about the meaning of what we are doing. This can be true of our Easter celebration too. I will share with you my own experience. There have been 55 Easters in my life time. The first ten, I have no real memory of because I was a kid. Of the other 45, I have to say that I have "celebrated" only about ten, and just "observed" the other 35.

Now there is a huge difference between observing an event and celebrating an event. Observance means a customary act, rite or ceremony; something that we automatically do, every day, every month or every year. Easter comes once a year, usually in April; it follows Good Friday, and we go to church wearing nice clothes, have family dinner and, basically that is it. We remain the same persons that we were before Easter Sunday, and will remain the same on the Monday after Easter. This is called observing Easter.

Celebrating Eater is a totally different activity. Celebration does not just stop with one day, it continues on, in such a way, that it goes beyond the day. The whole life becomes one big celebration. Easter is meant to be celebrated every day, it is meant for all times, where ever we are and whatever we do. We are called to be an Easter people.

We live in a Good Friday world, but we are an Easter people. Now, what does that mean? Yes we live in a broken, sinful and divided world. There are personal and national problems all around us. We may be going through pain, suffering, depression and illness, financial problems, relationship issues, and whole lot of other problems in our lives.

But in spite of all that, in the midst of sickness, suffering and death itself, there is hope, there is redemption, and there is room for peace and joy. That is what this Sunday is about. And it is not just meant for this day but for every day of our lives, and that is why I chose the sermon title today: "If Jesus is in your heart, notify your face."

A few years ago, I was pastor a small church, with about 20 families. The name of the Church was Resurrection National Catholic Church. Under the logo of our bulletin every Sunday was those words. Week after week, we printed it and gave to the people; *if you have Jesus in your heart, you have to notify your face.* Because the face is the mirror of your soul, and most of the time, that is the only way to judge how we are feeling inside.

Let me tell you something: **A gloomy Christian is a contradiction in terms.** If you really believe that Jesus is raised from the dead and is truly alive today, you have to smile. You have to experience the power of his resurrection in your life, starting with your face.

Many people, who claim to believe in the resurrection, do not behave as if they believe it. And I will tell you why. While preparing this sermon, I talked with a few people: "So next Sunday is Easter, what do you think it means? "It means Jesus rose from the dead." "I know that, but what does that mean for you on a daily basis? If Jesus is alive today, where is he now, where can I find him?" And almost all of them said, pointing to the heavens: "He is up there, way up there."

And I said to myself, this is the problem. Majority of Christians believe that Jesus died, rose from the dead, ascended into heaven and will come again to judge us at the end of the world. That is what the creed has taught you. You recite that and believe it, although no one I talked to could explain it. **They think that the risen Jesus is sitting in a nice chair somewhere up there, watching us from a distance.**

If that is what you believe, that Jesus is somewhere UP there, no wonder you feel miserable, you feel unhappy and life feels like a tale told by an idiot full of sound and fury, signifying nothing.

On this Easter Sunday, I want you to forget about the UP there, and seriously think about the DOWN here, within you and around you. Jesus is right here, in this church, in the streets, in the supermarkets, in the shopping mall. In prisons, in detention centers; on cruise ships, air planes, trains and automobiles; where ever there is a human being, there is Jesus.

Now if you don't believe me, look at the last verse of the last chapter of Mathew's gospel. Chapter 28: 20: After giving them the great commission, Jesus says: "And know that I AM with you always, until the end of the world." It does not say, I WILL be with you at a future date, I will be with you in church, or on Easter Sunday or any Sunday, but I AM WITH YOU ALWAYS.

According to Mathew, there was no ascension. Jesus does not ascend into heaven, he stays with us. Now there is a spiritual presence and a physical presence. The spiritual presence is what you feel inside; the physical presence of Jesus is the human being out there.

How could we see Jesus in the people we don't like, people of a different color, or religion or race, or people who treat us badly. For example, how do you see Jesus in Bin Laden? You might say it is impossible and don't even go there. But if you really believe that Jesus is alive today, you have to go there, you have no choice. He is with us even when we are not with him.

Let me show you how you can see the risen Jesus in everyone around you by inviting you to take a deeper look at today's reading. It says, early Sunday morning, while it was still dark, Mary Magdalene went to the tomb. She finds the stone moved away, and the tomb empty. So she ran off to Simon Peter and the other disciple, and tells them.

And so they run to the tomb, first side by side, but apparently the other disciple was in better physical shape than Peter so, he overtakes Peter, but stops short at the entrance of the tomb. Peter comes running and goes straight in. He sees the wrappings on the ground and the piece of cloth that had covered the head of Jesus in the corner. Then the other disciple went in.

Watch what happens next: The gospel reports just four words: "He saw and believed." Believed what? These are just four simple words. We don't know what he believed. In parenthesis, it says (remember, as yet they did not understand the Scriptures that Jesus had to rise from the dead). There was no excitement on the part of this disciple who apparently believed, there was no behavior on his part or that of Peter, to indicate that they believed that Jesus had risen.

We know that they believed later, but that day, when they saw the empty tomb they did not believe in the resurrection. Had they believed, they should have jumped up and down; they should have shouted with joy. Nothing; look at their behavior; look at what they did: Verse 10 says: "With this, the disciples went back home."

Their hearts were as empty as the empty tomb. Nothing happened to them, they just went home, like we do on most Sundays after service, we just go home. It is ironic that in my bible, the first part of chapter 20 is called the EMPTY tomb.

Look at the second part; it is titled: "Jesus appears to Mary Magdalene." Now focus on what Mary Magdalene did. She did not go back home like Peter and the other disciple. They were men; they came down, took one look, and did not find anything, so they left. They had no time to wait, they had no patience to ponder.

But Mary stood there weeping and even as she wept, the gospel says, she bent over to look inside, and when she bent down and looked inside, something beautifully miraculous happened. She saw two angels in dazzling robes.

The angels asked her: "Woman, why are you weeping?" She was weeping because the Lord has been taken away, and when she turned around, Jesus was standing right in front of her. First she thought it was the gardener, but it was really Jesus.

Now we should ask the question: Why didn't this happen to Peter and the other disciple? Peter was after all the leader of the pack, and the other disciple, John, was the beloved disciple. You know what? They were so depressed; they were angry that Jesus died like a criminal; they were upset that Jesus did not stand up and fight like a man; they were mad that their dreams of sitting on his right and left in his kingdom were dashed.

So they came with a negative attitude, a barren heart and an investigative mind-set. They were checking out the tomb of Jesus like a crime scene. They were doing a *CSI Jerusalem*; they had no patience to wait, they had no emotions to shed tears like Mary did, they were in a hurry, they had lost hope, and so they went home empty hearted.

So here is the clue to finding the risen Jesus around you: Study the experience of Mary Magdalene. Examine closely what she did. She waited; she did not give up easily; she did not leave in a hurry to get home. She took a second look at the tomb. Focus on how she looked into the tomb: the gospel says, **"She bent down and looked." She looked with a longing her heart, she looked with tears in her eyes, she looked with the hope of finding Jesus, hoping against hope, and she found him.**

Our problem is that most of the time, we are like Peter and the other disciple. We are in a hurry, we have no patience for people; we don't have the compassion to take a second look at people, beyond the surface. When we look at them, we usually look with suspicion rather than love.

We rarely have the humility to bend down in front of people like Mary bending in front of the tomb. I don't mean, physically bending, but the willingness to bend our views, opinions, our prejudices and judgments; we don't even expect to find Jesus here, because we think he is UP there, and no wonder we don't see Jesus in the people around us.

Mary saw Jesus in the gardener, because she had Jesus in her heart. What she saw in the gardener was a reflection of the Jesus who had already risen in her heart. **Jesus is the gardener, and the painter, the mailman and the UPS driver and the fellow driver on the road, the garbage collector, the foreigner and the native; He is every man, every woman, and every human being everywhere**.

When you start believing that in your heart, and behave as if you really believe it, there will be a smile on your face and peace in your heart. You will be celebrating Easter every day.

# 46. Faith Seeking Understanding

John: 20:19-21; 24-28

*Now Thomas (Called Didymus), one of the Twelve, was not with the disciples when Jesus came. So the other disciples told him, "We have seen the Lord!" But he said to them, "Unless I see the nail marks in his hands and put my finger where the nails were, and put my hand into his side, I will not believe it."*

A pastor while visiting a fifth grade religion class asked: "Who can tell me what Easter is?"

One boy raised his hand and said "Easter is a holiday in November when we all get together, eat turkey and we are thankful." Wrong." The pastor turned to a second student and asked "what is Easter? "Easter is a holiday in December when we put up a nice tree, exchange presents, and celebrate the birth of Jesus." The pastor said that he was wrong too. Then another boy raised his hand, saying, "I know, I know."

"Easter is the Christian holiday that coincides with the Jewish Passover. Jesus and his disciples were eating the last supper. He was later betrayed and turned over to the Romans by one of his disciples. The Romans put a crown of thorns on his head and crucified him between two thieves. He was buried in a tomb which was sealed by a large stone...." The pastor smiled broadly with delight and said to himself, 'this boy knows his religion; his parents taught him right.' "Go on my child, finish the story…

The boy continued: *"Every year, the stone is moved aside so that Jesus can come out, and if he sees his shadow, there will be six more weeks of winter."*

Like this little boy, we may know a lot of facts about our Christian faith and still miss the important point. We may know doctrines about Jesus but fail to follow Jesus. We know what Easter is but do we really know the deeper implications of that event, and do they affect all aspects of our lives?

In a recent survey conducted by the Center for Missionary Research, 90% of the respondents said that they have not studied about their religion or reflected on their faith, beyond what they learned in Sunday school as children. The same survey also revealed that 87% of Christians have not read the entire bible once. Many have read parts of the bible, and have memorized many verses, but they often don't know the real meaning or context of the passage.

This means that for majority of Christians, their religious education stopped at about age 15. They grow up in age and gather knowledge in other subjects and become up-to-date in all areas of life, such as communication, medicine, science, transportation, etc. For example, if you want to travel to New York, you get into a plane and fly. You don't say, I am going to walk there or travel on a donkey, because that is what people did in Biblical times.

Or when you want to talk to someone, you pick up the phone or send an email from the comfort of your room; you don't walk to up the house of the person and knock on the door because that is what people did 2000 years ago. You get the point.

We have caught up with the 21st century in all areas of life, except on issues pertaining to faith and religion. When it comes to matters of faith, we are still children; we have not grown up. Why is that? I can think of two main reasons for that: Ignorance and fear.

You may remember the story of Chief Justice Roy Moore of Alabama who wanted to display the Ten Commandments in all the courtrooms in the state. During a TV interview, the host asked him: “Can you recite the Ten Commandments?” He paused for a moment and asked: “All of them?” “Yes all of them,” but, he couldn’t. The host asked him another question:

“Suppose you get to post the Commandments in the courthouse, do you think the court should impose the punishment for breaking the Commandments?” The judge paused for a moment and said: “I guess so.” He had no idea that death was the punishment for breaking three of the Ten Commandments. For example Ex. 21: 17 says: “Whoever curses his father or mother shall be put to death.” We think we know everything about what we believe, but do we really?

Fear is the second main reason why people don’t grow up in their faith. We are afraid to raise doubts regarding what we were taught in Sunday school. We are afraid to ask questions regarding matters of faith, because we think it will be displeasing God. As a matter of fact, we were given answers first, before we even asked any questions. We should ask questions about our faith. God who gave us a brain is delighted when we use it.

As Mark Victor Hansen says: “**You were born rich with 18 billion bountiful, beautiful, totally available, and in all probability, under used brain cells awaiting your desire, decision and directional compass to take you onward, upward, goodward and Godward.”**

The Brain is this engine that God has placed in each one of us to navigate through the mess called life. He expects us to use it in all areas of our life, including our faith. Today’s Gospel story about apostle Thomas confirms this point.

Thomas is my favorite apostle for two reasons. First of all, I owe my faith to him. According to tradition, Thomas traveled to India and landed in the south east coastal state of Kerala, which happens to be my home state. This was in AD 52, 2000 years ago. India had trade relations with Persia during those times, and Thomas is believed to have traveled in one of those ships transporting spices and other goods.

According to tradition, he preached the gospel to the Hindus, converted them and established seven churches. He was martyred in the southern state of Madras in AD 60 and there is a huge shrine and pilgrimage center there today. Christians in the state of Kerala are called "St. Thomas Christians" and there is a tradition in Christian families to name one of their children, Thomas. My son Tommy is named after that tradition.

In 1968 Pope Paul VI officially proclaimed St. Thomas as the "Apostle of India" and he was added to the litany of saints.

The second reason I love Thomas is that he had a questioning mind. He did not take anything for its face value. He was loyal, fearless, adventurous and a free spirit. Now how do I know that? Look at the gospels. Jesus had 12 apostles. We don't know much about nine of them, except their names. We have some information about three apostles and Thomas is one of them.

We all know about Judas because he betrayed Jesus. We know about Peter because he denied Jesus three times. We also know that Peter was married because there is an incident in the gospel about Jesus healing Peter's mother in law.

Thomas is usually referred to as "doubting Thomas," but that is actually an unfair title. If you read the gospels closely, you will find that all the apostles doubted the resurrection. Read John 20, verses 3 -9 which talks about Peter and John coming to inspect the empty tomb. They came, they found the tomb empty and the bible says, "They went home." That is not the behavior of someone who believed in the resurrection. Or read Mt 28: 16 where it says, "All of them still doubted the resurrection."

I would rather call Thomas, the "honest Thomas" who was honest about his feelings, and did not pretend to understand things he didn't. He did not fake faith in something he did not experience himself. He had the courage to ask questions in front of his fellow disciples who must have criticized him for making such a demand on Jesus.

We can sketch the personality of Thomas from three incidents in the gospel of John. First is John chapter 11: When his friend Lazarus died, Jesus decided to go to Bethany, even though he would be in grave danger. Bethany was a dangerous place to go because his enemies were looking for Jesus. When Thomas heard this, he immediately said to the other disciples: "Let us also go and die with him?" He was not doubtful, or fearful or worried about his life. He was willing to risk his life with his master.

The second incident happened during the last supper when Jesus told the twelve that he would be leaving them soon (John: 14: 5-6). He added that they knew where he was going. I am sure they had no clue, but everybody was afraid to speak up or ask a question. After all, it was a solemn moment, because Jesus was talking about his death. But Thomas did not hold back or pretend as if he knew where Jesus was going. He spoke up and asked: "Master, we do not know where you are going; how can we know the way? You have to love this guy, so outspoken, and not afraid to ask a question when he did not know.

The third incident is the one in today's reading. When Jesus appeared to the disciples, Thomas was not with them. Where was he that Sunday night? When the other disciples were hiding behind closed doors for fear of the Jews, Thomas must have been walking the streets. I can visualize Thomas walking into a '7 Eleven' in Galilee to pick up a six pack. He was exhausted and frustrated about the events of the week. He had put his trust in this teacher called Jesus; He was at one point ready to die with him; now, all hope is lost, he died like a criminal. Thomas was devastated.

When the other disciples told him that they had seen the Lord, Thomas is not ready to believe them. He is not satisfied with second hand information. He wants to find out for himself, he wants to experience the risen Lord for himself and in his characteristic way, he says: "Unless I see the mark of the nails in his hand and put my finger into the nail marks and put my hand into his side, I will not believe." Sounds like an audacious attitude, an unflinching position, a stubborn demand, but that is Thomas.

Look at how Jesus responds to that seemingly arrogant demand: Jesus does not get upset with Thomas, criticize him, or punish him for his attitude. Jesus does not rebuke his disciple's questioning mind. He challenges him to explore and find out for himself.

**Thomas is the patron saint of those of us who are trying to live a critical faith. He is not satisfied with other people's accounts. He is not going to believe something just because everybody else before him believed that. In this way, Thomas approached religion critically. But Thomas is not an unbeliever, his religion is critical faith.**

Christians are usually tempted by two false options. On the one hand, there is faith without doubt, a kind of faith so impatient with Thomas that it would cast him out for asking impossible questions. On the other hand, there is criticism without faith. Thomas shows a better way. He doesn't deny his doubts. This Easter story tells us that there is room for each of us with our questions and with our proclamations. A critical faith has a fundamental place in religion.

As a matter of fact, St. Thomas could be the patron saint of our church. Let me read to you what Pastor Craig wrote about this in *Disciples Values promoted at Royal Palm Christian Church*. It is titled *Reasonable Religion*. "We celebrate both the heart and the mind; we do not believe faith needs to be at odds with reason or that science and good religion are incompatible. We encourage a probing, thoughtful faith rather than mindless belief. We are convinced that faith should seek understanding, and an inquiring mind is important for spiritual growth and effective service in the world."

Always remember that faith evolves and it is an ongoing process. A faith that is not personalized has no transforming value; in other words, if we just repeat what others have told us, that won't change our behavior. **Thomas challenges us today to question our assumptions, reflect upon them and explore the edges of our fears and our faith.** And just as he did for Thomas, Jesus will meet us where we are and will invite us to touch resurrection.

# 47. What If God Is One of Us?

Luke: 24: 13-35

*As they approached the village to which they were going, Jesus acted as if he were going farther. But they urged him strongly, "Stay with us, for it is nearly evening; the day is almost over." So he went into stay with them. When he was at the table with them, he took bread, gave thanks, broke it and began to give it to them. Then their eyes were opened and they recognized him and he disappeared from their sight. They asked each other "were not our hearts burning within us while he talked with us on the road and opened the Scriptures to us?"*

In March 1992, *Newsweek* published a letter from the Greenville County Dept of Social Services. The letter was written to a dead person. "Your food stamps will be stopped effective immediately, because we received notice that you passed away. May God bless you. You may reapply, if there is a change in your circumstances."

The only person that I know of whose circumstances changed after his death is Jesus Christ. It happened 2000 years ago. During the course of the past 20 centuries Christians have believed that Jesus is alive. We believe that Jesus is alive, and it is that faith which brings us together here every Sunday.

But where do we find Jesus today? Today's gospel story shows us where to find him. It is the story of two disciples who were on a journey from Jerusalem to Emmaus.

Have you noticed that some of the saddest words in our language begin with the letter D. Disappointment, doubt, disillusionment, defeat, despair, depression, despondence, and death. All of these emotions were summed up in the experience of Cleopas and his companion. They had left the confused band of disciples to go to Emmaus. The master they had loved and followed had been put to death. Not just any death, but death by crucifixion.

You are familiar with the expression that Life is a journey, not a destination. It has almost become a cliché. The Bible is filled with images of spiritual life as a journey. The first notion of journey comes from Abraham, leaving his native town and journeying to a place that God would show him. The prime example of spiritual journey in the Bible is the story of the exodus. The Israelites left their bondage in Egypt and went through the Red Sea and journeyed for 40 years before finally reaching the Promised Land. Jesus' life was a journey from Galilee to Jerusalem where he was crucified, buried and rose again.

Bible scholar Walter Breggman, says that our **faith journey goes through three phases: being oriented, becoming disoriented and being re-oriented.** Look at Abraham's journey. It started off fine, in the orientation phase, but he was totally disoriented when he was asked to sacrifice his only son, Isaac, the most painful thing a father could ever be asked to do. He accepted that challenge in faith and ended up as the father of Faith, the re-orientation phase.

Same with the exodus experience. When they left Egypt, the Israelites were excited that they were finally escaping slavery, the orientation phase. Then comes the hard part, being chased by Pharaoh's army, the 40 years of wandering in the desert, struggling for livelihood, fighting their enemies, etc. the disorientation phase, and finally, reaching the promised land, the re-orientation.

The same thing happened to Jesus in his journey. Three years of teaching, preaching and gathering disciples in Galilee: orientation phase; the betrayal, crucifixion and death: the disorientation phase, and finally, resurrection which is the re-orientation. It happened to the disciples in today's story.

They were in the orientation phase when they were following Jesus listening to him teach, perform miracles, and enjoying his company. Then came the hard part, the suffering and death of their master which completely disoriented them and they left, to go back home to Emmaus. Then came the re-orientation back to Jerusalem where they become fearless witnesses to his resurrection.

This is true of all of our individual life journeys. Until we understand the different phases of our journey and accept all three phases, our lives will be miserable. A lot of people are happy to have the orientation and re-orientation phases, but they don't want to deal with the disorientation part of the journey. It is hard and unpleasant, and often painful. But there is no shortcut; our life has to go through all three phases, without skipping any.

When I say this I am reminded of some of my patients. Let me share with you just one story.

Jim is a 96 year old man, in hospice care. He had a wonderful life. Lived and worked in Chicago as a Union leader, made a lot of money. Traveled many places, had a great marriage, his wife died five years ago, he has children and grand children and now he is on hospice. He is oxygen dependent and he has to wear a diaper. Every time I visit, he complains about his situation. "Why is God doing this to me, I can't walk, I can't breathe, I can't go shopping," I can't talk to anyone on the phone any more (because he is hard of hearing but refuses to wear hearing aid, because it is a nuisance).

Now, this is a clear case of a man who is unable or unwilling to go through the disorientation phase of his life journey. He refuses to realize that it is part of the journey of life, and he is miserable. When I visit him, I draw his attention to the wall where he has several photos. One of them is his baby picture; a beautiful black and white picture still in very good condition; pictures of his high school and college graduation. There are pictures of his wedding day with a young beautiful bride, his union days in Chicago. Nothing seems to change his feeling of depression and sadness.

Jim is stuck in the orientation phase of his life. Until he accepts the disorientation phase, he will not reach reorientation and achieve peace before he dies.

I want you to know that these three phases are not one time events. In other words, they don't happen just once, from childhood to old age, in a linear fashion. It can happen a thousand times during our life time, in a circular fashion. Every day we could have experiences of orientation, disorientation and re-orientation. In order to experience life fully and peacefully, we have to go through all three phases; you cannot avoid disorientation and get to reorientation; it just does not work that way. And that is why Jesus takes Cleopas and his companion back to Jerusalem.

When life became difficult, when their hopes were dashed, they wanted to run away from Jerusalem because that is where bad things happened. That is where Jesus was crucified. They just wanted to forget that memory and escape. But Jesus brings them right back to Jerusalem. Because even though bad things happened there, a good thing also happened there. Yes Jesus died in Jerusalem, but he also rose in Jerusalem.

Like the disciples in today's story, many people do not feel the presence of Jesus walking beside them in their life journeys. There were two reasons why Cleopas and his friend, did not recognize Jesus. First of all, they were too focused on themselves: their pain, their loss, and their lost dreams. I have seen that when people are sad and depressed and going through rough times; they don't feel the presence of God.

I have a client whose mother died a month ago and he is extremely depressed. He told me: "Don't talk to me about faith now, because I just don't have any." This is the case of disorientation phase where God seems absent. When you go through difficult times in your life and God seems far away, ask yourself, "Who moved? Because God never moves away, He cannot move away, because "In Him we live move and have our being." We move away from God and fail to recognize his constant presence, but he is with us all along, all the time, everywhere. Unrecognized may be, but always present.

The second reason the disciples did not recognize Jesus is because they must have been expecting the miraculous, like the splitting of the Red Sea, or the appearance of Jesus from the sky or a burning bush experience similar to that of Moses. **Avoid the miraculous, and focus on the ordinary, because Jesus is often the stranger right in front of us.**

Few years ago, there was a TV show called *Joan of Arcadia* and its theme song was: "What if God is One of Us?"

And the show was full of experiences where its character, Joan, is constantly meeting God in mundane circumstance and encounters with ordinary people such as the cable guy, the child playing in a yard, her teacher, the school janitor, etc. Make it a practice to look for the risen Jesus around you all the time. **When you see people on the street, in the super market, or the shopping mall, try to say in your mind, "this could be Jesus," and you will be amazed how that encounter changes.**

I try to practice this on a daily basis. I meet new people every day, especially in my new patients and their care givers. Before I visit with them, I say a prayer in my heart, "*Lord, help me see your face on their face*", and it always works. Because I believe in the promise of Jesus that he is with us always till the end of time. I believe the message of today's gospel where Jesus walks along with these disciples, unrecognized by them. My challenge is to recognize him.

The story says that they recognized him in the breaking of the bread. When Jesus broke bread with them, they knew him. Breaking of the bread was the symbol of ultimate sharing of his life with his disciples. It was a symbol of breaking his body. This means that the best way to feel the presence of Jesus in our lives and recognize him is, when we share our lives with others.

When we approach others with open minds, with compassion in our hearts and kindness in our words, we will recognize Jesus, because openness, love, compassion, and kindness are qualities of a sharing person. **When you become a caring and sharing person, every stranger you meet, transforms and becomes the risen Jesus. This is how you change the resurrection of Jesus from a first century event to a 21st century experience.**

# 48. Holy Spirit, the Invisible Translator

Acts 2: 1-13

*When the day of Pentecost came, they were all together in one place. Suddenly a sound like the blowing of a violent wind came from heaven and filled the whole house where they were sitting. They saw what seemed to be tongues of fire that separated and came to rest on each of them. All them were filled with the Holy Spirit and began speaking in other tongues as the Spirit enabled them.*

Today we celebrate Pentecost which is a Greek word, meaning 'fifty.' It is the day the Holy Spirit descended on the apostles, and it happened fifty days after Easter. When I think of the Holy Spirit, the word that first comes to mind is "Confirmation."

For Catholics, there are seven sacraments: Baptism, Confirmation, Confession, Communion, Anointing of the Sick, Holy Orders and Matrimony. Baptism is given seven days after birth and confirmation is given when children are about 12 years old.

Confirmation is supposed to supplant and enhance what happened at Baptism. Although the Holy Spirit is given at baptism, it kind of stays dormant, because the child does not consciously know that he has received the Holy Spirit. So at age 12 you get "confirmed" of the fact that you have in fact received the Holy Spirit and that is the day you officially become a "soldier for Christ."

Even at age 12, I was not aware of these implications. I knew confirmation was important, because in the olden days, only the bishop could confer the sacrament of confirmation. In the 60s, a bishop visiting a parish was almost like God himself visiting in person.

The nuns who prepared us for confirmation were nervous. They wanted to make a good impression on the bishop. So the nuns taught us the prayers by heart, gave us clear instructions about the protocol of the bishops' visit.

We were 15 children receiving confirmation that day. We had to stand in front of the bishop. The nuns had prepared us in advance for the questions the bishop would ask. The first question would be: "Who created you? The answer: "God created me." The second question would be: "Why did God create you?" Answer: "To love and glorify God." The third question would be "Who are the three persons of the Trinity?"

We were well coached and choreographed. The first boy would get the first question, the second boy, the second question, the third boy, the third question. Unfortunately, on the day of confirmation, the first boy who was supposed to answer the question "who created you" was absent due to illness. So the second boy got the first question. But he was programmed to answer the second question.

So when the bishop asked him, "Who created you?" he said: "To love and glorify God." The bishop asked again: "Who created you?" and the boy repeated like a robot: "To love and glorify God."

So the bishop corrected him and said: "God created you!" And the boy said: "*No, the boy whom God created is sick today!*"

As I said, confirmation is the most structured and choreographed sacrament. But the original coming of the Holy Spirit, on Pentecost, had nothing structured or choreographed about it. The spirit came freely and fiercely, like the blowing of a violent wind. The spirit came down like tongues of fire, descending on the apostles. The experience of that fire and heat jolted them from their sleep and totally transformed their lives.

The Holy Spirit completely changed the disciples. Their demeanor, attitude, behavior and their entire personalities were changed for the better. Let us just examine the change it brought in them starting with Apostle Peter.

Peter was a timid man. When Jesus was arrested, you see him hanging around the courtyard, like a coward, covering his head with a scarf so that no one would recognize him! But a maid recognized him, and Peter denied Jesus not once, but three times.

At another time, when Jesus was going to a hostile town to preach, the disciples held back. They did not want to go there because they were afraid of their lives.

After the crucifixion, the disciples were hiding behind locked doors for fear of the Jews. That is why, during each post resurrection appearance, the first thing Jesus told them was: "Do not be afraid." So how did these terrified and cowardly disciples suddenly become bold and courageous witnesses to the gospel, ready to lay down their lives for Jesus?

It was the Holy Spirit. The Holy Spirit took hold of their lives; they were empowered by the Spirit. When they were infused with the Holy Spirit, they became powerful witnesses for Jesus.

Pentecost is important for two reasons: First, it was the defining moment in the life of the disciples. It was more defining than Christmas, Epiphany, Crucifixion and Easter put together. Christmas did not change anybody's lives. Three years of fellowship with the historical Jesus did not change the disciples.

They still argued about who is greater among them. They still would not wash each other's feet; that is why Jesus had to do it. Even resurrection did not change them. After Jesus died on the cross, they were so disappointed that they went back to their old jobs. Pentecost changed all that.

Secondly, it is on Pentecost that Jesus became available to the whole world. During his earthly life, Jesus was limited to Palestine. He did not travel more than thirty miles beyond his home town. Only very few people had the opportunity to see him in person and experience his love.

**But Pentecost changed all that. On Pentecost, Jesus made himself available to you and me, and to all humanity**.

The Holy Spirit is the spirit of Jesus. When his disciples were upset that Jesus had to die, he comforted them by saying that he would send his spirit. In John 16: 7, Jesus says: "It is for your good that I am going away. Unless I go away, the Counselor will not come to you; but if I go, I will send him to you." Again, in John 14: 16, Jesus says: "And I will ask the father, and he will give you another Counselor, to be with you for ever - the spirit of Truth."

On Pentecost, the disciples spoke one language, but the people heard the message in their own languages. There were people from 15 nations gathered there, people from Mesopotamia, Judea, Capadocia, Egypt, Libya, Parthians, Romans and Arabs. Each heard the message in their own language. What does that mean?

**It means that God is not tied down to one religion, language or nationality; that God is accessible to all, through one's own culture, language and experience. It means that God is not an old man with a white beard somewhere up there, but God is a spirit dwelling in your heart. It means that God meets you where you are, through your language and your culture. You don't have to go looking for God; He comes to you.**

**It means the Holy Spirit is the "invisible translator."**

The spirit who lives in you will translate for you, the messages you hear. You have to go into your heart, figure out your life with the help of the Spirit and lead your life based on the prompting of the Spirit. In other words, don't look outside for all the answers, be it from a book or a teacher. Trust your inner spirit and the right answers will come from within.

You have to believe that the spirit is in you. The church does not exactly encourage you to trust in your spirit. It encourages you to trust outside sources or authorities. That is why a lot of people describe themselves as "wretched sinners." We often say I am "just human." We blame our weakness and inability to live as witnesses to Christ, on our being just human. We forget that we have the Holy Spirit in us.

**So the question today is, "Has Pentecost happened to you? If so, when did that happen?"** Protestants would say it happens when a person is baptized; Catholics would say it happens when someone is confirmed. Others might say, Pentecost happens when a person is "born again."

**I say Pentecost happens to everybody, at the moment of birth**. In Christianity, we may celebrate it, using different sacraments, but everybody has the Spirit embedded in them at birth.

Nobody comes into this world with just the 'human" part; we come with two parts: "human" and "being;" The flesh and the spirit, the body and the soul. The 'being' with the small 'b' shares in the life of the Being with the Capital 'B', which is the Supreme Being.

That is what the Bible means when it says: "God created man in his own image, in the image of God he created him; male and female he created them" (Gen: 1:27). This idea is emphasized in another context where God creates the first man. God took clay from the earth and shaped it like a man, breathed into his nostrils, and the human being came alive. Breath is another word for Spirit.

So the image of God, or the breath of God, or the divine spark in you, is the Holy Spirit. We don't see it or feel it, because we are too busy with life. We forget that we are spiritual beings first and human beings second. We forget that our spirit existed before our bodies came into existence. **We forget that our bodies are just external wrappings around our spirit, which is eternal.**

Because of this forgetfulness, we mostly engage in affairs of the body. We make sure that the body is cared for, decorated and demonstrated. Ninety nine percent of our efforts are geared towards the affairs of the body. We are driven by issues of bread and butter, not love, peace and unity, which are issues of the Spirit.

**The Spirit gets honorable mention when we are in church or when we say our prayers. At other times, the Spirit is ignored, forgotten or dormant.**

Pentecost reminds that we should bring forth that Spirit to the forefront of our consciousness and live our lives led by the Spirit. In Romans 8: 5, St. Paul reminds us: "Those who live according to the flesh are intent on the things of the flesh; those who live according to the Spirit, on those of the Spirit. The tendency of the flesh is toward death, but that of the Spirit, towards life and peace."

And what is the sign that your life is driven by the Spirit? You will manifest these qualities in your life: love peace, joy, patience, kindness goodness, faithfulness, gentleness and self control. They are called the fruits of the Spirit.

# 49. World Communion Everyday

John 17: 20-23

*My prayer is not for them alone. I pray also for those who will believe in me though their message, that all of them may be one, Father, just as you are in me and I am in you. May they also be in us so that the world may believe that you have sent me. I gave them the glory that you gave me, that they may be one as we are one: I in them and you in me. May they be brought to complete unity to let the world know that you sent me and have loved them even as you have loved me.*

Today we celebrate World Communion Sunday. The sermon is called, "World Communion Every Day," because our communion with the world does not have to be confined to just one Sunday. If we can internalize the meaning of this day and make it part of our everyday consciousness, our spiritual life will be much stronger and deeper.

What does World Communion mean? Well, there are two words in it: World and Communion. Pretty simple words, but are they as simple as they seem?

Everybody knows what "world" means in this context; the big world out there with all those countries, but on a practical level, for most people, world means their little world. The place they live, the people they know, the concerns they have, etc. Most of the time, we are not conscious of the wider world.

For example, just look at the words we use. We have 'Red States' and 'Blue States,' we have a 'Black America' and 'White America,' we have 'Republicans' and 'Democrats,' 'Anglicans' and 'Catholics,' 'Baptists' and 'Methodists.' These words indicate divisions not wholeness.

Most people don't know much about the world. If you want to prove this, try this exercise at home. Take a piece of paper and start writing the names of the countries of the world. Give yourself ten minutes to do it. I guarantee you that after about six or seven minutes, you will be stumped, you won't be able to come up with any more names. In that initial six or seven minutes, you might come up with 20-25 names, may be less. Unless you have majored in world history, you won't get more than that.

I am very aware of the world. When I did this exercise, I could come up with names of 93 countries, and that is less than half of the total of 214 countries on this planet.

In this day and age, we cannot afford to be isolated and separated from the cares and concerns of the world and live in our own little corner, because we live in a fast shrinking world.

In 1941, as Franklin Roosevelt was preparing his State of the Union speech, he was with his aides, Samuel Roseman, Robert Sherwood and Harry Hopkins. The president said to his secretary: "We must look forward to a world based on four essential freedoms. The first is freedom of speech and expression everywhere in the world. The second is freedom for every man to worship God in his own way, everywhere in the world. The third is freedom from want, and fourth is freedom from fear." At the end of that meeting, Hopkins objected to the phrase, "everywhere in the world."

"That covers an awful lot of territory, Mr. President; I don't know how interested Americans are going to be, say, in the people of Java." Roosevelt came right back at Hopkins and said: "I am afraid they will have to be some day, Harry. The world is getting small that even the people in Java are getting to be our neighbors now."

By the way, Java is an island in Indonesia, the most populated in the world per square mile, with 107 million people.

This was said in 1941, almost 70 years ago. Today, the world is even smaller. If you like to learn how small and interconnected the world has become, read book, *The World is Flat* by Thomas Friedman.

Martin Luther King understood our interconnectedness so well when he wrote: "We are tied together in the single garment of destiny, caught in an inescapable network of mutuality and whatever affects one directly, affects all, indirectly. For some strange reason, I can never be what I ought to be until you are what you ought to be. And you can never be what you ought to be until I am what I ought to be. This is the way God's universe is made; this is the way it is structured."

When we understand that truth, we are in communion with the world. When we can embrace the people of Java or Bangladesh or Darfur, as our neighbors and as our brothers and sisters, not just in a theoretical sense, but really deeply and sincerely in our hearts, we are in communion with the world.

**When we are in communion with the world, we are in communion with God, because God is always in communion with the whole world. God is everywhere; God loves everyone; God is in everyone. So, when we expand our consciousness to include everyone and embrace everyone, everywhere, we are actually practicing world communion and communion with God at the same time.**

I have been practicing this world communion for a while now, and it has brought great spiritual benefits for me. I have become more loving, peaceful and compassionate. Let me share with you a few ways in which I practice world communion.

As you know I am a hospice chaplain. We are about 25 chaplains in our program representing Buddhism, Judaism and Christianity, with its many denominations. Once a month, we have a meeting. One of the things we do is self introductions if there is anyone new to the group. In the interest of time, we introduce ourselves by name and denomination only.

So we started from one end: "I am Joe, and I am a Presbyterian;" "I am James, and I am Baptist;" "I am Mark, and I am Southern Baptist;" "I am Patrick, and I belong to Church of Christ," and the next one said, "I am Janice, and I belong to the United Church of Christ," then the next one said, "I am Nick, and I am Methodist" and the next one said, "I am Cathy, and I belong to the United Methodist Church." And it went on and on, 25 people in one room, belonging to 25 different groups. So when my turn came I said: **"My name is Paul, and I am a human being."**

Everyone chuckled and the meeting proceeded. During the break, the Rabbi who was new to the group that day, took me aside and said that she was intrigued by my introduction and wanted to talk more about it. I told her that I was not trying to be a wise guy or being flippant about it. That is exactly what I believe. God did not create all these denominations; we created them mostly for selfish reasons.

I told her that if I say I am a Catholic, which I am by baptism, I am connected to about 1.2 billion people because that is the total number of Catholics in the world. If I say I am an American, which I am by citizenship, my connection shrinks to 300 million people; if I say I am Indian, which I am by birth, I am connected to one billion people.

These three identifications connect me to a total of about 2.5 billion people, but leave me unconnected to about 4 billion people out there, because there are 6.5 billion people on this planet. **'Human' is the only title that connects me to everyone. Human being is the only label that brings me into communion with the whole world.**

John says, "God so loved the world that he gave his only son." We usually focus on the second part of that sentence about the 'only son' and forget the first part which says, 'the world.' It does not say God so loved America, or God so loved India, or any particular nation, or any particular group of people, but God loved the World. **So when you expand your mind to embrace the world, you are manifesting the godliness within you.**

Let me share with you another story where this awareness of humanity came into play. I received a telephone call in the evening. It was a call from a telemarketer. She was doing a survey about a computer we had purchased directly from Dell. At the end of that customer satisfaction survey, the caller needed three pieces of information: My age, sex and race.

So I said, "I am fifty years old, I am male," and I stopped. "And your race, sir," she asked; and I said: "Human." There was dead silence at the other end. Then she said, "But I don't have a box for that on this paper, I have 'white,' 'black,' or 'other' and I have to put you in one of those boxes." And I told her that I did not want to be in a box. I want to be outside the box.

**Celebrating world communion is about thinking outside the box and getting outside the artificial boxes we have created.** World communion is about seeing beyond boundaries and barriers; World communion is about knocking down walls and fences.

In the Second World War, a group of soldiers were fighting in the rural countryside of France. During an intense battle, an American soldier was killed. Instead of leaving his body in the battle field, his comrades decided to give him a Christian burial. They remembered a church a few miles behind the front lines whose grounds included a small cemetery surrounded by a white fence. They set out for the church arriving just before sunset.

An elderly pastor, responded to their knocking. "Our friend was killed in battle," they blurted out, "and we wanted to give him a church burial." "I'm sorry," he said, "but we can bury only those of the same faith here." Weary after many months of war, the soldiers simply turned and walked away. "But, the pastor called after them, "you can bury him outside the fence."

The soldiers were not too happy about their friend being not inside the cemetery, but dug a grave and buried him just outside the white fence. The next morning the entire unit was ordered to move on, and the group raced back to the little church for one final goodbye to their friend. When they arrived, they couldn't find the grave site.

Tired and confused, they knocked on the door of the church. They asked the old pastor if he knew where they had buried their friend. "It was dark last night and we were exhausted. We must have been disoriented." A smile flashed across the old pastor's face. "After you left last night, I was saying my night prayers, and I began to feel very troubled and full of shame. I could not sleep, so I went outside early this morning and I moved the fence."

Where do you have fences built to keep out those who are not your kind? What kind of fences have you built to keep the world outside? Of course these fences are not physical structures but they are fences in our minds and our hearts. Racism, sexism and homophobia are mental fences.

We have built them over the years, some built for us when we were children, which makes us believe that somehow we are different and perhaps better than other people. This is the type of thinking that World communion Sunday is trying to change.

The pastor in this story just moved the fence to include the soldier in the cemetery. World communion Sunday invites us, not just to move a fence but to tear down all the fences we have built in our minds.

Jesus had no fence around him. He embraced the lepers and the sinners, the prostitutes and the Samaritans, the least of the society whom the religious authorities of his time disdained and discarded.

During the farewell prayer with his disciples, Jesus prayed for unity. He prayed that all may be one, beyond the artificial boundaries that we create for ourselves.

St. Paul echoed that sentiment when he said: "There is neither Jew, nor Greek, neither woman nor man, neither slave nor free, we are all one in Christ Jesus."

Celebrating world communion Sunday means keeping that sentiment always alive in our hearts.

# 50. Doing Small Things with Great Love

Mark: 12: 41-44

*Jesus sat down opposite the place where the offerings were put and watched the crowd putting their money into the temple treasury. Many rich people threw in large amounts. But a poor widow came and put in two very small copper coins, worth only a fraction of a penny.*

*Calling his disciples to him Jesus said, "I tell you the truth, this poor widow has put more into the treasury than all the others. They all gave out of their wealth; but she, out of her poverty, put in everything—all she had to live on."*

Every year for the last 16 years, *USA Weekend* magazine has designated the last Saturday of October as MAKE A DIFFERENCE DAY. The thinking behind the celebration of this day is that all of us, regardless of how insignificant we consider ourselves to be, can make a difference in the world.

Your response might be: "What can I do to make any difference in this huge world of 6 billion people?" You may feel a sense of powerlessness and ignore the whole thing as insignificant.

You might say things like, "What can I do, I am just one person, nobody knows me, I don't have any power," I used to think like that and shrink into myself until the following incident five years ago.

In my job as a hospice chaplain, I used to visit a patient every Friday. Her name was Angela; she was 92 years old and lived alone. Every

Friday, she would wait near the window, looking through the blinds for my arrival.

One Friday, I found her to be extremely upset and distressed because her television had stopped working. Now you have to remember, TV is the lifeline for a lot of seniors. Some of them keep it on, just for the background noise, to mask the deadly silence of loneliness.

Angela was on a limited budget, and the thought of paying for a repairman bothered her so much. She began crying when I walked in and paced through the room. Angela said that there was a storm the night before and she was afraid the TV had blown out. She asked me if I could repair it.

Being totally mechanically challenged, I didn't dare. However, when Angela was busy making a cup of coffee, I just looked around the TV, and to my surprise, found out that the TV was not hooked up to the outlet. I plugged in the TV and voila, "Price is Right" came on. "Angela, it is a miracle", I cried out in excitement. She couldn't believe her eyes. She hugged and kissed me and profusely thanked me. "You made my day; thank you, thank you; you have no idea what this means to me; I thank God for sending you here."

That day I realized that a simple act as plugging in a TV can make a huge difference in some one's life. **I also determined never to judge the impact of my behavior on others based on my perceptions, because what I consider to be insignificant could be significant for somebody else.**

There is a saying that "when a butterfly flaps its wings in San Francisco, it causes weather change in Singapore." It is a poetic way of saying that every little act can make a difference somewhere in somebody's life, like the ripple effect of a small stone thrown in the middle of a lake causing waves all around.

There is a book by *New York Times* columnist, Thomas Friedman, called *The World is Flat: A Brief History of the 21st Century.* He explains how technology has shrunk the world so much that people in faraway places, people who have never met in person are really touching each other's lives. He talks about his 80 year old mother who lives in Minneapolis, playing checkers on internet with a woman in Romania, and how they make each other happy.

He describes how a mundane activity such as you shopping in Wal-Mart impacts millions of people worldwide. Listen to this passage and try to visualize what he is describing.

*I visited the Wal-Mart headquarters in Bentonville Arkansas. My host took me over to the 1.2 million sq. feet distribution center where we climbed up to a viewing porch and watched the show.*

*On one side of the building, scores of white Wal-Mart trucks were dropping off boxes of merchandise from thousands of different suppliers.*

*Twenty four hour a day, seven days a week, the suppliers' trucks feed the twelve miles of conveyor streams, and the conveyor streams feed into a huge Wal-Mart river of boxed products but that is just half of the show.*

*As the Wal-Mart river flows along, an electronic eye reads the bar codes on each box on its way to the other side of the building. There, the river parts again into a thousand streams. Electric arms from each stream reach out and guide the boxes ordered by particular Wal-Mart stores, off the main river and down its stream, where another conveyor belt sweeps them into a waiting truck, which will rush the particular products into the shelves of a particular Wal-Mart store somewhere in the country.*

*There, a consumer will lift one of those products off the shelf and the cashier will scan it, and the moment that happens, a signal will be generated. That signal will go out across the Wal-Mart network to the supplier of that product whether that supplier's factory is in coastal China or coastal Maine. That signal will pop up on the supplier's computer screen and prompt him to make another of that item, and ship it via Wal-Mart supply chain and the whole cycle will start anew.*

*So, no sooner does your arm lift a product off the local Wal-Mart shelf and on to the checkout counter, than another mechanical arm starts making another one, somewhere in the world. Call it the Wal-Mart symphony with multiple movements with no end.*

So the next time you pick up a pair of shoes, or a CD, or bath towels, or a toaster oven or any little things, remember that you are touching the lives of many people around the world. That $19.99 or $29.99 you paid, trickles down as pennies and nickels into the hands of thousands of people, whose hard work and co-ordinated effort made it possible for that item to arrive in your hands. Say a small prayer in your heart blessing them whoever and where ever they may be. They are all your brothers and sisters and members of the body of the Cosmic Christ.

The point is that everything we do, even our most ordinary and mundane activities, impact people. What is truer is that God notices everything we do, especially those things which we consider to be unimportant, insignificant or trivial.

That is the message of today's story about the Widows' Mite. In the ancient world, a widow was a nobody. It is the husband who brought value to the woman. Once the husband dies, the widow is forgotten and forsaken and exploited. In verse 40, Jesus talks about the Scribes "devouring the savings of widows."

Such a widow approaches the collection box. The story says that Jesus was watching a crowd that was putting money into the box. Many wealthy people were putting sizable amounts, but that does not impress Jesus. Jesus notices a poor widow putting two small copper coins which was worth only a fraction of a penny! Jesus was so touched by her action, that he made an example of her. He called his disciples and told them: “This widow has contributed more than all the others. They gave from their surplus, she gave all she had.”

Yes, Jesus observes everything we do: the mundane and the minutia, the smallest and simplest of our behaviors and gestures. He is not watching us as a ‘big brother,’ but to impress upon us that **everything we do is important in the eyes of God, so that we may do it with compassion and devotion; that we won’t look at anything casually, or treat any one callously; that we will pay attention to the event, embrace the moment and cherish the person.**

It doesn’t matter how much we give, what matters is HOW we give. When we give all we have, with love and dedication, it is pleasing to God, and it makes a big difference.

Mother Teresa is someone who really understood the deep meaning of the story of the widow’s mite. She had no worldly power, she was not a president or prime minister; she had no military at her disposal; she never made big speeches, nor donated millions to any cause.

All she did was patch up the wounds of the poorest of the poor in the slums of Calcutta. I had the honor of working with the sisters of her congregation. It was part of my seminary training, a week of field work with the sisters of Missionaries of Charity.

It was extremely hard and mind numbing work to walk around the slums, surrounded by stray dogs, wading through puddles of dirty water, bitten by mosquitoes and harassed by huge flies, suffering the stench coming from dead rats and human waste. Yes, human beings live in such inhuman surroundings in the slums of Calcutta and elsewhere.

We had to squat on the mud floor, give sponge baths, shave the older men, and feed soup to the hungry, all of them ravaged by sickness, and extreme poverty.

It was not a glamorous job by any stretch of the imagination. But it is that simple and ordinary job done with love and commitment which made Mother Theresa a symbol of holiness and Christian charity all around the world. The impact this one humble, diminutive woman, who did a very simple act of caring for the least of this world, is enormous.

It is Mother Teresa who said: **"All of us may not be able to do great things; but all of us can do small things with great love."**

Here at Faith Christian church, you don't have a mega church with thousands of people. But you have a small group of very dedicated people who want to worship God as a community: a group that wants to bear witness to the love and compassion of Christ. And the impact your Christ-filled lives have on others is beyond measure.

For example, just by attending church every Sunday, you are impacting others. Your mere presence and positive energy could serve as encouragement and inspiration for your fellow worshipers.

The other day, I came across a Peanuts cartoon strip. In the first frame, a sad Charlie Brown says to his friend Linus: "*You know why that little red-haired girl never notices me?*

In the second frame he answers his own question: "*Because I am nothing! When she looks over here, there is nothing to see! How can she see someone who is nothing*?

In the third frame, Linus says to Charlie Brown: *"You are depressed, aren't you?*

When you are depressed, distressed, dis-spirited, disheartened, or feel like a nobody, or a nothing, reflect on the story of the widow's mite and remember Mother Teresa's words: "*All of us may not be able to do great things, but all of us can do small things with great love."*

# 51. Is the End Near?

Matthew: 24:36-45

*No one knows about that day or hour, not even the angels in heaven, nor the Son but only the Father... So you must be ready, because the Son of Man will come at an hour when you do not expect him.*

During my seminary training, we were taught that sermons should be preached with the Bible in one hand and the newspaper in the other. It is advice taken from a famous theologian, Karl Barth and it means that the word of God has to have relevance to what is happening in the world. In other words, we have to connect the word to the world.

What is happening in the world today, especially in Israel and Lebanon, is of great concern. Millions of people are displaced and are suffering. Thousands are killed and there is so much fear and destruction, and interest in the 'end times' has spiked. Mainstream reporters and producers along with a growing number of U.S and foreign political leaders are fascinated by the issue. Look at some of the articles in recent days. In a *USA Today* article entitled "In the headlines: glimpses of Apocalypse" columnist chuck Raasch asked quite pointedly: "Are these the end of times?"

"With the war in Iraq persisting, with fresh fighting in Afghanistan, with missiles raining down on Israel, the world's most powerful government and the United Nations appear unable or unwilling to stop a chain of events that may be spinning out of earthly control," he wrote.

Raasch is not alone. A headline in the *Waco Tribune Herald* asked: "Are we living in the final days?" *The Columbus Dispatch* has this headline: "Is the Mideast Rupture a sign of the Rapture? I have seen several television channels dealing with this issue, for example MSNBC last Friday asked the question whether current events suggest, if we are living in the last days before the return of Christ?

When I watch ministers and TV preachers babbling on this topic, I ask myself, two questions: First, "why are these mere mortals trying to speculate on this issue, a question Jesus himself did not know the answer?" Secondly, "why do these television anchors treat this as 'breaking news?"

Setting a date for the end of the world is nothing new. Every time a natural disaster happens, or war breaks out in the in the Mideast, especially involving Israel, people talk about the end of the world. There is a website called *datesettersdiary.com* which has hundreds of dates for the end of the world. Some people thought that the world would end in AD 1000, the end of the first millennium. Others set the date as AD1033, a thousand years after the death of Christ.

Jehovah's Witnesses set the date twice: 1941 and 1975. When I was growing up, my mother told us that the world would end in the year 2000. We had a picture of the risen Christ on the wall, and his two fingers are raised. My mother thought that the two fingers symbolized the year 2000 and the end of the world. My mother is still alive and the world is still here. My father thought that the two fingers of Jesus meant that on Easter Sunday, he was allowed to drink two bottles of vodka!

People point to the book of Revelation, the predictions in Ezekiel chapter 38, and the book of Daniel, and connect them with the events in Israel and believe that these tribulations are a precursor to the glorious coming of Jesus on a horse. This event is called the *rapture.* At the time of rapture, Christians who have died will have their bodies reconstituted and will ascend through the air and meet Jesus Christ in the sky. That is why Jehovah's Witnesses bury their dead with a set of extra clothes. They keep a new set of clothes along with the body, which the person is supposed to wear at the resurrection.

The word *rapture* comes from the Latin word *rapare,* which means "to take away" or "snatch out." This would be a remarkable event. Pilots would disappear from planes, truck drivers from their trucks, drivers from their cars,, etc. Some 'born again' Christians believe that a family will be eating dinner, when some of the members will rise from their seats, pass through the roof and keep rising in the air. An associated event is Christ's imminent return also known as the 'Second Coming.'

Those who believe in Jesus will be taken up to heaven and the unbelievers will be 'left behind' and exterminated in a massive genocide. There is series of books called the *Left Behind Series*, written by Tim Lehay and Jerry Jenkins which deals with this subject, and they have sold millions of copies. There is a website called *Raptureready.com* which sells merchandise such as helmets, face masks, body armor, etc. to get people ready for the rapture.

Some people think the whole concept of rapture is funny. I have a friend who said that he cannot wait for the rapture to happen so that he could go into the street and pick up a Lexus or a BMW, whose driver was taken up to heaven and the car was left behind with its engine running!

Many people are concerned and confused. I have a 95 year old patient who watches religious TV all day. She watches this preacher of Cornerstone Church in Texas, John Hagee, who advises Christians to look up to the heavens each day and ask the question: "Lord, is this the day?" T.V. Evangelist, Charles Stanley says "the end will not happen until the Jerusalem temple is rebuilt and it will take time." My patient told me that she is very confused.

Dan Brown, author of the *Da Vinci Code*, says that "the ends times is the fantasy of paranoid minds."

As disciples of Christ, what are we to believe? How do we face these trying times? I want to share with you some personal reflections which have helped me process the events that are happening around us and make some sense out of them. These are my reflections and not the position of my Church. If you would like t to discuss further about these ideas, come directly to me, call me or email me.

First of all, Bible passages describing end times have to be understood symbolically, not literally. Secondly, I am abiding by the words of Jesus about the end of the world. When asked, Jesus said: "No one knows about that day or the hour, not even the angels in heaven, nor the Son, but only the father." In this context, it is very helpful to remember the Buddhist saying: **He who talks does not know and he who knows does not talk.**

There are about 1200 religions and about six billion people on this planet. Only one third of them are Christians. Why would God, who is the father of all, give this information about the end of the world to just one group of people and keep it as a secret from the rest of his children? **Moreover, if God takes into heaven only those who believe in Jesus, and leaves the rest behind, about 4 billion people will be annihilated. That will be the biggest case of divine ethnic cleansing in the history of humanity. I cannot fathom a loving God doing that.**

According to a *Newsweek* article, there is genuine excitement among some people that Jesus' return might be near. I feel that these people are totally missing the point of the message of Jesus and the basics of Christian faith. **By focusing their attention on the second coming, they are missing out on the life-giving implications of the first coming of Jesus**. They are depriving themselves of the fullness of life that Jesus promised us now. Jesus came that we may have life, and have it abundantly now, not later.

**Focusing on the second coming takes away any motivation to take care of the problems today**. For example, during the civil rights movement in 1963, after the March in Washington, Billy Graham said: "Only when Christ comes again will the little white children of Alabama walk hand in hand with the little black children." That one statement deflated the enthusiasm of so many people to do anything about eradicating racism because they left it for the second coming. Thank God, Martin Luther King did not heed those words.

By the way, Billy Graham, in his old age, has changed his thinking about the Bible. In a *News Week* interview, he said: "There are many things that I don't understand; sincere Christians can disagree about the details of Scripture and theology absolutely; I am not a literalist about the Bible in that every word is from the Lord. This is a little difference in my thinking through the years."

I have a client who is in a very bad marriage. They hurt each other, they are unfaithful to each other and they are miserable together. With a sigh, the wife would say, "I am a Christian and I believe that when the Lord comes, all this would be better." **Hoping that the 'second coming' would solve our problems, mostly created by our selfishness, is an excuse and a cope out from dealing with the painful realities of life now.**

And believe me; we don't have to solve our problems alone. Jesus is with us to help us, but we have to believe that he is with us now.

**Personally I don't worry about or anxiously anticipate the second coming. I am more engaged in living my life today with Jesus, who in fact has never left us.** The second coming almost presupposes that Jesus is not with us now, and that we have to wait. His last words to the disciples were: "I am with you always." He is always with us; his name is *Emmanuel*, which means, "God with us." **Our challenge is to recognize Jesus today in the least of his brothers and sisters, love them unconditionally and be a light in the world, instead of staring at the sky.**

So to answer the question, "Is the end near? I don't believe that the world would end. The earth has been around for 5 billion years. Human beings are the last to arrive on the planet, and we have been here only about 65 thousand years. The earth can survive without us; but we cannot survive without the earth. I don't believe God will destroy his creation; it will be like a father killing his children; Yes, some parents do kill their children, like Andrea Yates killed her six children, but she was mentally ill. I can't imagine God our loving father destroying his creation.

However, human beings by their fear and hatred of one another have the potential to destroy themselves. We humans have produced enough nuclear weapons to destroy the world many times over. My fear is that if they get into the wrong hands, such as Iran, they might use it to destroy Israel and that will be the beginning of the end. **Or, misguided leaders could use them in a war, and blame it as fulfillment of biblical prophecy and make it a self-fulfilling prophecy**.

So I encourage you to pray hard for leaders of nations so that they can settle their differences through negotiations and not war. Pray for the innocent victims of war and send our positive energies of love and kindness to our brothers and sisters around the world, especially in the Middle East.

**But never be afraid, because fear is not the quality of a disciple**. Every time Jesus appeared to his disciples, his first words were: "Be not afraid." That is why we sang that song today; "*Be not Afraid;*" because Jesus, who is always with us, walks before us. That is why I chose Ps 23 as our first reading today; "The Lord is my shepherd, I shall not want. Even though I walk in the valley of darkness, I fear no evil, for you are at my side." Feel the presence of Jesus, the good shepherd, in your heart and at your side every moment now, not in a distant future.

# 52. Die Before You Die

John: 11:17-27

*Martha answered, "I know he will rise again in the resurrection at the last day." Jesus said to her, "I am the resurrection and the life. He who believes in me will live, even though he dies; and whoever lives and believes in me will never die."*

Once, a preacher was giving a sermon on death. He began with this declaration: "Someday, everyone in this church will die." He saw a man in the front pew, laughing. So the preacher, repeated with force: "Someday, everyone in this church will die;" and the man laughed again. So the preacher asked him. "What is so funny, don't you think you will die some day?"

And the man replied: "You said someday, everyone in *this* church will die; I am not from *this* church."

We are smarter than that. We know that we will die but we don't really want to think about it. Comedian George Carlin who died few months ago said: "Thanks to our fear of death in this country, I won't have to die, I will pass away, or I will expire like a magazine subscription."

For most people, death is one of the scariest things in life. Woody Allen said: "I am not afraid of death, as long as I don't have to be there when it happens." A lot of my patients are afraid of death; I had a patient who had this idea that most people die in their sleep and so he refused to go to bed at night. He would drink several cups of coffee and stay up all night watching TV and go to bed in the morning. Ironically, he died in sleep, during the day!

Death denial is actually not healthy. According to Mother Theresa, "People who are unable to confront the fact of their own mortality are unable to fully appreciate life." So, it is good to think about death, so that we can appreciate the precious precariousness of our lives.

Since I started working in hospice, my life has become much more peaceful and joyful. I am not stressed out or worried, and it has become easy to love everybody. I have learned to live in the NOW because tomorrow is not guaranteed. Awareness of death gives perspective on every aspect of life.

When I tell people that I am a hospice chaplain, the usual reactions are: "that must be depressing," "Seeing death every day must be stressful," "Being near dead bodies must be scary." Death was dreadful, depressing, scary and dreary, until I understood the real meaning of death a few years ago. Since then I have been able to accept it, be comfortable with it and even embrace it.

It became easy, when I understood the meaning of the Buddhist saying: "Die before you die and find out there is no death." What does that mean?

When we face death, all the things that we normally consider to be important, become unimportant and irrelevant: our name, status, position, possessions, money, job, car, and house; things that we usually fight for and become upset about, turn out to be insignificant. At our deathbed, none of these things matter.

I have seen people dying, with millions of dollars in their brokerage account, precious jewelry in their safety deposit box, and cherished paintings on walls and designer clothes in their closets. Things they were so attached to and worried about losing and were reluctant to share, had to be left behind.

I remember the death of my next door neighbor, Greg, who died on March 13th this year. Greg was very fond of his house. He meticulously took care of it, both inside and outside. He had several things in the house that he cherished. He had a motorcycle he worshiped. Every Saturday, he cleaned and polished it, and on Sundays, he went on a ride with his buddies.

But when he died, it was left behind along with all the things he had cherished. I vividly remember the scene, where the undertaker placed the body in a plastic bag, covered it with a green blanket, placed it on a gurney, rolled it to the curb, and pushed it into the back of his white van and drove away in the middle of a humid Florida night.

It was an eerie sight. The man who owned his house, who was the head of his household, left alone and empty handed, never to return again.

**As the saying goes, nobody hooks up a u-haul to a hearse!**

So if we can live our lives as if the external and material things are unimportant, if we can live without enormous attachments to stuff and people, thus die to the world, and die to the self, as Jesus asks us to do, then at the time of physical death, we will find out that, death is not scary at all, because we have already died to everything that makes death difficult and scary.

Death is our re-joining with God. I did not understand it, until I got a chance to observe the dying process. I had that chance when I sat at the bedside and observed one of my patients die.

Helen was 80 years old. I had the opportunity to stay at her bed side, along with her daughter at the time of Helen's death. As death approached, her breathing began to slow down and the intervals became longer and then she took a last breath. That is why, when someone dies, we say: "She took her last breath."

Then I noticed something beautiful. Her facial skin seemed to become smoother and tighter with the wrinkles almost disappearing and the face of this 80 year old woman looked as if she were 60. There was this special glow on her face. I said to myself: "This glow must be the blush, when God kissed her on the cheek and said: "Welcome home my child."

Now, I want to take you to the creation story in the book of Genesis. I don't take that story literally, but it conveys a very profound truth. It says that "God formed man from the clay on the ground and blew into his nostrils, the breath of life, and the man became a living being."

From the moment of our birth until we take our last breath, it is the "breath of God" that keeps us alive. Breath is the spirit of God; that is why St. Paul says "our bodies are temples of the Holy Spirit."

We are Spirits and therefore, we are immortal. Body perishes, but spirit survives, because spirit by its very nature cannot die. Neale Donald Walsch puts it beautifully when he writes: "We are related to God, the Eternal Spirit, like the waves are related to the ocean. We are different from God, but we are not divided from God. The fact that we are not divided from God is why we can never die."

Jesus knew this truth so well and that is why he did not panic or rush to Bethany when he heard the news that his best friend Lazarus had died. The gospel says, "He stayed on where he was for two more days." Imagine you hearing about the death of someone dear to you. You will panic, become restless, drop everything and rush to the scene.

Jesus is very calm and collected. There is no fear or anxiety, because Jesus knew the deeper meaning of death. Jesus knew that physical death is not the final word about human life; he knew that all endings are also beginnings. Look at his reaction when he faced his own death: Jesus does not get agitated or aggravated or sink into a deep depression, but calmly surrenders to God saying: "Father, into your hands I commend my spirit."

Death is the biggest mystery of life. Nobody knows exactly what happens at the moment of death. Near Death Experience (NDE) studies have described death "as the most beautiful human experience." It must be, and, that is why nobody who has died has ever come back.

In his book, *Home with God in a Life that Never Ends*, Neale Donald Walsch describes it as "experiencing complete oneness with God." There are no words to adequately describe this feeling, partly because the feeling is huge: this is how he describes what happens at the moment of death:

*It might be characterized as a single, enormous, conglomerate of feelings that encompasses a thousand individual feelings, now slowly filling the soul.*

*A feeble attempt to describe it would call it the feeling of being warmly embraced, deeply comforted, dearly cherished, profoundly appreciated, genuinely treasured, softly nurtured, profoundly understood, completely forgiven, wholly absolved, long awaited, happily welcome, totally honored, joyously celebrated, absolutely protected, instantly perfected, and unconditionally loved - all at once.*

That is death. This description gives me much comfort in dealing with death.

If we live our lives in communion with God through prayer, scripture reading, worship, and loving others while we are still in the flesh, when death comes, whenever and where ever that may be, it will never come as a shock or a surprise, but merely as a continuation of the loving, joyful and peaceful life we currently have. That is what Jesus meant when he said: "I am the resurrection and the life, he who believes in me will never die."

# For Further Reading

Armstrong, Karen, *A History of God* (Alfred A. Knopf, New York 1993)

Armstrong, Karen, *The Battle for God* (Random House, New York, 2001)

Borg, Marcus J. *The God We Never Knew* (Harper, San Francisco, 1998)

Borg, Marcus J. *Reading the Bible for the First Time* (Harper, San Francisco, 2002)

Borg, Marcus J. *The Heart of Christianity: Re-discovering a Life of Faith* (Harper, San Francisco 2004)

Brown, Dan, *The Lost Symbol* (Doubleday, New York 2009)

Brussat, Frederic and Mary Ann, *Spiritual Literacy* (Simon & Schuster, New York 1996)

Camp, Lee C, *Mere Discipleship* (Brazos Press, Grand Rapids 2003)

Campolo, Tony, *Red Letter Christians* (Regal, Ventura, 2008)

Chopra, Deepak, *How to Know God* (Harmony Books, New York 2000)

Chopra, Deepak, The Third Jesus: The Christ We Cannot Ignore (Harmony Books, New York 2008)

DeMello, Anthony, *The Song of the Bird* (Doubleday, New York 1982)

Dowd, Michael, *Thank God for Evolution* (Viking, New York 2007)

Dyer, Wayne W. *Manifest Your Destiny* (Harper Collins, New York 1997)

Dyer, Wayne W. *Change Your Thoughts, Change Your Life* (Hay House, Carlsbad 2007)

Fox, Matthew, *Original Blessing* (Bear & Company Inc. Santa Fe 1983)

Friedman, Thomas L. *The World is Flat: A Brief History of the 21st Century* (Picador, USA 2007)

Gilbert, Elizabeth, *Eat, Pray, Love* (Penguin, New York 2006)

Hays, Edward, *Prayer for a Planetary Pilgrim* (Forest A. Publishing Co. Leavenworth 1989)

Irwin, Lee, *Awakening to Sprit* (State university of New York Press, New York 1999)

King, Barbara J. *Evolving God* (Doubleday, New York 2007)

Kopp, Sheldon, *If You Meet the Buddha on the Road, Kill Him* (Bantam, New York 1976)

Lerner, Michael, *The Left Hand of God* (Harper, San Francisco 2006)

McLaren, Brian D, *A New Kind of Christian* (Jossey-Bass, San Francisco, 2001)

O'Murchu, Diarmuid, *Reclaiming Spirituality* (Cross Road, New York 1998)

O'Murchu, Diarmuid, *Religion in Exile* (Cross Road, New York 2000)

O'Murchu, Diarmuid, *Our World in Transition* (Cross Road, New York 2000)

Pearson, Carlton, *The Gospel of Inclusion* (Altria Books, New York 2008)

Rossing, Barbara R. *Rapture Exposed* (Basic Books, New York 2004)

Taylor, Brian C. *Becoming Human* (Cowley Publications, Cambridge 2005)

Tippett, Krista, *Speaking of Faith* (Penguin, New York 2008)

Thich Nhat Hanh, *No Death No Fear* (Penguin, New York 2002)

Spong, John Shelby, *A New Christianity for a New World* (Harper, San Francisco 2002)

Spong, John Shelby, *Jesus for the Non-Religious* (Harper, San Francisco 2007)

Tolle, Eckhart, *The Power of Now: A Guide to Spiritual Enlightenment* (New World Library, New York 1999)

Tolle, Eckhart, *A New Earth: Awakening to Your Life's Purpose* (Penguin, New York 2005)

Walsch, Neale Donald, *Conversations with God*, Book 1 (G.P. Putnam's Sons, New York 1996)

Walsch, Neale Donald, *Conversations with God,* Book 2 (Hampton Roads, Charlottesville 1997)

Walsch, Neale Donald, *Conversations with God,* Book 3 (Hampton Roads, Charlottesville 1998)

Walsch, Neale Donald, *Communion with God* (G.P. Putnam's Sons, New York 2000)

Walsch, Neale Donald, *Home Wirth God in a Life That Never Ends* (Altria Books, New York 2006)

Walsch, Neale Donald, *Tomorrow's God (*Altria Books, New York 2004*)*

Walsch, Neale Donald, *What God Wants (*Altria Books, New York m2005*)*

Walsch, Neale Donald, *When Everything Changes, Change Everything* (EmNin Books, Ashland 2009)

Wright, Robert, *The Evolution of God* (Little Brown & Co. New York 2009)

Yong, William, *The Shack* (Windblown Media, Newbery Park 2007)